CW00542369

This Book Belongs To:

....

Anniversary Date:

....

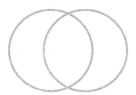

The Smiths are a testimony to the power of our loving God to work through the prayers of his people. Your marriage is bound to grow as they guide you into the depths of God's goodness and truth through praying intentionally for your marriage.

Ryan and Selena Frederick, founders of
Fierce Marriage and Fierce Families

The Marriage Gift felt like a guide to meaningful time with God and my husband. I believe couples who set out to make prayer together a first response will see radical shifts in all areas of their lives!

Chelsea Hurst, coauthor of *Marriage Minded*

We are so thankful for Aaron and Jennifer's powerful ministry to marriages. They have equipped and encouraged countless couples (including us)! *The Marriage Gift* is a beautiful culmination of their years of marriage ministry and practical wisdom.

Dave and Ashley Willis, authors; hosts
of *The Naked Marriage* podcast

Taps the timeless wisdom of Scripture to reveal how we can confidently talk to God about our most important relationship—every single day! Grab a copy for yourself and another for a friend; there is no better gift than prayer!

Jodie Berndt, bestselling author of *Praying
the Scriptures for Your Marriage*

Invitational and easy to approach yet filled with deep truths. Each day offers Scripture-based opportunities to engage in meaningful prayer for your marriage that will sincerely bless and refresh your connection.

Francie Winslow, host of the *Heaven in Your Home* podcast

If you're not sure where to start or are wondering, Where is God? *The Marriage Gift* will help you rediscover the power of prayer and strengthen your marriage through the peaceful presence of God.

Jeremy and Audrey Roloff, *New York Times*
bestselling authors of *A Love Letter Life*

365 PRAYERS
FOR OUR MARRIAGE

THE
MARRIAGE
GIFT

A DAILY DEVOTIONAL JOURNEY TO
INSPIRE, ENCOURAGE, AND TRANSFORM US
AND OUR PRAYER LIFE

AARON AND JENNIFER SMITH

ZONDERVAN
BOOKS

ZONDERVAN BOOKS

The Marriage Gift
Copyright © 2023 by Aaron Smith and Jennifer Smith

Requests for information should be addressed to:
Zondervan, *3900 Sparks Dr. SE, Grand Rapids, Michigan 49546*

Zondervan titles may be purchased in bulk for educational, business, fundraising, or sales promotional use. For information, please email SpecialMarkets@Zondervan.com.

ISBN 978-0-310-36708-6 (audio)

Library of Congress Cataloging-in-Publication Data

Names: Smith, Aaron, 1984– author. | Smith, Jennifer, 1985– author.
Title: The marriage gift : 365 prayers for our marriage: a daily devotional journey to inspire, encourage, and transform us and our prayer life / Aaron Smith, Jennifer Smith.
Description: Grand Rapids : Zondervan, 2023.
Identifiers: LCCN 2023015307 (print) | LCCN 2023015308 (ebook) | ISBN 9780310367062 (hardcover) | ISBN 9780310367079 (ebook)
Subjects: LCSH: Married people—Prayers and devotions. | Married people—Religious life. | Spouses—Prayers and devotions. | BISAC: RELIGION / Christian Living / Love & Marriage | RELIGION / Christian Living / Devotional
Classification: LCC BV4596.M3 S642 2023 (print) | LCC BV4596.M3 (ebook) | DDC 248.8/44—dc23/eng/20230622
LC record available at https://lccn.loc.gov/2023015307
LC ebook record available at https://lccn.loc.gov/2023015308

All Scripture quotations, unless otherwise indicated, are taken from the ESV® Bible (The Holy Bible, English Standard Version®). Copyright © 2001 by Crossway, a publishing ministry of Good News Publishers. Used by permission. All rights reserved.

Scripture quotations marked NIV are taken from The Holy Bible, New International Version®, NIV®. Copyright © 1973, 1978, 1984, 2011 by Biblica, Inc.® Used by permission of Zondervan. All rights reserved worldwide. www.Zondervan.com. The "NIV" and "New International Version" are trademarks registered in the United States Patent and Trademark Office by Biblica, Inc.®

Any internet addresses (websites, blogs, etc.) and telephone numbers in this book are offered as a resource. They are not intended in any way to be or imply an endorsement by Zondervan, nor does Zondervan vouch for the content of these sites and numbers for the life of this book.

All rights reserved. No part of this publication may be reproduced, stored in a retrieval system, or transmitted in any form or by any means—electronic, mechanical, photocopy, recording, or any other—except for brief quotations in printed reviews, without the prior permission of the publisher.

The authors are represented by Alive Literary Agency, www.aliveliterary.com.

Cover design: Studio Gearbox
Cover illustration: Patt Patt / Shutterstock
Interior design: Denise Froehlich

Printed in the United States of America

23 24 25 26 27 LBC 5 4 3 2 1

To the people in our lives who taught us the significance of prayer.

Thank you for being an example of what it looks like to pray faithfully. Thank you for responding to life's circumstances by praying to God with humble hearts. You have helped us lay the foundation of our marriage, showing us how to never give up hope, to trust God, and to never cease praying.

The prayer of a righteous person has great power as it is working. **(James 5:16)**

CONTENTS

INTRODUCTION

Prayer Matters More Than You Know

Prayer is not just a word to describe what religious people do in faithful duty. It also is not a frivolous word synonymous with wishful thinking. Prayer is much more than a word; it is a breath, a heartbeat, a sanctuary where one enters boldly before the throne of God to meet our Creator, our Father in heaven, our Savior. Prayer is a way of connecting and communing with the Lord, making our relationship with Him amazingly personal. Prayer is humbly acknowledging His lordship over all. Through the gift of prayer, we have the privilege of expressing our burdens, our praises, and our requests for God to move in our lives.

If we could permanently etch one thing into your heart from this book, it would be that prayer matters more than you know. The perfect and holy Creator allows His beloved creations, made in His image, to communicate directly with Him. The fact that He listens to us—and more than that, welcomes us into His presence—is utterly miraculous. What an extraordinary gift!

The purpose of prayer is not to bend God to our will, but rather to align our heart to His. God's will is revealed through His Word. As we abide in Scripture and as we pray, we are seeking God's will to be done. When we do this, we can be confident that He hears us!

This is the confidence that we have toward him, that if we ask anything according to his will he hears us. (1 John 5:14)

Even when we do not feel confident and do not know how to pray, we can still draw close to God in our weakness, knowing that we are not alone, that we cannot live in our own strength, and that our Savior understands our weakness. We can still rely on Him daily. The beautiful truth is that the Holy Spirit intercedes for us. Though we may lack the words to pray, the Lord never does.

> The Spirit helps us in our weakness. For we do not know what to pray for as we ought, but the Spirit himself intercedes for us with groanings too deep for words. (Romans 8:26)

In marriage, when pain and weakness overwhelm us, when the tension of love and frustration stirs within us, when it seems like there is no clear path forward, prayer is the bridge of peace that brings connection between the one offering up a prayer and the Lord, as well as between spouses. Prayer is always the next right step. Prayer is essential for everyone because we are all made of flesh, which is weak, susceptible to temptation, and inclined to sin. Scripture warns us to watch and pray, guarding ourselves from temptation and the deceitfulness of sin.

> Watch and pray that you may not enter into temptation. The spirit indeed is willing, but the flesh is weak. (Matthew 26:41)

In prayer, we have the opportunity to reveal our hearts to our heavenly Father. We get to offer Him our thoughts and feelings about what we are experiencing. We must trust the Lord in order to bring Him our worries and cares, our needs and our fears. We must lay aside our pride to appeal to the Lord and speak to the author of life. In doing so, we receive from Him the gift of relationship, answered prayers, met needs, life-changing transformation, and transcending peace.

So may we experience the breath and heartbeat of prayer as we bolster the courage to enter into the throne room of grace in faith, believing that He will move in our lives and marriages. May we have the assurance and fortitude to pray without ceasing.

> Praying at all times in the Spirit, with all prayer and supplication. (Ephesians 6:18)

The Power of Prayer

We hope that by sharing our journey of experiencing the power of prayer in our marriage, you will be inspired to build your own daily habit of prayer.

The impact of prayer in our lives and in our marriage has been extraordinary. Although we grew up learning how to pray and were committed to praying often, we did not know how vital prayer is to marriage until we were desperate for it. In the first few years of our marriage, we experienced the pain of hardship. Finances often brought us to our knees in prayer. The burden of school loan debt, the stress of searching for good-paying jobs during the recession, and the consistent daily demand of our responsibilities brought concerns we had to handle as a married couple. We also realized we needed to grow in the way we communicated with one another, especially during conflict. When we felt frustrated and hurt, we would surrender our hearts and our emotions to God in prayer, pleading with Him to help us understand each other. Countless times we have felt divided in how we feel, think, and perceive circumstances, and the only thing that helps us feel connected again is praying together.

In addition to struggles with finances, communication, and

challenging circumstances, we experienced a specific issue in marriage that lasted four years. Jennifer experienced physical pain every time we tried to have sex. This situation stirred up many doubts and insecurities within us. We relied on prayer more than we ever had before. When despair and hopelessness overwhelmed us to the point of heartache, and the temptation to separate from one another berated us daily, we cried out to the Lord in prayer. We begged and petitioned Him for an answer to our circumstances, for relief, and for hope that our marriage would survive. There were times we prayed alone, times we prayed together, and even times that only one of us had the courage to stand in the gap to pray for our marriage.

The Lord heard us and He answered. He helped us find a path to reconciliation and healing. Not only did He reveal a solution that helped Jennifer's body, but He also used our struggle to refine our character and help us get to know Him better. Through every circumstance we've faced as a couple, we have endured together with hope in our hearts because we choose over and over again to submit ourselves before the Lord in prayer. In humility, we have laid down our strong opinions, our hurts, and our burdens, asking the Lord to lead us through each situation.

We have witnessed the power of prayer draw us closer to God and closer to each other. When we approach the Lord in prayer together, we feel united, encouraged, and reassured. Our hope and desire is that you too would experience and witness the wonderful working power of the Lord in your marriage as you purpose to pray for your marriage.

Will you consider believing and hoping for good things to happen in your marriage?

Will you step into the throne room of grace and trust the Lord to lead you and your spouse through any and all circumstances?

Will you take time to petition the Lord for healing and restoration and for His will to be done in your marriage?

We encourage you to try.

What This Book Is

This book is full of prayers written for the sole purpose of encouraging your faith and supporting your marriage. This book has been written to inspire you to devote yourself to daily prayer for your life and marriage. The topics of each prayer have been curated and produced from the experience of praying for our own marriage. The varying topics are intended to remind you of the many different areas of your marriage relationship that need constant, fervent, and humble prayer. Praying for these areas of your marriage, praying for your heart and for your spouse's heart, will hopefully show you how transformative it can be to bring both of your needs to God. This book provides you with words to share with the Lord, a helpful tool when you are building confidence in praying. May these pages be a bridge to draw you closer to God and closer to your spouse.

What This Book Isn't

This book is not meant to be a replacement for your everyday prayer life. Nor is it meant to be a comprehensive list of topics that cover every part of your life and marriage. These prayers can't fully address the intimate details of *your* story, so we urge you to add those details as you pray. This book is also not meant to be divisive and shouldn't be used as a weapon against your spouse to show them the areas in which they are failing or have neglected. Please don't misuse these prayers with the motivation to control or manipulate one another in marriage.

These prayers are not magical, and praying them does not

guarantee you will receive all that you want in life and marriage. Ultimately, having a humble heart before the Lord is more important than having a prayer answered the way you desire it to be. This resource does not require you to read the prayers together with your spouse. You can agree to read together, or you can do it on your own. Lastly, this book is not intended to collect dust on the shelf, so use it regularly to prevent buildup.

How to Use This Book

Our goal with offering 365 written prayers is to embolden you to create a habit of praying every day of the year, not just when you have a need or the pressures of life seem unbearable. We also hope that each unique prayer topic would encourage you to consider the varying areas of your marriage to bring before the Lord. As you commit to establishing a daily prayer habit, we believe these prayers will encourage growth in your personal relationship with the Lord and with your spouse.

As you work through these prayers, we encourage you to add personal details as you go. Make these prayers your own! Also, if you find that a prayer topic doesn't quite fit your marriage, we encourage you to use it to pray for another married couple in your life who might be struggling in that area.

Don't get overwhelmed if you miss a day of prayer. Keep a steady pace by picking up where you left off.

The best way to utilize this book is to choose a time of the day that you and your spouse can read it together. But if your spouse can't read it with you, then choose a time that you can commit to reading it yourself. If your spouse also commits to reading the prayers on their own time, consider making room each week or once a month to talk about the impact you are experiencing.

We intentionally did not add dates to each prayer because we want you to be able to start from any point in the book on any day of the year. This also makes it easy to skip around to individual prayers and topics that may cover a pressing issue you'd like to address in prayer.

One more practical idea we suggest is keeping a journal nearby to record any encouragement or insight the Lord provides as you pray. You can also use this journal to keep a record of answered prayers that you can celebrate and praise Him for.

> Continue steadfastly in prayer, being watchful in it with thanksgiving. (Colossians 4:2)

The Marriage Gift

Years ago, the Lord planted a seed deep in our hearts for this specific book. We longed for it to one day break free from our hearts and be held in the hands of married couples who deeply desire to draw close to the Lord in prayer together. We knew this book needed time to grow its roots deep in our hearts if we wanted it to have a long-lasting presence and impact in the lives of believers. The conviction of praying over our own marriage led us through the development of each prayer we chose to include in this book. Over the years, the Lord faithfully watered this idea He planted in us, and in His timing He's brought it forth for His glory. We are grateful for the opportunity to share these prayers, and we hope they minister to you the divine message that God loves you and has a purpose for your marriage.

We felt inspired to title this collection of prayers *The Marriage Gift* as it holds a multilayered meaning. The first thing we want to point out is that prayer is a gift to marriage. Through lifting up praises, concerns, and requests to the Lord, spouses draw close to God and to each other. Prayer is a gift that blesses marriage. As we have prayed together over the years, we have been continually reaffirmed in our love for each other. This is the ministry of prayer! We discovered that prayer has a uniquely powerful way of bringing unity to marriage. Experiencing the ministry of prayer in our marriage convinced us to make prayer a significant part of our ministry to others.

You have the opportunity to experience the gift of prayer in your marriage. In times of hardship and in times of overflowing joy, in times of confusion and in times of clarity, in times of challenge and in times of rest, having a heart committed to prayer will support your marriage, encourage your faith, and be a catalyst for growth in your life. You can experience the extraordinary power of the Lord as He works in you and through you when you pray. And when you commit to pray for and with your spouse, you are ministering to them, reminding them of the importance to remain humble before the Lord. In doing this, you become a gift to your spouse!

When you and your spouse are unified and walk with the Lord, when you pray, obey His Word, and let Him lead you, your marriage is a gift to God! He finds pleasure in your marriage and can use your marriage to carry out His will as He pleases. For example, when you and your spouse are moved by God to pray for another couple, you experience the ministry of prayer. And in such a selfless and loving response of submitting to the Lord in prayer, you and your marriage become a gift to others!

Lastly, this book itself is the marriage gift, a resource that we hope becomes an extraordinary blessing to you that contributes to spiritual growth and marital intimacy.

Prayer is humbling.

Prayer is sanctifying.

Prayer reminds us we are not alone.

Prayer alleviates pressure and provides great peace.

Prayer is an extraordinary part of our journey with God that matures as we practice it faithfully. May this book inspire a lifelong pursuit of prayer and help you build such a strong prayer life that prayer becomes your first response to any circumstance.

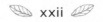

A Prayer for Your Marriage

From the Authors

Dear heavenly Father, Thank You for the couple reading this book and praying these prayers. We ask You to bless their marriage and strengthen their relationship as they recognize the truth that their marriage is a gift from You. In submitting their hearts to You in prayer, may they also recognize the truth that they are offering their marriage as a gift to You, in hopes that it would bless You and be used as You see fit. Holy Spirit, please be their navigator as You guide them to a place of greater spiritual maturity and deeper intimacy with You and with each other. Cover their marriage and protect them from the threats of the Enemy. Protect them from the dangers of their own flesh hindering them from continual growth. Holy Spirit, please convict their hearts of any sin they are struggling with, help them repent, and lead them to be reconciled with You and with each other. May these prayers inspire them to draw closer to You and each other in a way they have never known before. As they submit their hearts to You in prayer, please let them experience Your wonderful working power. Sanctify them and build them up in love. We pray that their marriage is a beacon of light and hope in this dark world as they choose to reflect Your love. May they bring You glory as they chase boldly after You together in Jesus's name. Amen.

365 Prayers

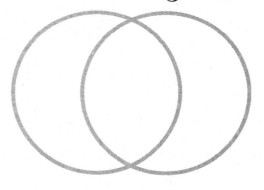

FOR OUR
MARRIAGE

LOVING EACH OTHER
LIKE CHRIST

Dear Lord,   Thank You for the gift of marriage and for leading us to a season of intentional prayer so that we may keep You at the center of it. Help us hold fast to the commitment of praying for our marriage, and draw our hearts closer to You and to each other every day. Heavenly Father, will You transform the areas of our relationship that need maturing? We want to grow in our desire to be like Christ and to love each other like He loves. We want to love one another unconditionally. Please help us love with a sacrificial, compassionate love, Lord. May we be peacemakers in our marriage, kind to one another, and quick to forgive as You are quick to forgive us. May Your love abound in us as we abide in You, and may Your will be done in us and through our marriage. In Jesus's name we pray. Amen.

A new commandment I give to you, that you love one another: just as I have loved you, you also are to love one another. **(JOHN 13:34)**

RESISTING THE ENEMY

Dear Lord, Thank You for being our defender, our refuge, and our strength. Thank You for equipping us by Your Word to do what is right. God, we give You this day, and we surrender our plans so that Your will is done. Help us to resist the Enemy, to shut out his lies, and to believe only what is true. May we resist temptation and choose to walk confidently in righteousness. In moments of weakness, when the Enemy tries to whisper his lies or throw flaming arrows our way, please protect us. Tune our hearts and minds to hear Your truth above any lies. Holy Spirit, remind us of all that Your Word says. We pray the Enemy would not prevail in our marriage. Please help us to share our weaknesses with each other and encourage one another through challenging times. Lord, strengthen our souls, and help us to flee from the Enemy every day. May Your name be magnified as we submit to You. In Jesus's name we pray. Amen.

Submit yourselves therefore to God. Resist the devil, and he will flee from you. **(JAMES 4:7)**

3

IN GOD'S HANDS

Dear Lord, We invite You to be present in our relationship, to teach us how to thrive in our marriage, and to show us how to glorify You with our marriage. Our relationship is in Your hands. May we experience unity and know the joy of a peaceful relationship. Please watch over us and guard our hearts as we follow You. Help us find our security in You and to trust You more. We humble ourselves at the foot of Your throne and submit to You in all Your ways. Please be our comfort in times of distress, our security in times of confusion, and our refuge when circumstances are challenging. God, when our relationship feels unstable and our hearts are insecure, thank You for holding us up with Your mighty hand. Help us to have hearts full of gratitude so we never forget all You have done for us. In Jesus's name we pray. Amen.

Humble yourselves, therefore, under the mighty hand of God so that at the proper time he may exalt you. **(1 PETER 5:6)**

PRESERVE OUR LOVE

Dear Lord, Thank You for Your gift of love. Thank You for showing us in Your Word how to love. Please help us choose to love each other every day, just as You love us. Will You give us fresh eyes to see when we are not loving one another well? Lord, transform us to be responsive to Your Holy Spirit so that You can guide us to be quick to apologize when we do wrong and forgive when we need to forgive. Show us ways to fulfill each other's needs. Season our love with creativity. Fortify and preserve our love so it will stand the test of time. Holy Spirit, please guard our marriage from the attacks of the Enemy and the temptations of our flesh. May we bear the weight of one another's burdens, believe in each other's abilities, hope in a beautiful future together, and endure side by side, all in love. We pray that our love for each other never ends. In Jesus's name we pray. Amen.

Love bears all things, believes all things,
hopes all things, endures all things. Love
never ends. **(1 CORINTHIANS 13:7–8)**

MARRIAGE IS A TESTIMONY

Dear Lord, Thank You for the way Your love has covered our sins. Your love is transforming, and Your kindness is beyond measure. We lift up our hearts to You and ask You to show us how to love each other earnestly. We pray we would have a sincere and intense conviction about how we are supposed to treat one another in marriage. May Your Holy Spirit help us to be self-controlled, not quick to get angry with one another. Please infuse our hearts with grace to pour out over one another when we sin against each other. We pray we would repent and forgive each other as we pursue reconciliation. Please help us never to shame each other for our sins. Heavenly Father, will You show us how to gently restore each other after sin is exposed? We pray our love would cover sin just like Your love covers us. Lord, we know the marriage relationship is a picture of Christ's love for His bride, the church. We pray that those who see into our marriage see Your love reflected in the way we love each other. Our hearts' desire is that our marriage would be a testimony of Your loving-kindness and that others would witness Your wonderful working power in our lives. In Jesus's name we pray. Amen.

Above all, keep loving one another earnestly, since love covers a multitude of sins. **(1 PETER 4:8)**

REFINE US

Dear Lord, We exalt You! Thank You for giving us life. We know You have made us new creations in Christ. Lord, cleanse us and sanctify us in truth. Purify our hearts and minds so that we may be holy as You are holy. We rejoice knowing that You allow us to experience various trials that test our faith. Lord, fill us with understanding during these times, and help us respond to these tests and trials in a way that honors You. Our desire is that we would encourage and support one another through every hardship that comes our way. We pray You would use us to sharpen each other, to inspire each other, and to affirm each other. God, will You please refine our thinking, refine our communication, refine our belief, and refine every part of our lives? May we remain steadfast in faithfulness and abide in Your Word and walk in faith so we can continually bring You glory. In Jesus's name we pray. Amen.

In this you rejoice, though now for a little while, if necessary, you have been grieved by various trials, so that the tested genuineness of your faith—more precious than gold that perishes though it is tested by fire—may be found to result in praise and glory and honor at the revelation of Jesus Christ. **(1 PETER 1:6–7)**

OUR PURPOSE

Dear Lord, We know You created marriage as a testimony of Your power and grace, and that our marriage is a vessel for Your good will. Our greatest desire is to be unified in marriage to faithfully live out our days to please You. We pray You would give us a clear understanding of our purpose together. As we pursue our purpose, we ask You to strengthen our hearts and give us confidence to accomplish all that You have for us. No matter what circumstances we face together, we pray that we would trust You to work all things together for good. Thank You for the time we get to spend together: the conversations we have, the memories we make, and even the simplest moments of connection we share. Will You remind us to take advantage of the opportunities we have today to love each other in big and small ways? Please remind us that a significant part of our purpose in marriage is to encourage one another with the truth that You love us deeply. As we chase boldly after You together, may our love reflect Your love to a broken world. In Jesus's name we pray. Amen.

We know that for those who love God all things
work together for good, for those who are called
according to his purpose. **(ROMANS 8:28)**

SUPPORTING EACH OTHER

Dear Lord, Thank You for the gift of companion-ship. We are grateful to share life together, to support each other, to persevere together, and to grow alongside one another. Help us to be strong pillars of steadfastness and fountains of encouragement for one another. May our words be sincere and uplifting. May our hearts be tuned in to each other, capable of knowing what the other needs before a word ever expresses it. Holy Spirit, inspire us to know how to respond quickly to one another's needs and may we have the capacity to assist each other when possible. Will You stir up motivation in our hearts to love each other by praying for each other even when we don't know exactly what to pray? Please bless our marriage as we walk in obedience to Your Word. Please give us eyes to see where You are already working and the wisdom we need to join You in that work. May we cheer one another on as we keep in step with You. In Jesus's name we pray. Amen.

Let us consider how to stir up one another to love and good works. **(HEBREWS 10:24)**

FINDING HEALING

Dear Lord, We crave healing and restoration in our marriage. Will You open our eyes to the struggles of our pasts and help us find healing from anything hindering our growth or that has been left unresolved? In Jesus's name, remove any roots of bitterness or unforgiveness in our hearts. Lord, we desire to see each other as You see us. We pray You would heal us from any wounds we may have from our childhoods, anything that negatively affects how we live today. We invite You to purify our hearts, cleanse our minds, and heal us in any and every way we may need. We want to grow in our marriage, to be closer than ever before. Help us to remain strong in our relationship, knowing that You are our anchor. Thank You, Jesus, for healing us from our sin and covering us in Your righteousness. Thank You for the gift of salvation. May we remember daily the wounds You have already bound up and healed. Lord, make Your testimony evident in our lives and in our marriage so others would be encouraged to turn their eyes toward You. In Jesus's name we pray. Amen.

He himself bore our sins in his body on the tree, that we might die to sin and live to righteousness. By his wounds you have been healed. **(1 PETER 2:24)**

Help us to relearn what we have not learnt correctly. Uproot any wrong mindset, attitude, idea from us. Cast out any lies.

BUILDING CONFIDENCE

$Dear\ Lord,$ We acknowledge that our sufficiency in this life is from You. Thank You for adequately supplying our needs and blessing us with all You have given us. We desire to grow in confidence of Your provision, trusting You more. We also desire to grow in confidence of our understanding of Scripture. Please fill us with Your holy assurance so that doubt cannot flourish in our minds. Will You also build our confidence in our love for each other? Help us to intentionally affirm one another, and inspire us with words of encouragement to build up each other's confidence in our marriage. Lord, please help us to speak the truth in love with one another and in our conversations with others. Please increase our confidence in sharing Your gospel with others. May our faith expand as we recognize our security is in You alone. In Jesus's name we pray. Amen.

Not that we are sufficient in ourselves to claim anything as coming from us, but our sufficiency is from God. **(2 CORINTHIANS 3:5)**

11

BEING ON THE SAME PAGE

Dear Lord, Thank You for the unity we experience in marriage. Thank You for the way You have created the marriage covenant to bless us. We confess that we are not always on the same page with one another, which causes hurt. Because of our different perspectives and emotions on varying topics, we sometimes encounter tension in our relationship. Please help us navigate these moments with maturity, walking in the Spirit and not the flesh. We pray we will grow in our understanding of each other. Please help us to communicate respectfully, especially when tensions are high. May Your Holy Spirit intercede on our behalf and diffuse the intensity of our emotions in those hard moments. Please keep us united, even when we experience disagreement. Lord, we ask that You keep at the forefront of our minds the truth that we are one—help us to remember that we are not enemies, but rather teammates. Please show us how to lay aside our pride so we can be unified in marriage. Please help us recover during dissension and get back on the same page quickly. Let resolve and reconciliation be our aim. In Jesus's name we pray. Amen.

I appeal to you, brothers, by the name of our
Lord Jesus Christ, that all of you agree, and
that there be no divisions among you, but
that you be united in the same mind and the
same judgment. **(1 CORINTHIANS 1:10)**

SEEING GOD MOVE
IN OUR HEARTS

Dear Lord, Thank You for always moving, even when we don't see it. Thank You for caring for us in big and small ways. You consider every detail of our lives, and You know us better than we know ourselves. Open our eyes to all You are doing in us and in our marriage. We desire to grasp the full picture of how You are weaving together our love story. We want to see You move in our hearts so that we can give You glory. Once our eyes are opened to all You are doing, we can focus on all the good that is unfolding in our relationship instead of being consumed with the areas of marriage that frustrate us. May Your Holy Spirit teach us what we need to know to thrive in our relationships with You and with one another. Please reveal the parts of our lives and the parts of our marriage that You desire to transform, the parts we still need to surrender in faith. Please show us the sin in our lives so we may repent. Holy Spirit, lead us through each day as we pursue You and one another in love. In Jesus's name we pray. Amen.

The Helper, the Holy Spirit, whom the Father
will send in my name, he will teach you all
things and bring to your remembrance all
that I have said to you. **(JOHN 14:26)**

13

FORGIVENESS

𝒟*ear* ℒ*ord,* Keep our hearts tender to the grace You have gifted us. We know You have forgiven us for our countless sins—please help us to forgive ourselves. Will You remove the gut-wrenching shame and guilt we feel for the choices we've made? Holy Spirit, help us to continually forgive each other. We can't do it without You. We desire the courage to forgive and let go of the offenses that cause us pain. Lord, help us understand that our forgiveness should not be contingent on the other person confessing or changing their behavior first. Stir our hearts to freely forgive just as You have forgiven us. During reconciliation, we ask You to mend our hearts and pour Your peace over our thoughts toward each other. Humble us and remind us daily of the love You have for us. May Your name be magnified as we walk with one another in humility, faith, and love. In Jesus's name we pray. Amen.

Be kind to one another, tenderhearted,
forgiving one another, as God in Christ
forgave you. **(EPHESIANS 4:32)**

BEARING ONE ANOTHER'S BURDENS

Dear Lord, Thank You for the beautiful gift of our marriage relationship. We are blessed to share joys and sorrows with one another, to enjoy each other's company, and to endure life's circumstances alongside each other. Lord, we pray for the burdens concerning our hearts and consuming our thoughts today. We need help trusting You to lead us through them and to show us how to be a strong support to bear one another's burdens. Give us the stamina to persevere through any storm. Our hope is that we would be quick to encourage each other by sharing the wisdom from Scripture, whether we share it with our words in person, in a hand-written letter, or even in a brief text message. May we take advantage of every opportunity to remind each other of the truth from Your Word. Please give us the gift of gentleness as we face difficult situations, relationship strain, internal struggles, or any other burden that comes our way. May our hearts be open to receive affirmation from each other as we try to comfort each other when hard times persist. In Jesus's name we pray. Amen.

Bear one another's burdens, and so fulfill the law of Christ. **(GALATIANS 6:2)**

BEING CONTENT

Dear Lord, We confess we sometimes struggle with discontentment. When we are tempted in this way, please show us how to shift our perspectives and search for reasons to be grateful. In challenging moments, may we not dwell on our frustrations, but rather share with You our praises. We want to be quick to recognize the good in our lives and in our marriage. We don't want to take for granted all the simplest of miracles You have already given to us. Lord, we ask You to help our hearts be secure in You and in our marriage. Please help us to throw out our desire for things we don't need, and keep envious thoughts from taking root in us. May true peace fill our minds and joy fill our hearts. In Jesus's name we pray. Amen.

I have learned in whatever situation I am to be content. **(PHILIPPIANS 4:11)**

PUTTING GOD FIRST

Dear Lord, As we consider our day, we ask You to help us prioritize time spent abiding in Your Word. Please help us to keep You first above all other priorities. If there are idols in our lives, we ask You to remove them. Examine our hearts, God, and teach us to guard ourselves from making idols out of things such as work, social media, or even ideals like personal achievement and perfectionism. Tear down anything inside of us or in our lives that hinders us from loving You. May we put You first when we make decisions together, and help us to submit to Your will in everything. Lord, help our minds stay on You as we choose to keep in step with Your Spirit! Learning how to love You encourages growth in how we love each other. When we put You first in our lives, our marriage also reaps the benefit of walking in faithfulness. In Jesus's name we pray. Amen.

You shall have no other gods
before me. **(EXODUS 20:3)**

REFLECTING ON THE GOOD

Dear Lord, Thank You for Your goodness. Thank You for all the good You have done in our lives and in our marriage. We praise You for the incredible moments of intimacy we have experienced with each other. We have had the privilege of feeling deeply connected, experiencing the oneness You intended when You designed marriage. We ask You to bless us with new experiences of incredible emotional intimacy, as well as extraordinary physical intimacy. Please help us to lay aside any pride or selfish ways so that we can fully engage with one another. When we encounter difficult moments, will You help us to remember and reflect on all the good we have experienced in our relationship? Give us a clear perspective of the many seasons our marriage has endured and how You have used it all for good. Fill us with hope to cling to as we share with one another the vision we have for our future together. Lord, please motivate our hearts to seek after You and to seek Your presence continually. In Jesus's name we pray. Amen.

> *Seek the Lord and his strength;*
> *seek his presence continually!*
> *Remember the wondrous works that he has done.*
> **(PSALM 105:4–5)**

RECONCILING WITH
EACH OTHER

Dear Lord, We are grateful for the time You have given us to spend together. Please help us not to waste it by being angry or upset with one another. When there is tension between us, we ask You to destroy it. We want our unity to be indestructible. May peace continually overflow from our hearts and minds. Lord, we ask You to help us love each other better every day. During times of conflict, we ask You, Lord, to guide us toward reconciliation. Give us the courage to expose any sin affecting our relationship so we may repent and reconcile. Lord, when we walk in humility and apologize for any hurt we caused, will You help us to listen to one another? Our desire is to receive each other's apologies and truly forgive one another. Please help us hear, see, and comprehend the pain that exists in conflict. In those moments, we ask You to lead us to quickly lay down our pride and courageously seek restoration in our relationship. Give us the right words to speak and actions that prove our desire to reconcile. Strengthen our bond of unity as we choose reconciliation. In Jesus's name we pray. Amen.

If your brother sins against you, go and tell him his fault, between you and him alone. If he listens to you, you have gained your brother. **(MATTHEW 18:15)**

LIGHT IN A DARK WORLD

𝒟ear ℒord, Thank You for the creation of the world. We can clearly see the contrast between light and darkness. In the same way, help us to clearly know the difference between right and wrong, righteousness and sin. Although there is a vast amount of good that can be measured and experienced in this world, there is also a great amount of darkness. Help us to be a light in the darkness, and do not let the darkness overcome us. As we choose righteousness over sin, we are confident our faith will be evident to others. We pray for an increase of courage to stand boldly for Your truth. We know Your light in our lives will continue to grow brighter as we abide in Scripture. Please continue to transform our character so that we would be an honest representation of Your work in this world. Lord, we want our marriage to be a light that leads others closer to You. In Jesus's name we pray. Amen.

The light shines in the darkness, and the darkness has not overcome it. **(JOHN 1:5)**

LIFE-GIVING WORDS

𝒟ear 𝒧ord, Thank You for the gift of words and the ability to use them to understand each other. Our words are so powerful. We know they can build up or tear down. Help us use our words to build each other up, build up our marriage, and build up Your kingdom. We want to speak life-giving words every day to remind one another of the truth. Please help us to choose our words wisely and to hold back words that could be a source of destruction. Please guard us from the pain of miscommunication as we grow in our ability to understand each other. When there is miscommunication or words are used to tear each other down, please help us to humbly walk with each other and use our words to get back to a place of understanding. May our words be seeds of life that we sow to produce fruitfulness in our marriage. Give us words of encouragement and affirmation for each other every day. Lord, help us to be quick to use our words in a way that honors You. In Jesus's name we pray. Amen.

Death and life are in the power of the tongue,
and those who love it will eat its fruits.
(PROVERBS 18:21)

LIVING DEBT-FREE

Dear Lord, Thank You for the times of abundance and for the leaner times when we have experienced Your faithfulness. You have always carried us through. We want to be good stewards, wisely caring for everything You've given us. We submit all that we have and ask You to use it to do Your will. Give us wisdom as we consider how to spend within our means. We long to live debt-free and to owe no one anything, except our indebtedness to love others well. Holy Spirit, please help us not only to pay attention to our bills and stay on top of our accounts, exercising wisdom, but also to be openhanded with our money, giving generously. When we want to make purchases that don't align with living debt-free, please help us to lovingly and respectfully encourage each other to stick to the plan. Make us a couple who trusts You with our finances and who works together as a team for Your glory. In Jesus's name we pray. Amen.

Owe no one anything, except to love each other, for the one who loves another has fulfilled the law. **(ROMANS 13:8)**

MARRIAGE GOALS

Dear Lord, Thank You for the opportunity to consider our marriage and how we hope to grow together. As we think about our relationship goals, we invite Your Holy Spirit to lead us to aim for things that build up our marriage. Help us focus on key areas such as communication, finances, and intimacy. We pray that our plans to be diligent in these areas would lead to abundant blessing in our marriage. Our hope is to set our eyes and hearts on ways we can mature in our relationship. We are confident that as we grow together, our marriage will reflect Your amazing love. Please help us to listen to and respect one another's dreams and desires for our marriage. We submit to You the goals we are aiming for. We believe these marriage goals will bless our union and help us fulfill the work of ministry You have for us. Will You show us how to prioritize the goal of reading Your Word daily, hoping to find comfort in it and striving to obey it? May all our goals align with Your will as we diligently seek to fulfill Your purpose for our life together. In Jesus's name we pray. Amen.

> *The plans of the diligent lead surely to*
> *abundance,*
> *but everyone who is hasty comes only to*
> *poverty.* **(PROVERBS 21:5)**

TAKING EVERY
THOUGHT CAPTIVE

Dear Lord, Like a blanket that brings comfort and warmth, we ask You to cover our minds with Your remarkable peace. Lord, help us take every thought captive to obey Christ. Plenty of things in this world try to consume our thoughts. Every day, we are tempted to worry over our lives and concern ourselves with what might come. In Jesus's name, we ask You to keep us from dwelling on thoughts that stir up anxiety, fear, or doubt. Protect us against the bombardment of fearful thinking, and guard our every thought. Our marriage relationship is often the place our thoughts are exposed, whether intentionally or unintentionally. And our actions often reflect what we have been thinking or what we believe. May our interactions with and responses toward each other be based in faithfulness, love, and trust. May our thoughts toward each other be pure and true, affirming our commitment to love unconditionally. Thank You, Lord, for affirming Your love for us in the Bible. Let our minds dwell on Your Word, Your goodness, and Your promises throughout today. In Jesus's name we pray. Amen.

We destroy arguments and every lofty opinion raised against the knowledge of God, and take every thought captive to obey Christ. **(2 CORINTHIANS 10:5)**

MARRIAGE IS AWESOME

Dear Lord, Thank You for guiding us in Scripture and showing us how we should walk together in marriage. We love our marriage! Marriage is awesome! Marriage is awesome because it is an intimate relationship that shows the power of unity. Although we don't always feel unified, we know the truth that we are one. Thank You for helping us through tough moments and humbling us and helping us choose to reconcile. We have been through a variety of seasons together, and we long to see our marriage as an incredible blessing from You through all the highs and lows. May we always treat one another as a gift from You. When we are tempted to think negatively of each other, we ask You to protect our marriage and shift our perspectives. Humble us! Holy Spirit, please remind us every day that we are one flesh, brought together by You. May Your will be done in us and through us. In Jesus's name we pray. Amen.

"And the two shall become one flesh." So they are no longer two but one flesh. **(MARK 10:8)**

BEST FRIENDS

Dear Lord, Thank You for the gift of friendship in our marriage. We ask You to show us how to cultivate our friendship and inspire us to find creative ways to spend time together. Help us enjoy each other and increase our desire to be fully present with each other, and present more often. May we be willing to try new things for each other, not letting self-ishness determine how we spend our time. Lord, transform our hearts so that we consider the other person more highly than ourselves. We want to outdo each other with kindness. Show us of the value of playing, being silly, and laughing with each other. And as good as it is to be playful, we also pray our friend-ship deepens as we comfort and support one another as needed. Strengthen our friendship as we seek to bless one another, trust one another, and build each other up. May our love help us stick close and walk together in confidence and in truth. We yearn to be each other's best friend. In Jesus's name we pray. Amen.

A man of many companions may come to ruin,
but there is a friend who sticks closer
than a brother. **(PROVERBS 18:24)**

COMPASSION FOR
EACH OTHER

Dear Lord, We want to be a couple who always seeks peace in our relationship and who has compassion for each other. Help us walk with one another in an understanding way, a humble way, a patient way. Please fill us with wisdom and help us to understand what the other is enduring. In addition to giving us greater insight, please show us how we can support one another emotionally and physically. Holy Spirit, we invite You to remind us of the ways we can bear patiently with each other. In moments when we have frustrations or complaints with one another, would You help us to forgive just as You have forgiven us? Our desire is that compassion would be a deeply rooted part of our character and a defining mark of our marriage. May we be kind and loving toward one another just as You have been toward us. We love You and we pray our marriage honors You. In Jesus's name we pray. Amen.

Put on then, as God's chosen ones, holy and beloved, compassionate hearts, kindness, humility, meekness, and patience, bearing with one another and, if one has a complaint against another, forgiving each other; as the Lord has forgiven you, so you also must forgive. **(COLOSSIANS 3:12–13)**

RECONNECTING AFTER CHALLENGES

Dear Lord, Thank You for the challenges we experience as a couple. As much as we wish we could experience a pain-free, perfect life together, we know the challenges we experience test our hearts and give us the opportunity to grow. Keep our hearts humble so that You can work through us in those difficult situations. Help us improve at reconciliation as we practice sincere apologies and forgiveness. Conflicts and disagreements are strenuous to our relationship, but we pray we develop our ability to reconnect after challenges. Holy Spirit, during contentious times, immediately guide us to come to You in prayer for our marriage. We submit our wills to You and plead for greater understanding of each other. May we live in such harmony that we glorify You with one voice. Lord, we ask You to bind us together so that our marriage is stronger than ever and able to endure through any challenge. In Jesus's name we pray. Amen.

May the God of endurance and encouragement grant you to live in such harmony with one another, in accord with Christ Jesus, that together you may with one voice glorify the God and Father of our Lord Jesus Christ. **(ROMANS 15:5-6)**

LIVING WITH UNDERSTANDING

Dear Lord, Thank You for loving us, even when we feel unlovable. Your love continues to transform us. Sometimes we struggle to feel loved and understood by each other. Will You help us courageously share our hearts with one another? Holy Spirit, please urge us to be more transparent, connecting more regularly with each other. Please remove any temptation to hide or keep secrets from each other. Give us the strength to bring everything into the light so that the Enemy does not have a foothold in our relationship. Lord, please help us to create a safe and comfortable environment so we can be honest with each other. We humbly ask You to make us better at communicating with each other. We confess we aren't always quick to listen and slow to speak. Lord, will You increase our ability to listen? May we give each other the benefit of the doubt and support each other in every circumstance we encounter together. In Jesus's name we pray. Amen.

Husbands, live with your wives in an understanding way, showing honor to the woman as the weaker vessel, since they are heirs with you of the grace of life, so that your prayers may not be hindered. **(1 PETER 3:7)**

MAKE US ACTIVE

Dear Lord, Thank You for the life in our bodies. Please make us a couple who encourages one another toward intentionally healthy lifestyles so that we are fit and able to do ministry for Your kingdom. Use our family and friends to send us encouragement to eat well and take diligent care of our bodies. Lord, show us how to make exercise a priority so that we keep our bodies strong. We yearn to be an active couple who enjoys doing activities together, knowing that these types of experiences affirm healthy living. Holy Spirit, remind us that we were bought with a price, the price of Christ's sacrifice that He made in His body for us. Please motivate our hearts to endure when our flesh is tempted to give up. Instill in us self-discipline so that in every choice we make, we glorify You in our bodies. In Jesus's name we pray. Amen.

Do you not know that your body is a temple
of the Holy Spirit within you, whom you
have from God? You are not your own, for
you were bought with a price. So glorify God
in your body. **(1 CORINTHIANS 6:19–20)**

FEELING REJECTED

Dear Lord, Thank You for receiving us as adoptive heirs. Thank You for Your gracious love. Lord, please help us never to doubt Your love for us. We don't want to wrestle with insecure thoughts of feeling rejected by You. We know these feelings are a lie because You have not rejected us. When we think You have rejected us, please quiet all those thoughts by Your transformative love. May Your peace fill us up and comfort us. Please help us to stand firm on the Word of Your testimony. Lord, will You also help us not to wrestle with insecure thoughts of rejection in our marriage? And help us not to reject each other, even in the simplest of things. Everything we choose to do and say sends a message about what we think of each other. Remind us that we are one in marriage. Affirm our love for each other every day. In Jesus's name, may our actions and our words make clear the love we have for each other, and may our relationship become strong. Develop confidence in us of the love and devotion we have for each other. In Jesus's name we pray. Amen.

The LORD your God is in your midst,
a mighty one who will save;
he will rejoice over you with gladness;
he will quiet you by his love;
he will exult over you with loud singing.
(ZEPHANIAH 3:17)

PATIENCE WITH
EACH OTHER

Dear Lord, Mature us in areas where we are weak—specifically we ask You to give us more patience toward one another. May we be slow to speak, slow to become angry, and not quickly offended by each other. In moments that catch us off guard, where sin is present, or something hurtful is done, we ask Your Holy Spirit to help us not to explode with emotion, and instead fill us with self-control. When there is an offense, help us to patiently wait for each other to process the wrong and be ready to reconcile. We also pray we would not put off reconciliation, but instead, be mindful of what needs to take place to feel unified again. Being patient with each other is a way to show true love. We hope that as we encourage each other and help each other patiently, we would bring You honor. Make us a couple who listens well to one another and responds with an outpouring of amazing grace and patience, blessing each other in this way. In Jesus's name we pray. Amen.

We urge you, brothers, admonish the idle,
encourage the fainthearted, help the weak, be
patient with them all. **(1 THESSALONIANS 5:14)**

REFLECTING GOD'S LOVE

Dear Lord, Thank You for the deep, never-ending love You have poured out over us. Your unconditional love has radically changed us, and Your amazing grace has transformed us. Our marriage would not be where it is today if we did not know Your true love. Please make us a couple who is just as faithful and devoted in the way we love. Just as Jesus Christ loves His bride, the church, we hope our unity, faithfulness, and affection toward each other reflect that same awe-inspiring love. Our prayer is that we would choose to love each other sacrificially as You have loved. Help us to be deeply devoted to each other with sincerity and truth. Please write Your Word on our hearts so that we never forget how to love each other. May our marriage be a testimony to the world of the power of Your love. In Jesus's name we pray. Amen.

We have come to know and to believe the
love that God has for us. God is love, and
whoever abides in love abides in God, and
God abides in him. **(1 JOHN 4:16)**

TRUTH TELLING

Dear Lord, May we never take for granted the access we have to the truth, Your Holy Word. Please help us study Scripture and know it well. Lord, make us truth tellers, proclaiming Your gospel to one another, especially when we feel weak, struggle with sin, or have a difficult day. Holy Spirit, please bring Your words to the front of our minds so that we can encourage one another with Scripture. As we stand firm on Your Word, trusting it to guide us, our desire is that we would always be honest with one another. If we are tempted to lie, we invite Your Holy Spirit to convict our hearts to only tell the truth. In Jesus's name, make us resolute to put away falsehood. When we are tempted to hide information or mislead each other, will You encourage us to share openly? If we lie, fill us with courage to expose the truth and seek reconciliation. Humble us so that we live honest lives that represent Your truth. In Jesus's name we pray. Amen.

Having put away falsehood, let each one of you
speak the truth with his neighbor, for we are
members one of another. **(EPHESIANS 4:25)**

CELEBRATING VICTORIES

Dear Lord, Thank You for every big and small way You are faithfully moving in our marriage. Thank You for the record of miracles You have shared with us in Scripture that encourages us to believe in what You are capable of doing. We trust You are still working miracles in this world every single day. We acknowledge that our marriage has benefitted from the way You lead us to victory, growing our desire to pray together, unifying us, and giving us the strength to persevere during challenging times. Please continue to develop our relationship, Lord. Please make us humbler, gentler, kinder, and more patient with one another. Thank You for the victories over sin You have helped us to overcome. Lord, we praise You for setting us free from the bondage of sin. Open our eyes to the spiritual milestones we have reached so that we don't overlook Your power in our lives. Help us take time to celebrate the growth we have experienced—for every victory won, every prayer answered, every hardship overcome, every stronghold defeated, and every goal achieved deserves celebration. We praise You for every win. In You, we are more than conquerors! In Jesus's name we pray. Amen.

In all these things we are more than conquerors through him who loved us. **(ROMANS 8:37)**

PROTECTION AGAINST EVIL

Dear Lord, We know the Enemy prowls around like a lion looking for a way to devour us. Keep him far from our marriage. Thank You for being our refuge. Thank You for protecting us from the Evil One. Lord, please guard our relationship and destroy the Enemy's attempts to have a stronghold in our marriage. You are our faithful defender! We praise You for keeping us safe from the attacks of the Enemy. May our marriage be resilient to endure this harsh world. No matter what circumstances we face, we petition Your Holy Spirit to equip us to remain steadfast. Please strengthen our faith and show us how to protect one another's hearts. In Jesus's name, we pray the Enemy does not win in tempting us to do wrong in our marriage. Lord, if our union is rocked, making it difficult to trust each other or feel close to one another, will You please hold us together? Help us to stay alert and remain prayerful. In Jesus's name we pray. Amen.

The Lord is faithful. He will establish you and guard you against the evil one. **(2 THESSALONIANS 3:3)**

GUARDING OUR HEARTS

Dear Lord, Will You show us what it fully means to guard our hearts? Help us understand the spiritual and practical ways of guarding our hearts. Holy Spirit, please speak to us about areas of our lives where we leave our hearts unguarded. May we not leave any doors open for sin to come in and take root in our lives. Please help us to be sensitive to the way You are sanctifying us. When idols or priorities in our lives are a detriment to our relationship with You or our marriage, please eliminate them, God. For any areas of our lives we haven't submitted to You, we submit them to You now in reverence. Make us quick to respond to Your Holy Spirit as You help us navigate righteous living. May we never tempt each other to sin. Please teach us how to guard one another's hearts by directing each other to follow Your Word. In Jesus's name we pray. Amen.

Above all else, guard your heart,
for everything you do flows from it.
(PROVERBS 4:23 NIV)

SUPPORT FOR OUR MARRIAGE

Dear Lord, Our hope is that whatever we go through as a couple, we would be surrounded by others who cheer us on, creating a pillar of support for our marriage. Please send people to encourage us in our marriage. We plead with You to help us build a strong community of believers who will affirm our relationship. Lord, we pray that those we trust would flood us with marriage wisdom and encouragement to never give up hope. Remind us daily that we are not alone in our marital struggles. May no challenge or trial tear us down or separate us. Lord, help us to have a healthy marriage, as well as a healthy perspective of the reality of marriage. Some days we seem to complement each other, with peace and unity abounding. Other days we find ourselves in strife, fighting against each other and holding our marriage in contempt. Please help us to embrace these marriage moments, having confidence that You established our marriage and have equipped us to endure through every season. Especially during difficult times, we hope others will come alongside us, rallying with us to believe what is true and to remain steadfast. In Jesus's name we pray. Amen.

Where there is no guidance, a people falls,
but in an abundance of counselors there
is safety. **(PROVERBS 11:14)**

DIFFICULT SITUATIONS

𝒟ear 𝓛ord, Experiencing difficult situations is never easy. Yet You sustain us. You equip us to walk through hard times, and You give us peace that guards our hearts and minds. Thank You for Your peace that transcends all understanding. Lord, when we go through hard circumstances, we ask You to help us to love one another well, supporting each other and intentionally pointing each other's hearts back to You. When we are tempted to be short with each other, please show us how to take the next right step, maintaining self-control over our emotions. When we share how we are feeling with each other, will You please help us to have compassion? May the challenges we face and the way we respond in the moment strengthen the bond of our marriage, giving us hope for the future. We continue to grow in our confidence that with You, we can make it through anything! Please increase our faith. Keep us aware of how You can use all our circumstances for Your good. May our hearts never waver in trusting You, and may fear be far removed from our thoughts. Thank You for extending Your arm to uphold us. We want our faith in You and our faithfulness in marriage to be a light in this world, illuminating who You are and all that You are doing. In Jesus's name we pray. Amen.

Fear not, for I am with you;
be not dismayed, for I am your God;
I will strengthen you, I will help you,
I will uphold you with my righteous
right hand. **(ISAIAH 41:10)**

CONNECTING WITH FAMILY

Dear Lord, Thank You for family—our families of origin, our in-laws, our extended family, and our chosen family. Please help us make it a priority to connect with them, check on them, visit with them and host them if we can, and share Your love with them. With every opportunity You provide, may we have the courage to share Your gospel with them. We want our families to see You in our marriage, and we want our marriage to be an encouragement to them. Please help us to find time to spend together and build up our relationships with our loved ones. Lord, we ask You to help us not to be easily offended by our families. If any of these relationships experience brokenness or strain, we ask Your Holy Spirit to lead us in the way of reconciliation. May peace and unity dwell among us. In every moment we spend with our family, we hope and pray we would have a truly enjoyable experience. Please use us to bless our loved ones and to draw them closer to You each day. In Jesus's name we pray. Amen.

Behold, how good and pleasant it is
when brothers dwell in unity!
(PSALM 133:1)

GOD'S LOVE FOR US

Dear Lord, Your love is steadfast, and Your mercy and grace are gifts. Thank You for sending Your Son, Jesus Christ, and allowing Him to endure what He did on the cross so that we could be set free from sin. Thank You for salvation. Thank You for eternal life. We worship You! Lord, remind us daily of Jesus and all that He accomplished in His death and resurrection. When persecution comes our way, please strengthen our hearts and help us not to be shaken. Holy Spirit, show us how to walk in humility, meekness, and compassion, just like Jesus walked. We want to love like He loves. Lord, transform our hearts and implant Your character within us. We ask that our love for one another be sacrificial. May our love be evident in the way we serve one another. In our obedience and devotion to You, Lord, help us walk in Your example of how to love. In Jesus's name we pray. Amen.

For God so loved the world, that he gave his only Son, that whoever believes in him should not perish but have eternal life. **(JOHN 3:16)**

CRY FOR HELP

𝒟ear ℒord, We have continually relied on You in our faith and in our marriage. It would have been impossible to make it this far without You. Thank You for being faithful and reliable. We praise You for hearing our prayers and responding. Thank You for the gift of prayer, allowing us bring our needs before You. Right now, we cry out to You and ask You to help us overcome the challenges in our relationship. We know we will go through difficult times, and we know our flesh will be tested. Please rescue us when the pain threatens to undo us. Lord, will You please meet us right where we are and tell us what next step to take to restore our relationship? Humble us! Revive us! We beg You to intercede in our marriage. Lord, deliver us from our current troubles. We love each other and long for our marriage to be in a better place. Fill us with Your hope, anchor our hearts through this storm, and cover our minds with Your peace. In Jesus's name we pray. Amen.

When the righteous cry for help, the LORD hears
and delivers them out of all their
troubles. **(PSALM 34:17)**

HEALING FROM OUR BROKENNESS

Dear Lord, Thank You for freeing us from the snare of sin. Thank You for reminding us of who we are, especially when our pasts tempt us to feel insecure. Parts of our pasts are broken. Parts of our character are broken. Some of our ways of thinking are broken. Parts of our marriage are also broken. But despite our brokenness, we identify with Christ and Him crucified. When we feel shattered or discouraged, may we lay down our thoughts and feelings about it and instead dwell on how Christ was broken and redeemed to save us. Please remind us of all the ways You have healed our brokenness and have saved us in moments when we felt unbearably crushed. Continue to heal us from past wounds and hurts, especially the ones we have experienced in marriage. Lord, transform our lives so that our past experiences no longer define us or impact the way we think of one another. In Jesus's name we pray. Amen.

The Lord is near to the brokenhearted
and saves the crushed in spirit.
(PSALM 34:18)

HAVING MORE FUN

Dear Lord, Thank You for Your beautiful creation. Thank You for the many opportunities You give us to enjoy Your world and enjoy one another. We want to be intentional about having fun together, which cultivates friendship in marriage. Please help us prioritize going on dates and spending quality time together. Inspire our hearts to consider the ways we can enjoy each other's company, such as exploring nature, trying new foods, or finding a hobby to do together. May we laugh more, interact more, and converse more as we discover ways to incorporate fun into our work and daily life. Lord, encourage our hearts to be light and flexible. Help us make each other smile, especially when we experience consistently heavy days. Lord, will You help us make room in our schedules and our finances to take pleasure in this life together? Please help us to pursue one another in extraordinary ways. Our hope and prayer is that our willingness to have more fun will affirm our love for each other. Fill us up with Your utmost joy, and may it flow out of us. Make us into a couple full of life and light. In Jesus's name we pray. Amen.

Everyone should eat and drink and take pleasure in all his toil—this is God's gift to man. **(ECCLESIASTES 3:13)**

LORD, WE NEED YOU

Dear Lord, In this moment, we humble ourselves and draw near to Your throne of grace in confidence. Thank You for mercy and grace in our times of need. Lord, we need You as our provider. We need You as our protector. We need You as our healer. We need You as our redeemer. We need You as our peacekeeper. We need You as our navigator. We need You as our Savior. Lord, we need You in every capacity that exists, and we praise You for being our helper. Lord, teach us how to love and how to communicate better. Transform our hearts and continually refine us. Lord, we need You every day. Please cover us with Your peace and fill us with Your strength so that we may persevere in every way. Lord, we ask You to use us today to fulfill Your purpose. In Jesus's name we pray. Amen.

*Let us then with confidence draw near to the throne
of grace, that we may receive mercy and find
grace to help in time of need.* **(HEBREWS 4:16)**

WORKING TOGETHER

𝒟*ear* ℒ*ord,* Thank You for the opportunities You have given us to work. Thank You for bringing unity of mind in what we aim to achieve together, whether that be financial goals, relationship goals, or ministry goals. We acknowledge the beauty and gift of working alongside one another in marriage. We are grateful that we are not alone and appreciate the companionship we share. Thank You for Your design of marriage. Thank You for creating us uniquely, with abilities that complement one another. Lord, open our eyes to the ways we help each other. Fill us with gratitude for the talents we are able to exercise when we work together. Will You give us more opportunities to work together so that we may reflect Your testimony of love? Please continue to mature and develop our communication so we avoid contentious arguments. While working together, we want to respect one another, including how each one of us thinks the work should get done. May unity and peace overflow from our hearts as we pursue all that You have for us to do together. In Jesus's name we pray. Amen.

Then the LORD *God said, "It is not good that*
the man should be alone; I will make him
a helper fit for him." **(GENESIS 2:18)**

SOFTEN OUR HEARTS

Dear Lord, We confess we have sometimes let frustration and anger toward one another crowd our hearts and minds. We acknowledge we have let our emotions, including bitterness, harden our hearts toward each other. Yet this is not our desire for marriage. We want to grow in this area of our relationship. Lord, please show us how to resolve and remove our frustrations and to tear down any walls that keep us from experiencing true intimacy. In Jesus's name, soften our hearts toward each other. Help us to be transparent as we share our thoughts and feelings. As we make ourselves known, we ask Your Holy Spirit to guide us in our communication. Destroy any pride in our hearts, and keep our hearts from being hardened again. Please keep them tender, believing the best about each other, so that we aren't quickly offended by each other. May our love for each other grow deep and wide, leaving no room for bitterness to take root. In Jesus's name we pray. Amen.

I will give you a new heart, and a new spirit
I will put within you. And I will remove
the heart of stone from your flesh and give
you a heart of flesh. **(EZEKIEL 36:26)**

TRUSTING IN GOD

Dear Lord, You are trustworthy. Our hope is to be trustworthy and reliable like You are. May our character reflect Your character. At every opportunity, may we prove we are trustworthy by walking in integrity. In circumstances that challenge our beliefs and make us feel spiritually uncomfortable, please help us to seek the truth in Scripture and trust You more. Sometimes our weaknesses get in the way of trusting You with our lives, our relationships, our finances, and our possessions. We often convince ourselves that we are in full control of our lives, even though we know we actually aren't. We fret, we worry, and we get frustrated by our circumstances. Holy Spirit, please remind us every single day, regardless of our circumstances, to trust in You. Don't allow us to grow weary or fainthearted. We yearn to honor You with our lives and believe You are for us and for our marriage. We praise You, and we praise the goodness of Your Holy Word. In Jesus's name we pray. Amen.

> When I am afraid,
> I put my trust in you.
> In God, whose word I praise,
> in God I trust; I shall not be afraid.
> What can flesh do to me?
> **(PSALM 56:3-4)**

PURSUING HOLINESS

Dear Lord, Will You uncover sin in areas of our lives that we need to repent of? Will You refine us and shape us into Your image? Holy Spirit, as we read the Word, please guide our hearts, impart Your wisdom, and lead us in the way of righteousness. Help us pursue holiness in our lives and in our marriage. When we are struggling with sin in any area of our lives, when we are failing to live in purity, when we are resisting Your leading away from sin, please convict our hearts. Take control of our thoughts. Break through the barrier of pride that hinders our walk with You. We invite You to help us live in obedience to Your Word. As we abide in Your Word, we pray we grow in our understanding of all that You have commanded us. Holy Spirit, teach us, correct us, and train us up so that we are equipped for every good work. We believe our marriage is a good work You have set before us. May it be a testimony of the work You are doing in us and through us. In Jesus's name we pray. Amen.

All Scripture is breathed out by God and profitable for teaching, for reproof, for correction, and for training in righteousness, that the man of God may be complete, equipped for every good work. **(2 TIMOTHY 3:16–17)**

TRUE WORSHIP

Dear Lord, Thank You for the art of worship and the unique way it brings You glory. Thank You for providing a means of expressing our love and admiration for You. May we worship without hindrance of sin or insecure thoughts. God, we want our whole lives to reflect true worship. Worship requires submission, ardent adoration, and love. Lord, captivate our hearts as we praise You. Our desire is to worship You every day. Please help us encourage one another to exalt You readily. Inspire us with new praise and worship that is true. If we use worship in a way that glorifies ourselves or fulfills our own needs, please change our hearts. Purify our worship. We humbly pray that our worship would be done in spirit and in truth. May we confess Your name and Your good deeds before others. May Your name be magnified in our lives and in our marriage as we worship You with pure hearts. In Jesus's name we pray. Amen.

God is spirit, and those who worship him must worship in spirit and truth. **(JOHN 4:24)**

WALKING IN THE SPIRIT

Dear Lord, Thank You for Your Holy Spirit, who convicts our hearts and gently draws us toward repentance and reconciliation. Help us walk according to Your Holy Word while keeping in step with Your Holy Spirit. As we abide in Your Word and consider how Jesus walked, help us walk in that same way. Lead us to choose righteousness over sin. Refine our thinking and intentions so that we love one another as Jesus loves. Lord, we ask You right now to show us how to walk with each other in a compassionate and caring way. Sometimes we aren't in sync with each other and can't seem to find a good rhythm. Please renew our hearts and help us to take the next right step with each other. May the fruit of Your Holy Spirit be evident in our lives, and may it bless our marriage relationship. In Jesus's name we pray. Amen.

Whoever says he abides in him ought to walk in the same way in which he walked. **(1 JOHN 2:6)**

INTIMACY

$Dear$ $Lord,$ Thank You for the intimacy You created to exist in the bounds of marriage. Thank You for the moments of intimacy we have experienced in our relationship and for the ones we will experience in the future. We are grateful to know we belong to one another. We have a responsibility to fulfill some of each other's needs that no one else in this world has the right to fulfill. Establish our commitment to marriage firmly in our hearts. May our pursuit of an intimate marriage be dynamic and encompass both the emotional and physical elements of this gift. We desire to give our full attention and full affection to one another. Give us courage to embrace togetherness, sharing our hearts, minds, and bodies, even sometimes when we don't feel like it. Holy Spirit, show both of us how to be initiators of intimacy, and prepare us to join in and participate when one of us bravely takes that step of initiation. We want to use our time together to understand each other better so that our intimacy reaches a place we have never experienced before. May our closeness, our unity, and our oneness increase and contribute to a thriving marriage. In Jesus's name we pray. Amen.

My beloved is mine, and I am his.
(SONG OF SOLOMON 2:16)

OUR JOBS

Dear Lord, Thank You for instilling in us the desire to work. Please help us honor You with our jobs, what we choose to do to make a living. Lord, make us content and diligent in our jobs and to be grateful for the opportunity to work. Make us a couple who is a light to those we work with. May we never compare our responsibilities with those of others, complain about what is required of us, or covet the job of another. Fill us with integrity. Help us grow in our knowledge about the work we do. Show us how to invest our efforts so that we continually progress in our work and in our understanding. Please help us trust You and rely on You to help us navigate decisions that have to do with our employment. We pray our jobs never become a hindrance or source of contention in our marriage. Please teach us how to joyfully support and encourage one another in our jobs. May Your favor be upon us and upon our marriage as You establish the work of our hands. In Jesus's name we pray. Amen.

Let the favor of the Lord our God be upon us,
and establish the work of our hands
upon us;
yes, establish the work of our hands!
(PSALM 90:17)

ENCOURAGEMENT
FOR TODAY

Dear Lord, Help us remember to run to You more
often and sooner than we have in the past. We want to seek You
every day, with our eyes open to all the ways You are working in our lives—especially in our marriage. Align our hearts
with Your will. Lord, please humble us and help us to remain in
submission to You. No matter what today holds, we claim Your
Word as an encouragement to us. Holy Spirit, lead us to share
Scripture with one another to extinguish any lies or insecurities that might rise up in us. May the passage we share hold a
specific message that would encourage us for anything we face
today. Lord, inspire us to encourage each other as well as those
we interact with today. May our marriage be an encouragement
to our family, friends, and even strangers. We long for love,
unity, and peace to abound. In Jesus's name we pray. Amen.

Every word of God proves true;
he is a shield to those who take refuge
in him. **(PROVERBS 30:5)**

READING SCRIPTURE TOGETHER

Dear Lord, Thank You for Your Holy Word. Thank You for the admonition in Your Word to let Your Word dwell richly in us. Lord, please write Your Word on our hearts, and help us have excellent memory of Scripture. Thank You for the opportunity to read the Bible together. In moments when we don't know what to read, let Your Holy Spirit impress upon our hearts where to start. In moments when our flesh is tempted to choose other priorities over reading Your Word, convict us and keep us close to You. Please help us keep You at the center of our marriage, and make reading Your Word and praying together a habit we refuse to break. We lay aside the reasons and excuses we make for not doing these things on a regular basis. We know that reading Scripture will remind us of Your will and Your ways. We desire to grow closer to You and closer to each other in this way. May You be glorified as we read Scripture together. In Jesus's name we pray. Amen.

Let the word of Christ dwell in you richly,
teaching and admonishing one another in
all wisdom, singing psalms and hymns and
spiritual songs, with thankfulness in your
hearts to God. **(COLOSSIANS 3:16)**

THANKFULNESS

Dear Lord, Thank You for sending Your Son as a propitiation for our sin. You have forgiven us and reconciled us to Yourself. We are grateful for the way You love us and for the love we share in marriage. We are also thankful for the many circumstances we have experienced together. Please help us remain humble, thankful, and aware of all You have done for us and in us. May we acknowledge Your wonderful works and praise You every day as we remember the miracle and mystery of how You have made us new creations in Christ Jesus. Thank You for the promises in Your Word and for the promised gift of eternal life. Our marriage is another gift. Will You help us to be grateful for one another? Please fill our minds with thoughts of goodness and thankfulness for the things we appreciate about our marriage. We also ask You to motivate us to tell each other aspects of our marriage that we're thankful for. This will greatly affirm our love for each other. May thankfulness and gratitude be evident in our marriage as we follow You and fulfill Your will. In Jesus's name we pray. Amen.

Give thanks in all circumstances; for this is the will of God in Christ Jesus for you. **(1 THESSALONIANS 5:18)**

OUR BODIES ARE
FOR EACH OTHER

Dear Lord, Thank You for the way we get to express our love for each other in marriage. Thank You for the gift of physical touch. The way You designed our bodies to feel close to each other through touch is amazing. Help us to show more physical affection with one another. We want to take the time to hold hands, hug, and cherish one another in more intimate ways. Please make our hearts receptive to physical touch when one of us initiates, and grow our understanding of the importance of engaging with each other through physical touch. We know how affirming affection can be, and our desire is to experience more physical intimacy in our marriage. Thank You for sharing in Your Word the truth that in marriage we do not have exclusive authority over our own bodies. We are accountable to one another. In marriage we have a responsibility to care for our bodies and share them with each other. Please help us to walk this out with grace. Remind us that our bodies are a gift for each other to enjoy. Lord, please help us respect one another's bodies and find joy in using our bodies to bless each other. In Jesus's name we pray. Amen.

The wife does not have authority over her own body, but the husband does. Likewise the husband does not have authority over his own body, but the wife does. **(1 CORINTHIANS 7:4)**

EXPLORING TOGETHER

Dear Lord, Thank You for this beautiful world You have created. Thank You for the opportunities You give us to explore nature, whether it is a brief walk or a longer hike. We love being able to see and experience all that You have made. Being outside reminds us of Your creativity and Your power. Soften our hearts to be receptive when one of us plans an outdoor activity. We want to prioritize going outside together and to take advantage of those opportunities to explore. Give us creativity as we plan fun outdoor activities and marvel at the beauty we discover. Make us flexible when unplanned and spontaneous adventures come up. Please help us to unplug from technology so it doesn't hinder us from getting outside. We long to explore together more often and desire it to be one of the many ways we enjoy each other's company and make memories together. We pray that our open-air adventures would cultivate and bless our friendship. In Jesus's name we pray. Amen.

What can be known about God is plain to them, because God has shown it to them. For his invisible attributes, namely, his eternal power and divine nature, have been clearly perceived, ever since the creation of the world, in the things that have been made. So they are without excuse. **(ROMANS 1:19–20)**

CELEBRATING MILESTONES

Dear Lord, Thank You for equipping us to navigate marriage. You've shown us that we can endure any situation when we put our trust in You. Sometimes when we get through a difficult circumstance or mature in an area of struggle, we tend to move quickly past it all to get away from the pain. We convince ourselves that quickly moving on, pushing through our thoughts and feelings, is the best way to move away from any pain endured during those challenges. We must not overlook the importance of processing what we went through. Lord, please insist that we slow down, take time to consider how You help us through every victory, and process what we learn through every circumstance You lead us through. Help us to take a moment to celebrate the milestones in our marriage. Inspire us with creative ways to rejoice in all the ways we have grown together. Show us how to acknowledge the maturity we see in each other's lives, as well as celebrate a job well done in the goals we have accomplished together. Please help us to commit to celebrating the milestones, in big or small ways, so that we can rejoice knowing You are moving in us. In Jesus's name we pray. Amen.

I will remember the deeds of the LORD;
yes, I will remember your wonders of old.
I will ponder all your work,
and meditate on your mighty deeds.
(PSALM 77:11-12)

FOLLOWING GOD

Dear Lord, Thank You for being our Good Shepherd. Thank You for Your Holy Word, which tells us the ways in which we should walk. As we read Your Word, make us more and more familiar with Your voice. As we abide in You, may we be known by You. Even though You have the power to know everything, please help us reveal ourselves to You through prayer. We never want to neglect communing with You. Help us choose to follow You every single day and to spur one another to read Your Word and pray. Strengthen our prayer life and impress on our hearts what we should lift up to You in prayer. Please increase our faith and our trust in You. When discouragement comes knocking on the door to our hearts, will You transform our perspective and provide what we need to persevere? We hope to grow in our knowledge of You so that You can use us to tell others of Your saving grace. Please help us to pick up our cross every day. In Jesus's name we pray. Amen.

My sheep hear my voice, and I know them,
and they follow me. **(JOHN 10:27)**

LIFE AND GODLINESS

Dear Lord, We know that pursuing godliness starts with us reading and gaining knowledge of Your Word. Thank You for helping us to escape the corruption of sin, find reconciliation through repentance, and walk in faith in Christ alone. Being confronted with our weaknesses, failures, and sins can be painful, but it also brings to light that You are our strength and righteousness. In moments when we doubt ourselves, feel like we can't continue, or feel discouraged by our sin, please draw us back to You and to repentance. Please help us never to give up having faith in You and pursing godliness. May following You, Lord, produce fruit in each of us that benefits our marriage. Holy Spirit, please use us to encourage one another to walk in righteousness. May we affirm the good we see in each other and receive those words into our hearts. Lord, please keep our hearts tender toward each other. As we pursue life and godliness, may Your name be magnified. In Jesus's name we pray. Amen.

His divine power has granted to us all things that pertain to life and godliness, through the knowledge of him who called us to his own glory and excellence, by which he has granted to us his precious and very great promises, so that through them you may become partakers of the divine nature, having escaped from the corruption that is in the world because of sinful desire. **(2 PETER 1:3-4)**

OUR MARRIAGE
BELONGS TO GOD

Dear Lord, Thank You for creating marriage. Everything You created is Yours. Our marriage is Yours! We will put our trust in You alone. Keep a tight grip on us, and be our strength in times of weakness so that we will not be shaken. No matter what we face, may we submit ourselves to You and build our marriage on You as our firm foundation. Lord, please grow our knowledge and understanding of who You are and what Your Word says about marriage. Please fill us with Your wisdom about our relationship, and may we honor You as we walk in Your Spirit and obey Your Word. During challenges, may encouragement be our first response. We yearn to operate in Your Spirit and not our flesh. Our marriage belongs to You, and we desire Your purpose and will to be fulfilled in us and through us. In Jesus's name we pray. Amen.

The earth is the Lord's and the fullness thereof,
the world and those who dwell therein.
(PSALM 24:1)

62

AMBASSADORS OF
THE GOSPEL

Dear Lord, Thank You for the good news of Your Son, Jesus Christ. Thank You for all He has done in His death and resurrection, atoning for our sin. Thank You for revealing Your gospel to us and giving us the opportunity to surrender our lives to You and believe what is true. Please help us remind one another regularly of the power of the gospel. In times when we doubt Your goodness or our insecurities hinder us from receiving Your love, may we be quick to share the truth with each other that You are good, You are faithful, You are near, and You do love us. Fill us with boldness and courage so that we can speak the truth in love. Make us ready to share Your testimony with each other, even when we have heard it a thousand times before. Holy Spirit, please help us to rely on You to lead us every day. Make us ambassadors of Your gospel, and show us how to willing share Your Word with others. Let the testimony we give fall on softened hearts that need to hear the good news. In Jesus's name, we ask that those who hear what Jesus has done would turn to You and be reconciled. Lord, our hope is that You would continually make Your appeal through us. In Jesus's name we pray. Amen.

We are ambassadors for Christ, God making his appeal through us. We implore you on behalf of Christ, be reconciled to God. **(2 CORINTHIANS 5:20)**

MORE SELF-CONTROL

Dear Lord, Thank You for Your Holy Spirit, who ministers to us and helps us live according to Your Word. Thank You for the fruit of the Spirit. We pray for the fruit of self-control to be evident in our lives. Fill us with self-control, especially in areas where our flesh is weakest. Holy Spirit, guide us in growing in self-control. Please convict our hearts when we fail in this area. We repent of the times we have lacked self-control. Instead, we choose to walk righteously. We lay down our wills and submit to all that You have for us. We desire to live in a way that honors You so that You may be pleased and glorified. We know having more self-control will be a blessing to our marriage, so help us be disciplined with our bodies, our emotions, and our minds. Please help us to have self-control in the areas where we are prone to sin, and continue to transform us for Your glory. In Jesus's name we pray. Amen.

For God gave us a spirit not of fear but of power and love and self-control. **(2 TIMOTHY 1:7)**

NO MORE HIDING

Dear Lord, You have called us out of the darkness and into Your glorious light. Thank You for equipping us with everything we need to run the race of faith with endurance. Thank You for surrounding us with other Christians who believe in the ministry of reconciliation and encourage us to live according to Your Word. Help us lay aside every weight and sin that hinders our walk with You or hinders our marriage relationship. Holy Spirit, convict us of sin, leading us to the foot of the cross, where we are reminded of the price Christ paid to set us free. Lord, please help us be transparent with one another. Give us courage to be honest about where we are emotionally and what we struggle with. Drag our sin into the light and expose it so that we repent and heal from it. Please help us not to hide our hearts from one another. May our lives be full of light so that our marriage can be a beacon of hope in this dark world. Our hope is that others would find You through us. In Jesus's name we pray. Amen.

Since we are surrounded by so great a cloud of witnesses, let us also lay aside every weight, and sin which clings so closely, and let us run with endurance the race that is set before us. **(HEBREWS 12:1)**

BEING INTENTIONAL

Dear Lord, We confess we aren't always mindful of how we spend our time. This world offers many things that consume our time and waste it on pointless distractions. Please give us wisdom regarding how best to use our time so that we do not regret our choices. We desire to be intentional with the time You've gifted us, both in how we use it to serve You and to serve each other. Lord, please show us how to creatively pour into our marriage with the time and opportunity we are given. May we be intentional whether we are planning date nights or simply staying up late to chat in bed. Lord, we want our souls to delight in our time together. Help us be diligent in our intimacy so that we feel filled up and content. Please help us to build up our friendship in marriage by spending time together doing things that bring us joy. In Jesus's name we pray. Amen.

The soul of the sluggard craves and gets nothing, while the soul of the diligent is richly supplied. **(PROVERBS 13:4)**

ADJUSTING TO TRANSITIONS

Dear Lord, Thank You for all the ways You help us navigate making decisions as a couple. As we make decisions that stir up our regular routines and cause life transitions, please prepare our hearts to handle the changes and the unforeseen situations that lay just beyond the horizon. Please brace us to receive what is to come, knowing that we can trust You in any circumstance. In every transitional experience we encounter as a couple, we invite You to help us adjust quickly and smoothly. Transitions are often a catalyst for stress, and stress is usually a source of contention in marriage. Please make us a couple who supports each other in the decision-making process, determined to persevere through stress with self-control and good communication. We desire to help each other be less burdened by stress. We desire to be patient with one another. Please remove any pride that tries to convince us that we know best. Lord, we ask You to help us communicate respectfully with each other. Please help us to endure any transitions by encouraging each other through them, serving one another in any capacity we can. In Jesus's name we pray. Amen.

> *Better is the end of a thing than its beginning,*
> *and the patient in spirit is better than the*
> *proud in spirit.* **(ECCLESIASTES 7:8)**

SEEING WHAT WE CAN BE

Dear Lord, Thank You for not giving up on us, but instead pursuing us and loving us continually. Please help us chase boldly after Your purpose for us. May Your Word transform us and our marriage so that we can grow in maturity, in our understanding of who You are, and in our recognition of who You created us to be. Please help us to see how You are moving in us. Open our eyes to see what we can be, instead of dwelling on who we used to be. Thank You that our mistakes don't define us. We identify with You and the redemption You have provided through Jesus Christ. Thank You for making us into a new creation. Help us grasp the incredible gift of being cleansed from our sin, and help us offer that gift to each other as well. We want to see each other as You see us, and we desire to see who we will become as You continue to work in our lives. Show us how to support each other as we aim to keep in step with Your Spirit. In Jesus's name we pray. Amen.

Nothing will be impossible with God. **(LUKE 1:37)**

HAVING INTEGRITY

Dear Lord, We never want to be resistant to Your correction or to extinguish the conviction of Your Holy Spirit. Grow us into unwavering believers, devoted to reading Your Word and faithful to our marriage. May integrity mark our character as we walk righteously alongside You. Please help us to be always alert to what is right and wrong. May we have integrity in our jobs and in our ministry, in our finances, and in our time alone. Lord, make our hearts aware of sin, and help us to choose to do what is right. We yearn to be trustworthy. Help us trust each other with the use of devices, social media, and other forms of entertainment. Lord, make us an honest couple determined to live each day in uprightness. May our integrity guide us to stay pure, fortifying our marriage. In Jesus's name we pray. Amen.

The integrity of the upright guides them,
but the crookedness of the treacherous
destroys them. **(PROVERBS 11:3)**

ADDICTION

Dear Lord, You have set us free from the power of sin and death! We are no longer under the yoke of slavery or the bondage of sin. Thank You for breaking the chains that once ensnared us. Please open our eyes to any habit that is an addiction or threatens to become one. We acknowledge that addiction is a lack of self-control, a sin that brings death and destruction to our lives and to our marriage. Whether we struggle with a big addiction, a small one, an addiction that is impossible to hide from others, or one that has been veiled in darkness, we lay it at the foot of the cross. Let us not quench Your Holy Spirit when You reveal the areas of our lives in which we allow ourselves to be enslaved. Help us walk in the freedom You have already given us in Christ. Lord, will You show us how to rely on Your strength and to trust in Your Word to transform our minds? When we are tempted to sin, we are enticed by our own desires, so in Jesus's name, remove our desires that lead to sin, and replace them with Your desires. We petition You right now to help us believe the truth that You have set us free from addiction and that we can walk in that freedom by Your strength. In Jesus's name we pray. Amen.

Let no one say when he is tempted, "I am being tempted by God," for God cannot be tempted with evil, and he himself tempts no one. But each person is tempted when he is lured and enticed by his own desire. Then desire when it has conceived gives birth to sin, and sin when it is fully grown brings forth death. **(JAMES 1:13–15)**

THE OVERFLOW OF
OUR HEARTS

Dear Lord, Thank You for giving Your Holy Spirit as a seal upon our hearts. Thank You for dwelling in us. Thank You for teaching us in Your Word that our mouths will reveal what is in our hearts. Will You give us deeper understanding of Your Word when it says that good treasure in someone's heart will produce good? Lord, will You continue to shape our character and fill our hearts with goodness? Search our hearts, and if there is any wicked way in us, please quickly make it clear to us and help us to repent. May the overflow of our hearts be words and actions based in Your truth. Our desire is that our response in every situation—whether well thought out or a quick reaction—would be reflective of Your character. If anything in our hearts is not of You, please prune us, in Jesus's name! As we commit to walking in uprightness, may deep love and compassion pour out and bless our marriage. In Jesus's name we pray. Amen.

The good person out of the good treasure of his heart produces good, and the evil person out of his evil treasure produces evil, for out of the abundance of the heart his mouth speaks. **(LUKE 6:45)**

PRAYING TOGETHER

Dear Lord, Thank You for the gift of prayer. Thank You for giving us a way to make ourselves known before You. Prayer is not always easy, especially in the presence of another. Yet Your Word is clear that we should pray without ceasing. Please show us how to pray continually and fervently. Lord, humble our hearts to submit to You in prayer. Fill us with boldness and faith as we pray for the things we yearn to see. Help us not to get tripped up on our words or what to pray for. We long to grow closer to You and to each other by praying together. As we make ourselves known to You, expressing our thoughts, feelings, praises, and desires, we also long make ourselves known to each during prayer. We want to benefit from hearing each other's perspectives on what we are going through. Will You please help us learn to love praying together? Holy Spirit, please help us to rejoice always, to give thanks to You, and to pray in all circumstances. In Jesus's name we pray. Amen.

Rejoice always, pray without
ceasing. **(1 THESSALONIANS 5:16–17)**

JEALOUSY

Dear Lord, We confess that we are tempted to become jealous of one another in marriage. There are moments when we envy each other and for different reasons. Lord, protect our hearts from jealousy in marriage. Help us to honor one another and not desire each other's position or opportunities. When one of us has the privilege of doing something or going somewhere that does not involve the other, we ask You, Lord, to guard our minds from negative thoughts. Help us not to entertain selfish ways of thinking that stir up bitterness or resentment. Our relationship needs to be secure and strengthened through one another's genuine support. Please keep our hearts and minds free of any bitter root of jealousy. May Your peace guard our hearts, and may we be so secure in the way we think that jealousy has no place to grow. In Jesus's name we pray. Amen.

Where jealousy and selfish ambition exist, there will be disorder and every vile practice. **(JAMES 3:16)**

GROWING IN WISDOM

Dear Lord, Your Word encourages us to ask for wisdom when we lack it, so we humbly come before You right now and ask You to fill us with Your wisdom. Equip us to walk rightly, securely, and confidently in every situation. We know that the way we operate influences each other and others, so we ask You to grant us impact in the lives of those who need Your wisdom. Help us to be good stewards of the responsibilities You have given us. Root our decision-making in Your wisdom and our thoughts in Your insight and intelligence. Please help us to encourage each other to operate wisely in every area of our lives, stimulating growth that will mutually benefit our marriage. Lord, make us prudent, astute, and balanced in how we make judgments on what we see as wise and how we communicate those insights. Establish our marriage on a strong foundation, built on wisdom, and centered on You. In Jesus's name we pray. Amen.

If any of you lacks wisdom, let him ask God,
who gives generously to all without reproach,
and it will be given him. **(JAMES 1:5)**

OUR CONDUCT

Dear Lord, We desire for our behavior to reflect our love for and trust in You. God, please help us to conduct ourselves in a way that shows the world that we know You, believe Your Word, and obey it. May our words and actions bring to light our devotion and submission to You as sovereign Lord. When we are tempted to behave in a way that is against Your will, please help us to deny our flesh and be above reproach. When we fail to deny ourselves, please don't let the discouragement of sin and the heaviness of shame burden us with condemnation. Rather, may we repent and rejoice in Your grace, choosing better the next time we are tempted. Let our conduct also bless our marriage as we honor one another respectfully. Please remind us that holiness is not achieved through works, but rather through our belief in You and choosing to abide in Your holiness. Lord, we bless Your holy name. In Jesus's name we pray. Amen.

As he who called you is holy, you also be holy in all your conduct. **(1 PETER 1:15)**

MERCY

Dear Lord, Thank You for the compassion You have shown us. We praise You for the mercy that triumphs over judgment. Thank You for washing us clean, removing our shame, and clothing us in Your peace. Lord, create in us the ability to love one another with the same transforming love You have for us. Show us how to extend mercy when one of us does something wrong. Help us to truly understand the importance of reconciliation and forgiveness. Sometimes it feels hard to truly forgive and be reconciled in marriage. We hold on to the hurt, convincing ourselves that if we forgive, the same hurt might happen again. But in our relationship, we want to be merciful, not judgmental. Please help us not to fear. Grant us the compassion to give each other another chance to do what is right. May we let go of offenses and allow grace to abound. If that wrong is done again, will You soften our hearts and help us to forgive again? We pray that the beauty of mercy and the gratitude of being truly loved, despite our sin, is evidence of Your presence in our marriage. In Jesus's name we pray. Amen.

Judgment is without mercy to one who has shown no mercy. Mercy triumphs over judgment. **(JAMES 2:13)**

HEALING FROM PAST HURT

Dear Lord, Our hearts can take a long time to heal. Sometimes the pain of past hurt springs up when we least expect it. Lord, will You please heal us from any hurt we have caused each other? Reconcile our hearts to each other, and restore any brokenness. Will You also heal us from the pain of past sin, choices we have made that seem to haunt us and stir up feelings of insecurity in our relationship? Will You show us how to forgive each other so that we can move forward and build trust again? We need You to transform our minds so that we don't define each other by our offenses. Please help us to love unconditionally, keeping no record of wrongs. Lord, when we do offend one another, please help us to wipe the slate clean again and again. In moments when we are tempted to bring up past wrongs, please humbly remind us how much You have forgiven us. We ask You to replace our pain with Your peace. In Jesus's name we pray. Amen.

> *He was pierced for our transgressions;*
> *he was crushed for our iniquities;*
> *upon him was the chastisement that brought us*
> *peace,*
> *and with his wounds we are healed.*
> **(ISAIAH 53:5)**

SERVING EACH OTHER

Dear Lord, Thank You for Christ's perfect model of how to serve others. Help us to live up to His example as we serve one another in our marriage. Give us eyes to see each other's needs and insight on how to fulfill them. Embolden us to care for each other to the best of our ability, and make us sensitive toward each other, recognizing the language of love in every small act. May we build a marriage that is based in serving and not selfishness. Please help us be considerate as we offer assistance to one another, never expecting anything in return. Lord, show us in Your Word the ways that Jesus served others and teach us to serve our spouse in similar ways. Our desire is to love sacrificially and compassionately, blessing each other in ways both large and small. God, show us how to honor each other and show our love through actions and words. May our enthusiasm to serve each other bless others around us, including family, friends, people at church, neighbors, and even strangers. In Jesus's name we pray. Amen.

The Son of Man came not to be served but to serve, and to give his life as a ransom for many. **(MARK 10:45)**

NO MORE PRIDE

Dear Lord, Please destroy any bit of pride that arises in our hearts and minds so that it doesn't get in the way of loving each other. When we let pride rule in our hearts, we experience turmoil in our marriage. Keep pride from dictating our decisions in life or distorting our perspectives of each other. Please help us to overcome the temptation of pride so that it does not have a place in our relationship at all. Lord, we come before You to ask You to transform our hearts and keep us humble. We know that when pride comes, so does disgrace. We have experienced this in marriage when we communicate disrespectfully and listen half-heartedly. Destroy any lofty thoughts we have of ourselves, and replace them with thoughts concerning the well-being of each other. We desire to thrive in marriage and to act in wisdom. We know this is only possible as we rely on You to help us grow in righteousness. May we bless You as we choose to lay down our pride. In Jesus's name we pray. Amen.

When pride comes, then comes disgrace,
but with the humble is wisdom.
(PROVERBS 11:2)

CONTENTMENT IN MARRIAGE

Dear Lord, Thank You for teaching us in Your Word the significance and value of contentment. Whether we are rich or poor, experiencing good health or struggling with our health, You are with us! Help us to be content in all circumstances, because in every circumstance, we have You, the greatest gift of all! We know we can experience true contentment only when we trust and hope in You for everything. Lord, shape our hearts by carving out discontentment and filling us with Your peace. We submit our thoughts to You and ask You to retrain our minds to dwell on things we are grateful for instead of things we are dissatisfied with. Remind us to share our gratitude, telling one another what we're grateful for in our lives and in our relationship, as this will cultivate an atmosphere of peace and thanksgiving in our home. Lord, will You continue to show us how to be content in our lives and in our marriage? We desire to experience contentment no matter what we endure together so that our eyes aren't on ourselves, but rather on You. In Jesus's name we pray. Amen.

Godliness with contentment is great gain,
for we brought nothing into the world, and
we cannot take anything out of the world.
But if we have food and clothing, with these
we will be content. **(1 TIMOTHY 6:6-8)**

PROTECTING EACH OTHER'S HEARTS

Dear Lord, We know that with the gift of marriage, we have also been given the responsibility of protecting our relationship and one another's hearts. May we protect and honor each other by being loving and respectful toward each other. Lord, please show us how to support each other with words of affirmation. We pray Your Holy Spirit would help us to act as protectors as we walk in integrity and humility, considering each other's needs above our own. In times of distress, we pray You would help us to comfort one another so that comfort is not sought after elsewhere. Show us ways we can guard each other's hearts to protect them from the negative impact of sin. When we are tempted to sin, we pray You would show us a way of escape and help us to overcome temptation. We pray we would not allow any room for our flesh to gratify what it desires. Instead we ask You, Lord, to remind us in the moment to turn our eyes toward Christ. In the moment of temptation, reveal the consequences and impact our sin would have on our marriage. May we be diligent to protect our marriage in this way. May You bring our hearts even closer together as we draw near to You and to each other. In Jesus's name we pray. Amen.

Put on the Lord Jesus Christ, and make no provision for the flesh, to gratify its desires. **(ROMANS 13:14)**

PEACEFUL REST

𝒟ear ℒord, Thank You for the rest and peace You offer so freely. We hope for the eternal life we have in You, and we trust You to provide for us until that true rest of eternity comes. Thank You for showing us the importance of rest. Please help us find time each week to rest in You and in Your Word. May the circumstances we face not distract us, overpowering our peace—protect us from anxious thoughts, God. Teach us how to find ways to rest and recuperate, and show us our limits so we don't overextend ourselves. Give us eyes to see when we are pushing each other too hard so that we can instead encourage one another to replenish our energy and find ways of slowing down that will bless our marriage. May we have deep, calming sleep at night so that we can wake up ready to do Your will each morning. In Jesus's name we pray. Amen.

It is in vain that you rise up early
and go late to rest,
eating the bread of anxious toil;
for he gives to his beloved sleep.
(PSALM 127:2)

OUR HEALTH

𝒟*ear ℒord,* The older we get, the more precious our health is to us. May You bless us with good health, Father, so that we are able to use our bodies to serve You in kingdom work. Please help us make good choices about food and exercise, lessening the risk of illness or injury. As important as it is for our bodies to be healthy, we understand the significance of having a healthy mind and soul. Lord, we ask You to help us maintain a strong and stable emotional state of mind. May we make healthy living a priority in our marriage, and may we have the kindness to encourage one another daily. Whether in sickness or in good health, we want to look after each other with tender hearts. If we make choices that will negatively impact our health, please reveal this to us and help us to correct our choices. Heal us where we are unwell, Lord, in both body and soul. May our healthy bodies and strong minds enable us to care for one another in the years to come. Heavenly Father, please provide the strength, determination, focus, and energy we need to cultivate a healthy lifestyle. May You be glorified as we endeavor to be healthy—in mind, body, and soul—ready for every good work. In Jesus's name we pray. Amen.

Beloved, I pray that all may go well with you and that you may be in good health, as it goes well with your soul. **(3 JOHN 1:2)**

LETTING GO OF FRUSTRATIONS

Dear Lord, When we encounter tension in marriage, please help us let go of our frustrations. When we irritate each other, let humbleness rule in our hearts so that we can reconcile. Make us a couple who forgives and does not hold on to the things that frustrate us. When we do bother each other, please help us resist sinning in our anger. Lord, remind us to communicate our feelings respectfully and effectively. Prevent us from giving the Enemy an opportunity to tear down our marriage relationship through offenses that we can overlook in love. On one hand we ask You, Lord, to help us not be overly sensitive toward each other, yet on the other hand, please help us to be quick to recognize when feelings are hurt and restoration is needed. Heal any pain we've caused one another, and help us to be easygoing, lighthearted, full of joy, and covered in peace. In Jesus's name we pray. Amen.

Be angry and do not sin; do not let the sun go down on your anger, and give no opportunity to the devil. **(EPHESIANS 4:26–27)**

LOVING-KINDNESS

Dear Lord, Thank You for Your loving-kindness, which never ceases. Thank You for Your offer of unlimited mercies. Your love is unmatched! We also thank You for every new day we get the opportunity to walk with You in faith. Your love is unending. Help us model that same unending love for one another, and encourage us to start each new day considering and appreciating the love we share. Let us be quick to lay down our selfishness and quick to show mercy. May we bless each other in extravagant and special ways that fill us with hope and joy. Help us to be kind, compassionate, and gentle in everything we do and say. We are motivated to share the love we have received from You, because it is powerful. And because Your loving-kindness has transformed our lives and impacted our marriage for the better, we want our interactions to be evidence to the world that we love You. May our marriage be a picture of Your transforming love, for Your glory. In Jesus's name we pray. Amen.

> *The steadfast love of the LORD never ceases;*
> *his mercies never come to an end;*
> *they are new every morning;*
> *great is your faithfulness.*
> **(LAMENTATIONS 3:22-23)**

OUR IDENTITY

Dear Lord, We often base our identity in wealth, appearance, music, hobbies, work, or even marriage. But we don't always recognize or see clearly that we've attached our identity to these things until our life is impacted by change. Our negative responses to a financial hardship, an inability to get what we desire, a conflict in relationship, or a transition at work can reveal where we've placed our identity. However, when we received salvation, we immediately received the privilege of identifying with Christ and Him crucified. Heavenly Father, please remind us daily that our identity is found in You alone. Instead of placing our identity in wealth or anything else, we want to trust You as our security. May our identity be placed firmly in You so we aren't tossed back and forth like a wave. Our hearts are overwhelmed with gratitude for the sacrifice Christ made so that we can live by faith. As we find our identity and security in You alone, please help us to alleviate the pressure we place on each other to meet our every need. You are our provider and our everything. In Jesus's name we pray. Amen.

I have been crucified with Christ. It is no longer I who live, but Christ who lives in me. And the life I now live in the flesh I live by faith in the Son of God, who loved me and gave himself for me. **(GALATIANS 2:20)**

LEAVING A LEGACY

Dear Lord, You have authored a miraculous legacy of faithfulness through Jesus Christ and Your Word, and we want to be mindful of the legacy we leave in this world as well. As our family and friends see You in us, may our lives be a light to draw others closer to You. Give us a vision and a hope for the future so that we clearly see the right steps toward building a legacy that glorifies You. Lord, please help us to consider the generations of family that will come after us. Let our faithfulness in serving You be a catalyst that inspires others to serve You in kingdom work as well. As we invest in our family by spending quality time together and nurturing one another, we also ask You to show us how to invest our finances to support the ministry work that will be done through us and through our family. May our strong marriage and family point others toward You. Holy Spirit, please help us to walk humbly, remaining faithful and steadfast according to Your Word. In Jesus's name we pray. Amen.

One generation shall commend your works to another,
and shall declare your mighty acts.
(PSALM 145:4)

CHERISHING EACH OTHER

Dear Lord, Thank You for the encouragement in Your Word to live in harmony with one another. One way we can do that is to take time every day to cherish each other and to affirm our love. Please inspire creative ways to express our love and to prove it through our actions. Stir in us a desire to share notes of encouragement with each other, and give us the words that would be most uplifting to hear. Impress upon our hearts the necessity to cherish each other through physical acts of service, such as giving massages or holding each other's hands. May our intentional encouragement lead us to admire each other more. Lord, will You also give us the gift of recognition so that we are aware of when our spouse is cherishing us? May we see when the other is going out of their way to care for us. If there is anything getting in the way of our cherishing each other, would You please help us to identify it? Our desire is that nothing would hinder us from living in harmony with one another, protecting and caring for each other in love. We long to experience an even deeper relationship, which we know is possible if we walk in Your wisdom and cherish one another. Lord, help us to love like You love. In Jesus's name we pray. Amen.

> *Live in harmony with one another. Do not be*
> *haughty, but associate with the lowly. Never*
> *be wise in your own sight.* **(ROMANS 12:16)**

SHOWING AFFECTION

Dear Lord, Thank You for Your loving affections toward us. You comfort us and lead us through this life with encouragement. We are grateful for the way Your Holy Spirit ministers to us every day, reminding us of Your truth. Please help us to yield our hearts to You and to walk according to the wisdom You give us. Lord, please grow our affection for each other, and inspire our hearts to find new ways of nourishing our marriage relationship. We want to be a couple who goes out of the way to show each other how deeply we love each other. Lord, teach us how to creatively express our fondness for one another. Encourage us to say "I love you" more often and to go even further and share what we like about each other. May our physical touch affirm our affectionate love for each other. May our soft touches, hugs, and kisses send a message of love to strengthen our bond of unity. Help us to pursue date nights and prioritize spending quality time together so we have more opportunities to show affection toward each other. Lord, may our marriage thrive as we choose to love each other in these ways. In Jesus's name we pray. Amen.

In the same way husbands should love their wives as their own bodies. He who loves his wife loves himself. For no one ever hated his own flesh, but nourishes and cherishes it, just as Christ does the church. **(EPHESIANS 5:28–29)**

MONEY MANAGEMENT

Dear Lord, Thank You for all You have given us and how You provide for our every need. Thank You for trusting us with money and for guiding us on how best to use it. Please shape our perspectives and beliefs about money. May we not wrestle with a love of money or a craving for wealth or material things. May financial security not take the place of You in our hearts, but rather help us to see money as a resource to care for our family and bless others. We pray our money management brings You glory. Teach us Your ways about money, and show us how to manage our finances as we work together to budget well. Help us communicate respectfully so that we can hear each other's hearts on the matter of money management and can stick to the boundaries we set as a couple. May we always hold our money loosely so that it is not an idol in our lives. Heavenly Father, please help us live with radical generosity, giving away our resources to fulfill needs as You see fit. Be magnified as we steward our money well. In Jesus's name we pray. Amen.

The love of money is a root of all kinds of evils. It is through this craving that some have wandered away from the faith and pierced themselves with many pangs. **(1 TIMOTHY 6:10)**

NAVIGATING THE INTERNET

Dear Lord, Thank You for all the resources and tools You have given us to gather information and communicate with others. God, we know the greatest tools can sometimes be the most dangerous, so please help us to navigate the internet wisely. Keep our hearts pure and help us escape any temptations online. Please help us to safeguard our relationship by agreeing to and setting up boundaries that will protect our marriage. May we not use the access we have online to sin, and may we not foster any interactions online that could hurt our marriage. Please remind us that we can't hide our sin. Eventually, our choices will be exposed, and what we do online will be dragged into the light. May we keep nothing hidden from each other. Let us never leave an open door for the Enemy to come in and cause destruction in our marriage. Lord, please give us wisdom in using the internet, using it for good and not for evil. In Jesus's name we pray. Amen.

Nothing is covered up that will not be revealed,
or hidden that will not be known. **(LUKE 12:2)**

NO MORE SELFISHNESS

Dear Lord, We confess that selfishness is something we continue to struggle with. We know that being selfish never benefits our relationship. We desire to destroy our selfish ways and replace them with acts of humility. Thank You for showing us the significance of being selfless. Christ lived a selfless life, giving Himself for all. Thank You for Your sacrificial love. Show us how to abide in Christ so we can learn from His selflessness. As we grow in our knowledge of Christ's love, we hope and pray it becomes second nature to love deeply and sacrificially in our marriage. Please continue to teach us how to put the interests of others above our own. May we never be motivated by selfish ambition or vain conceit. Give us Your desires for our relationship, and help us walk in submission to Your design for marriage. Our hearts' desire is that our love for one another would deconstruct any insecurities about our relationship and any fears about our marriage falling apart that may be holding us back from deeper intimacy or holding us back from fulfilling Your purpose for us. In Jesus's name we pray. Amen.

Do nothing from selfish ambition or conceit,
but in humility count others more significant
than yourselves. **(PHILIPPIANS 2:3)**

LONELINESS IN MARRIAGE

Dear Lord, Thank You for the companionship we share. Thank You for the way marriage challenges us and gives us opportunities to grow. We have been through so much together. We have experienced good days and difficult days. In future hard times, we ask You, Lord, to strengthen us so that we do not lose hope for better days. When we are frustrated with each other, are dealing with stress, or just feel disconnected, will You keep us from the sting of loneliness? Will You be our comforter and encourager? Lord, when conflict creates emotional distance in our marriage relationship, please help us to recognize it and take steps to strengthen our emotional intimacy, setting aside quality time to spend together, praying together, and sharing our hearts openly. Jesus, we implore You to intercede for us and unify our hearts. When we feel lonely in marriage, we ask You, Lord, to give us the courage to address those feelings immediately. Please help us to be fully present, to listen well, and to take responsibility for any hurt caused, and please banish any insecurities we may have about our marriage. When we are lonely, please remind us that we are not hidden from You, remind us of all we've been through together, and remind us to seek Your presence daily. In Jesus's name we pray. Amen.

O Lord, all my longing is before you;
my sighing is not hidden from you.
(PSALM 38:9)

GIVING AFFIRMATION

Dear Lord, Thank You for the affirmation we receive from Your Word, from each other, and from others in our lives. Affirmation makes us feel good and combats the lies we tend to believe about ourselves. May You open our eyes and our hearts to all the ways You encourage us. May gratitude fill our hearts as we recognize the overwhelming amount of love You pour over us every day. In the same way, Lord, help us to encourage one another in marriage. Give us words to express the admiration we have for each other's hard work, the tasks we each accomplish to keep our home running smoothly, and the intention we put into building up our family. May we supply emotional support that lifts each other up on especially difficult days. When our hearts feel empty and need affirmation, please help us to communicate those needs to one another respectfully. When we feel despair, may Your Holy Spirit comfort us and stir in us a desire to be close to You. May we choose to pursue one another as we look forward to growing together. Lord, thank You for the amazing power of our words to affirm each other. Please use us as a force of encouragement in marriage. In Jesus's name we pray. Amen.

> *Let us consider how to stir up one another to love and good works, not neglecting to meet together, as is the habit of some, but encouraging one another, and all the more as you see the Day drawing near.* **(HEBREWS 10:24–25)**

THE GIFT OF ONENESS

Dear Lord, Thank You for Your unique design of two becoming one flesh. Oneness in marriage is an extraordinary gift. Remind us that we belong to one another, that we influence one another, and that our love is intimately shared between us. We understand that we are two individuals woven together as one in a holy covenant. This intimate union involves laying ourselves down in humbleness to embrace unity, and we ask You, Lord, to impress this truth upon our hearts every day. Remind us that we are on the same team, working together to bless Your name. Please continue to mature us, increasing our desire for unity and guiding us to make choices that support our oneness. Show us how to walk humbly, to love deeply, and to honor one another fully. May we hold fast to one another, protecting our bond of unity. If anything comes against us or tempts us to sever our intimate bond, Lord, will You be our strength and firmly secure our marriage? May You be glorified as we remain steadfast and faithful, clinging to one another in true love. In Jesus's name we pray. Amen.

> *Therefore a man shall leave his father and*
> *his mother and hold fast to his wife, and they*
> *shall become one flesh.* **(GENESIS 2:24)**

BEING TESTED

Dear Lord, We praise You and thank You for testing our hearts to refine us. Please help us endure through tests and to learn the areas in which You desire us to mature. In challenging or painful moments, we ask that Your Holy Spirit bring to our minds all that Your Word proclaims. Please convict our hearts and show us how to make adjustments in our lives that would transform our character. As You sanctify us individually and together in our marriage, we hope to gain a deeper understanding of Your love for us. Remind us that You test our hearts just like a refiner's fire tests gold. Lord, as we are tested and tried, please increase our faith. We know You use our marriage to help refine us. May our responses to each other and situations we go through be full of faith and encouraging to each other. Will You also use our marriage to encourage others in the faith? Our desire is that anyone looking at our relationship would see a reflection of You and Your faithfulness. Like a lighthouse on a hill, may our marriage direct others to You. In Jesus's name we pray. Amen.

> *The crucible is for silver, and the furnace is*
> *for gold,*
> *and the Lord tests hearts.*
> **(PROVERBS 17:3)**

CONTRIBUTING AS A TEAM

Dear Lord, Thank You for the way You designed marriage partners to be like a team. Please help us see each other as teammates, working together to carry out Your will. We feel so blessed to have each other to lean on for support and to experience friendship through all that life offers. Holy Spirit, gently lead us in taking turns contributing to the maintenance of our marriage and home so that the weight of responsibility does not rest solely on one person's shoulders. Please help us to be considerate of the stresses we each carry and how we can help each other persevere through them. Show us ways we can alleviate that stress in each other's lives rather than contributing to it. Lord, Your Word explains how two are better than one and how a threefold cord is not quickly broken. With You we are not quickly broken! Let the way we work together, contributing as a team, be a testimony to others about You and Your wonderful working power in our lives. We praise You for our marriage, and we ask You to continue growing us closer together. In Jesus's name we pray. Amen.

Two are better than one, because they have a
good reward for their toil. For if they fall, one
will lift up his fellow. . . . A threefold cord is not
quickly broken. **(ECCLESIASTES 4:9–10, 12)**

WORDS MATTER

Dear Lord, Thank You for the ability to articulate our thoughts and feelings. Thank You for the way our communication has grown over time. Please continue to help us get better at sharing our words with each other. Slow down our thoughts so we can consider the impact of our words. Lord, remind us every day that our words influence each other. What we say and how we say it matters significantly. Our words are powerful. Make us a couple who uses our words to edify and uplift each other, bringing You glory. As we share Scripture with one another, may the power of Your words strengthen our faith and encourage our relationship. Holy Spirit, please help us to know how to affirm each other, especially when the need is greatest. Lord, please help us not to be critical of each other, but rather help us to communicate clearly in love and respect. May we bless each other and honor You with our words every day. In Jesus's name we pray. Amen.

A soft answer turns away wrath,
but a harsh word stirs up anger.
(PROVERBS 15:1)

JOYFULNESS

Dear Lord, Thank You for the fruit of the Spirit. Thank You for working in our lives and producing Your fruit in us. We know that joy, one of the fruits of the Spirit, is much more than just happiness. It is a deep well of contentment and pleasure that bubbles over within us because of our faith in You, regardless of what we face in life. Joy reveals our ability to trust You in every way. Joyfulness is expressed through our countenance and through our responses to life circumstances. It is light in our eyes and hope in our hearts. Lord, make our joy contagious. Let others ask why we have deep delight and how they can have it too. Inspire us to remind each other of the joy within us, that we may see more joyfulness expressed in each other. Make joy a defining mark of our marriage—the first thing others notice in us. May joy be an experience we share together regularly, even on the most difficult of days. Lord, help us serve You with gladness as we serve one another in love. Increase Your joy in us. In Jesus's name we pray. Amen.

Serve the LORD with gladness!
Come into his presence with singing!
(PSALM 100:2)

EATING HEALTHY

Dear Lord, Thank You for the food You provide that nourishes our bodies. Thank You for the amazing gift of the variety of flavors we get to enjoy. We praise You for the way You created food—some that taste amazing right off the plant and others that are a joy to prepare in countless ways. Your thoughtfulness in food and how it provides nutrition to our bodies is spectacular. We praise You for food! Please give us a strong understanding of how different foods support our bodies and overall health. We desire to do all that we can to maintain our health for each other in marriage. The healthier we are in mind, body, and soul, the better the overall health of our marriage will be. Please help us avoid foods that harm or inflame our bodies. Give us the determination to choose to eat healthy. Make us thoughtful of what we consume and how much we eat. We also ask You to help us be generous to share what we have with others and to show hospitality, inviting family and friends so we can share good food together. As we pursue hospitality, please show us how to use our time together to share Your truth. In Jesus's name we pray. Amen.

Whether you eat or drink, or whatever you do, do all to the glory of God. **(1 CORINTHIANS 10:31)**

REPENTING OF SIN

𝒟ear 𝓛ord, We know You have transformed us and will continue to transform us! We pray we would humbly receive from You the change Your truth brings to our lives as You sanctify us. We know we still struggle with sin. We ask Your Holy Spirit to reveal to us every single day the areas of our lives where we struggle so we can name the sin and repent of it. Draw any sin within us to the surface of our hearts so that we can repent and be reconciled to You and to each other. Help us choose righteousness over sin, God. In moments of temptation, may Your Holy Spirit show us how to escape from that situation and remind us of the freedom from sin we have received because of Christ's sacrifice on the cross. May we hate our sin. May we be willing to remove the sin in our lives that entangles us. Please give us fresh eyes to see clearly the truth that we are indeed set free. Help us to be gentle in the way we encourage each other toward purity. We plead and petition for Your Holy Spirit to help us overcome every sin our flesh craves. May we abide in You daily by diving into Your Word, letting it wash over us. In Jesus's name we pray. Amen.

No one who abides in him keeps on sinning;
no one who keeps on sinning has either
seen him or known him. **(1 JOHN 3:6)**

ALL OUR CARES

Dear Lord, We often allow cares to build up inside of us and overwhelm us. Lord, please remind us to come to You in prayer to lay all our cares at the foot of Your throne. Thank You for understanding the weight of our burdens. You know us so well! You know our hearts' concerns, and You comfort us with Your peace. You console us by reminding us of Your promises. Thank You for alleviating the pain that comes from having too many worries. Lord, help us trust You with the burdens we carry. Make our marriage a similar place of sanctuary and solace where we listen to each other's cares. Help us to comfort one another. Encourage us with creative ways to cheer each other up. Holy Spirit, when we struggle, ignite a response within us, quickly reminding each other of Your promises. In Jesus's name we pray. Amen.

> *When the cares of my heart are many,*
> *your consolations cheer my soul.*
> **(PSALM 94:19)**

DEEPEN OUR RELATIONSHIP

Dear Lord, Thank You for always pushing us to grow deeper with You. Thank You for also encouraging us to deepen our marriage relationship. As our relationship with You matures and we grasp Your truth in greater ways, we are confident You will transform us. We are grateful that the influence of a deep relationship with You overflows into our marriage and helps us love each other better. One way to experience more connection in our marriage is to dive into meaningful conversations, so we ask You, Lord, to give us courage to share the things we wrestle with and the things we win victory over. Give us boldness to share our opinions on current events and hot topics. Inspire us to share about what-if scenarios, inventions, a new job prospect, dreams, what we are studying, or anything else that consumes our thoughts. Being transparent is a beautiful way to get to know one another. Please help us to expose our hearts, but also help us create a safe place to do so. May our responses toward one another be coated in love and compassion. God, never stop sending us encouragement through Your Word and the words of others to care for our marriage, to fight for our marriage, and to pursue one another in marriage. May You be glorified as we seek to deepen our relationship with You and with each other. In Jesus's name we pray. Amen.

Beloved, let us love one another, for love is
from God, and whoever loves has been born
of God and knows God. **(1 JOHN 4:7)**

GIVING GLORY TO GOD

Dear Lord, Thank You for Your goodness. You are holy and worthy to be praised! We praise You for our lives, our marriage, and the gift of salvation. While we deserved nothing, You gave us everything when You gave us eternal life and freedom from sin. We give You glory! Thank You for transforming our hearts through the power of the gospel. Please continue to renew our minds so we think like Christ. May the light of Christ shine brightly in us, and may it be evident in our marriage. Lord, we give You glory for the growth we have experienced in our marriage and the understanding we have of love. We know we are able to love each other well only because You first loved us and continue to shower us with Your love. Will You please continue to shape us and work in our marriage? May Your light only get brighter within us as we live in submission to You. In Jesus's name we pray. Amen.

God, who said, "Let light shine out of darkness,"
has shone in our hearts to give the light of
the knowledge of the glory of God in the face
of Jesus Christ. **(2 CORINTHIANS 4:6)**

OUR FAMILY

Dear Lord, Family is an incredible gift. We are grateful for our immediate and extended families. We ask You to use our marriage to impact those closest to us. May we be a light and beacon of hope pointing our family to look to You for life and salvation. Will You please bless our family, Lord? Protect them from the threats of the Enemy. Keep the Enemy far from each of us, in Jesus's name! Please help our families to live in unity and peace with each other. As we hang out with our families, may our time together put smiles on all our faces. Please help us to cultivate these special relationships, caring for family members and providing for them in any capacity we can. Heavenly Father, may the things of this world, including challenging circumstances or difficult relationships, never burden our family. Our hope and trust remain in You. We ask You to remove worry and fear far from us. Lord, we also thank You for the family we have in the body of Christ. Please help us to care for Your family, using our marriage and our faith to bring glory to Your name as we seek to care for others. In Jesus's name we pray. Amen.

If someone does not know how to manage
his own household, how will he care for
God's church? **(1 TIMOTHY 3:5)**

BUILDING EACH OTHER UP

Dear Lord, Thank You for the opportunities You give us to build bridges of connection in our marriage. In Jesus's name, please keep us protected from anything that aims to tear down those bridges, whether it be the Enemy, someone or something else, or even our own flesh. Lord, show us how to maintain our connectedness when we are busy. Inspire us to build up our marriage by remaining connected emotionally, physically, and spiritually. We confess that expressing encouragement or showing our love through actions can feel overwhelming if we don't know what to say or do. In those moments of uncertainty, please give us courage and lead us in what to do and how to do it. May we use our time today to build one another up with our words. Lord, keep our words pure and uplifting. If we start to say something critical or unkind, please stop us in our tracks! Remind us of the impact of our words. May You be glorified as we seek to honor each other, support each other, and build each other up in all areas of our lives. In Jesus's name we pray. Amen.

Encourage one another and build one another up,
just as you are doing. **(1 THESSALONIANS 5:11)**

BEING GOOD TO EACH OTHER

Dear Lord, We desire to grow in our understanding of the richness of Your love. Lead us to search the depths of Your love and receive it fully. In moments when doubt steals our confidence, prompt us to remind one another of Your good love for us. In Jesus's name, we ask that Your goodness would be a character trait in us as well. Please help us to be good to each other. Lord, will You please shape us into good listeners and good communicators? Will You bless us with the ability to speak kindly and respectfully, even when our flesh doesn't want to? Our hope is that Your goodness would pour out of our hearts during our conversations. We also invite You to help us be thoughtful of each other's needs, aware of the challenges we face daily and the ways we can support one another. Lord, may our good intentions to love each other lead us to embrace each other more often. Even when a disagreement or conflict arises, please help us to be good to each other. May You be magnified as we choose to walk in goodness all the days of our lives. In Jesus's name we pray. Amen.

> *So then, as we have opportunity, let us do good*
> *to everyone, and especially to those who are*
> *of the household of faith.* **(GALATIANS 6:10)**

MARRIAGE IS TO MAKE US HOLY

Dear Lord, Thank You for the unique way You created marriage to refine us. Lord, will You please continue to use our marriage to transform us? Show us how to embrace the trials and challenges we experience as a couple in eager expectation, trusting You to use those situations to mature us. Even though testing stretches us, we know it will produce steadfastness. Our desire is to be more like You! We know that all our interactions affect each other either positively or negatively, and it is wild to consider how often we hurt or offend each other despite truly loving each other. We are sorry for this! Yet we believe the experience of humbling ourselves to apologize and forgive is transforming us, stimulating our growth. Please increase our desire and ability to reconcile with each other as we practice obeying all You have taught us through Your Word. As You sanctify us, may You also make us better spouses for each other. When we experience the pain of sin or conflict, restore us, God, and heal us from the hurt we have caused one another. Please use our marriage to make us holy. In Jesus's name we pray. Amen.

"You shall be holy, for I am holy." **(1 PETER 1:16)**

GOD'S PROVISION

𝒟*ear* ℒ*ord,* We are grateful for Your incredible provision! Time and time again You have provided for us and supplied our every need. You provide financially, but You also give us opportunities to experience extraordinary things. You provide talents, wisdom, strength, support, and so much more. All of Your ways of providing for us equip us with the ability to do all that You purpose for us. You care about the details of our lives and show us that we can trust in You. Lord, increase our belief in You as our provider for everything, especially when the pressures of the world wear us down. In Jesus's name, we ask You to remove any doubt from our minds that You are not enough! Or that Your provision is not good enough! Whether it's money, food, clothes, confidence, or the right words to share in pivotal moments, please remind us that in You we have enough! Flood us with secure thoughts of who You are, all You have done, and all You can do. Lord, we ask You to help us encourage one another during times of exhaustion and weakness—not to keep going in our own strength, but to trust You for our needs. Make us a couple who wisely manages all that You provide so that, having all sufficiency, we are ready and willing to abound in every good work You have purposed for us. In Jesus's name we pray. Amen.

God is able to make all grace abound to you, so that having all sufficiency in all things at all times, you may abound in every good work. **(2 CORINTHIANS 9:8)**

THE GIFT OF MARRIAGE

Dear Lord, Please help us recognize what an extraordinary gift our marriage is, and help us use it to bring You glory! Give us eyes to see one another as a gift from You. Show us how to cherish our relationship and prioritize quality time together. May we lay aside our selfishness so that we serve one another in love. Make our love immovable so that nothing in this world distracts us or keeps us from loving each other well, in Jesus's name! We pray we would remain steadfast in our marriage and maintain a solid foundation so that we can confidently encourage other couples, sharing where our hope lies. Please give us a clear vision of the purpose of our marriage. Thank You for the mystery of the gospel being represented through our unity and love as we reflect Your love in us. May the way we treat one another be a testimony of Your power in our lives. Lord, take us to new depths of understanding and new heights of experience as we use our marriage to spread hope to others and impact this world for You. In Jesus's name we pray. Amen.

Be steadfast, immovable, always abounding in the work of the Lord, knowing that in the Lord your labor is not in vain. **(1 CORINTHIANS 15:58)**

COMPANIONSHIP

𝒟ear 𝓛ord, We are blessed to have each other as companions. Thank You, Lord, for our friendship. We are glad we are not alone! We invite You, Lord, to show us how to support each other, especially in moments of dire need. Give us the courage to pray together more often. Stir in us a desire to support each other simply by being present. Impress on our hearts the importance of pursuing one another regularly. In our companionship, inspire us to be playful when one of us wants to play and a comfort when one of us is overwhelmed with sadness. May Your wisdom guide us to know how to be good company for each other. Lord, will You deepen our relationship by helping us confide in each other and make ourselves truly known to one another. Holy Spirit, please bring to mind the benefits of building up our friendship with one another and our friendships with others. Make us a couple who walks with wise friends who are quick to encourage us to grow in our marriage. Surround us with people who value wisdom and desire to grow themselves. Lord, we ask You to make us wise so that we can support each other and our friends. In Jesus's name we pray. Amen.

Whoever walks with the wise becomes wise, but the companion of fools will suffer harm. **(PROVERBS 13:20)**

PRAISING GOD IN HARDSHIP

Dear Lord, You are our refuge and strength. We praise You in the valleys and on the mountaintops! We praise You when we experience comfort and when we experience pain. We trust Your plan for our marriage. Lord, please help us never to forget Your benefits and every good gift You have bestowed on us. We desire to have hearts of worship that praise You continually as we acknowledge all the ways You are working in our lives and marriage. Lord, will You help us keep a heavenly perspective of our relationship and remind us of the good that can come from hardship? Praising You in hardship can produce an abundance of fruit in our lives if we yield ourselves to You. Boost our belief in this truth. Send affirmation through family and friends that directs us to wait on You and rely on You to bring us through every circumstance. Please help us submit our wills and to be grateful no matter what we face, and remind us to keep our eyes fixed on You through it all. Strengthen our marriage foundation as we surrender ourselves in worship. In Jesus's name we pray. Amen.

> *Bless the LORD, O my soul,*
> *and forget not all his benefits.*
> **(PSALM 103:2)**

SUBMITTING TO GOD'S WILL

Dear Lord, Thank You for Your Word, which affirms the truth that You desire to do Your will. Although our flesh often opposes Your will, making it challenging to follow You, we strive to surrender those desires and walk in a way that pleases You. Sometimes we desire to submit to You and serve You as a couple, but one or both of us choose to be foolish and disobey You. Lord, help us not to be judgmental of each other, but rather to gently and earnestly admonish each other to turn toward You. We ask You to fill us with patience as we seek to follow Your ways. We humble ourselves and ask You to align our hearts with Yours. Reveal Your will so that we may act in confidence, and bend our thoughts, our motives, and our actions to conform to Your will so that we can fulfill the purpose You have for us. We desire others to see the reverence we have for You and for them to be close to You. May our marriage stand as a good example of how submitting to You blesses the marriage relationship. Please help us to continue on the path You have for us, without growing weary or giving up. In Jesus's name we pray. Amen.

Do not be foolish, but understand what the will of the Lord is. **(EPHESIANS 5:17)**

PRAYING FOR EACH OTHER

Dear Lord, What a beautiful and intimate gift You have given to us in prayer. We praise You for the way You make Yourself available to us! Thank You for the privilege and opportunity to come before You right now. Today, we pray for our marriage. We invite You to motivate us to regularly share what is on our hearts—how we feel, needs we have, what we're struggling with—so that we know how best to pray for each other. We also ask You for the gift of understanding each other in a profound way. Let us come to You in confidence and ask only what is in Your will. Lord, will You bolster our faith and give us the courage to initiate prayer together? Make us brave to pray for each other, without being concerned with messing up our words or not praying perfectly. Please inspire our hearts with what to say so that our prayers uplift and comfort each other. Give us a deep desire and strong will to pray for one another daily. Bless our marriage with unity as we commit to praying for each other. In Jesus's name we pray. Amen.

> *This is the confidence that we have toward him, that if we ask anything according to his will he hears us.* **(1 JOHN 5:14)**

BEING GOOD STEWARDS

Dear Lord, We praise You for our lives, our marriage, our family, our possessions, our jobs, our church, and our finances. We recognize that in all You have given us, You have also trusted us to manage it well. Lord, our desire is that You would be pleased with what You see. We consider it an honor to have the responsibility of being good stewards. We hope to use our resources for Your glory and ask Your Holy Spirit to help us to care for them well. Open our eyes and our hearts to what You are doing in this world and how we can use what we have to support Your work and fulfill Your will here on earth. We surrender to You our finances, our time, our talents, and our belongings. May we tune in to and accept Your direction and leading as we make decisions regarding our resources. Make us honest with each other in how we spend our money, and give us wisdom in how to share our possessions to bless our family, friends, and others. Please continue showing us how to be good stewards, faithfully building Your kingdom. In Jesus's name we pray. Amen.

One who is faithful in a very little is also faithful in much, and one who is dishonest in a very little is also dishonest in much. **(LUKE 16:10)**

RESPONDING TO CONFLICT

𝒟*ear* ℒ*ord,* Thank You for our marriage and for the precious memories we've made together. We ask You to mature us, especially in the way we communicate with each other. Lord, transform our hearts so that we respond to each other with love and respect. Renew our minds, especially in the way we view each other, focusing our eyes to see the good in each other. Fill us full of grace when we struggle to have patience with one another. Please help us grow in our faith and in our love for one another so that when we experience conflict, we respond in a way that honors You. We yearn to be reconciled quickly, not letting pride get in the way of the restoration of our relationship. Destroy our pride, in Jesus's name! Create in us a clean heart, Lord, and renew a right spirit within us. Please help us to apologize and forgive one another regularly, and use the power of reconciliation to help us understand You in a deeper way. Restore our relationship after conflict, and help us move forward. In Jesus's name we pray. Amen.

> *Create in me a clean heart, O God,*
> *and renew a right spirit within me.*
> **(PSALM 51:10)**

RELYING ON GOD

Dear Lord, Our Rock, who is faithful and true, thank You for being reliable. We depend on You for guidance, wisdom, and provision. We don't know where we would be without You! In humility we ask You to remind us to rely on You every moment of every day. We also thank You for the way we can rely on one another in our marriage. Make us a couple who is trustworthy and full of integrity. Strengthen our commitment to support each other and fortify our faith in You so that our marriage foundation is like a rock firmly planted in its place. When times are difficult or we experience conflict in our relationship, equip us to endure as we lean on Your Word, which reminds us to pursue peace and to pray. You are our true peace! As we rely on You for everything, please make us resilient as we wait on You to act. We praise You for being immovable. Lord, we put our trust in You forever. In Jesus's name we pray. Amen.

> *Trust in the LORD forever,*
> *for the LORD GOD is an everlasting rock.*
> **(ISAIAH 26:4)**

ENCOURAGING EACH OTHER

Dear Lord, Thank You for another day, another opportunity to be strong encouragement in each other's lives. Lord, keep our hearts tender and soft, able to receive exhortation as we urge each other to walk righteously. Please give us the courage to say hard things in love. As we support one another, reminding each other of the importance of turning away from sin and repenting, may Your Holy Spirit speak to us of Your amazing grace. Lord, use our words to build each other up and not tear each other down. May we affirm that we are on the same team. Inspire us to find creative ways of reassuring each other of our commitment to love one another throughout the day. We pray that our intentional solacing would be a catalyst to also encourage those around us. Holy Spirit, please help us prioritize the daily reading of Your Word so that our hearts are encouraged by You and are never hardened by the deceitfulness of sin. In Jesus's name we pray. Amen.

Exhort one another every day, as long as it is called "today," that none of you may be hardened by the deceitfulness of sin. **(HEBREWS 3:13)**

RESTORATION AFTER TRUST IS BROKEN

Dear Lord, Thank You for the blessing of participating in the ministry of reconciliation. Thank You for Your miraculous grace, which covers us and comforts us. Instead of allowing us to feel buried under the weight of condemnation, You restore us. Despite our sin, You love us, forgive us, and make it possible to be reconciled to You. We praise You for the power of forgiveness! Holy Spirit, give us understanding of how deep, how wide, and how high the Father's love is for us. Mature us and grow our ability to apologize and forgive each other. May we be willing to reconcile so that the Enemy does not gain a foothold in our marriage. We specifically pray we would experience restoration after trust is broken. Lord, direct our steps in how to repair the damage done in the wake of our choices. Give us hope to fully trust each other again. God, will You keep us from breaking each other's trust? Will You help us to be trustworthy, holy, blameless, and pure? Transform us and help us turn away from sin and do good—to seek peace and pursue it. May our future be extraordinary as You restore and heal us. In Jesus's name we pray. Amen.

> *Whoever desires to love life*
> *and see good days,*
> *let him keep his tongue from evil*
> *and his lips from speaking deceit;*
> *let him turn away from evil and do good;*
> *let him seek peace and pursue it.*
> **(1 PETER 3:10–11)**

FEELING OVERWHELMED

Dear Lord, We know life is temporary, so we appreciate the valuable time we get to spend together. Our desire is to take every opportunity to live our lives to the fullest. In our pursuit of enjoying life and marriage, may we refuse to allow our circumstances to overwhelm us. Lord, protect our minds from being burdened by anxiety. When undesired circumstances come our way, we ask Your Holy Spirit to lead us to respond in a positive and hope-filled way. As we encounter situations that stir up crushing feelings within us, please help us to remain respectful and loving toward each other. May Your peace cover us like a thermal blanket, keeping the truth of Your promises from escaping our hearts. Heavenly Father, will You please help us to continually exercise self-control over our thoughts and emotions? Help us to understand the sufficiency of Your grace and to trust that You make Your power perfect in our weakness. When we feel overwhelmed, Holy Spirit, please teach to rely on You, enduring without panic. Give us Your perspective and patience as You lead our hearts and ease our restless thoughts. In Jesus's name we pray. Amen.

> He said to me, "My grace is sufficient for you,
> for my power is made perfect in weakness."
> Therefore I will boast all the more gladly of
> my weaknesses, so that the power of Christ
> may rest upon me. **(2 CORINTHIANS 12:9)**

THE BODY OF CHRIST

$Dear Lord,$ Thank You for the support, unity, and camaraderie of faithful people who make up Your church. It is amazing to consider the impact of Your testimony reaching around the world, creating a beautiful and diverse body of believers. Thank You for the sweet fellowship of meeting with the body of Christ. As we engage with one another, get to know each other, and worship You together, we hope You are glorified. Thank You for the way Your Word describes the body of Christ, teaching that each one of us has a significant role and is a valuable member of the body. Reveal how our lives influence the body and the ways You desire us to participate in the life of the church. Show us how we can work as a couple to serve the church. Use us to help other believers, encouraging them to walk in faith. Lord, grow us up in every way so that we are equipped to work together to magnify Your name and be unified with other believers. In Jesus's name we pray. Amen.

Speaking the truth in love, we are to grow up in every way into him who is the head, into Christ, from whom the whole body, joined and held together by every joint with which it is equipped, when each part is working properly, makes the body grow so that it builds itself up in love. **(EPHESIANS 4:15–16)**

FAMILY VALUES

𝒟ear 𝓛ord, Thank You for our family. We also thank You for inviting us into Your heavenly family. We acknowledge the importance of relationships, as well as our responsibility to maintain them. We appreciate the opportunities we receive to care for and nurture our relationships. We praise You for the people in our lives! We seek to honor You as we aim to love our families well. Lord, establish core values and standards in our home that align with Your Word. Motivate us to carefully consider how we operate in our everyday lives, choosing to be honorable in our communication, our work, and in every small or large goal we pursue. Help us to be not just hearers but also doers of Your Word. May Your values become our values. We long to pass down a love of Your Word to the next generation, which can happen only if we both commit to upholding these values, leading to fruitful lives. Lord, move in our home and show us any area where we have misplaced our values. When we cast a vision for our home and decide a major direction for our marriage and family, we pray Your Holy Spirit leads us. Teach us to establish strong biblical values that are founded in Christ, and unify us in marriage as we live them out faithfully. In Jesus's name we pray. Amen.

Be doers of the word, and not hearers only,
deceiving yourselves. **(JAMES 1:22)**

CHANGES IN OUR BODIES

Dear Lord, Thank You for the way You designed our wonderful bodies. Thank You for creating us, giving us life, and giving us to one another in marriage. Lord, please help us to take care of our bodies by eating healthy and staying active. Stir our hearts to encourage one another to make good choices that benefit our health. Despite striving to keep our bodies healthy, we know change is inevitable. Please help us embrace the way our bodies shift over time. Lord, keep us from entertaining negative thoughts about our bodies and from comparing our bodies with those of others. May we not lose heart and fret over our bodies, knowing that our value in Your eyes does not diminish as we age and deteriorate over time. No matter how our bodies change, we ask You to help us remain confident that our inner self is being renewed, built up, and refined by You. God, please keep us humble and respectful in the way we think and talk about each other's bodies. May we see our bodies as a gift from You to carry out Your purpose and as a gift to each other. In Jesus's name we pray. Amen.

Do not lose heart. Though our outer self is wasting away, our inner self is being renewed day by day. **(2 CORINTHIANS 4:16)**

BALANCING LIFE

Dear Lord, Thank You for our marriage and all the responsibilities You have entrusted to us. Thank You for the ebb and flow of life. Just when we feel like we are doing too much, You are faithful to remind us to rest. And once we have carved out enough time to recuperate, You often invite us to participate in something You are doing, giving us a new goal to aim for. Lord, we ask You to help us keep our life in balance. Keep us mindful of our schedules and all that we have going on. Make us aware of how much time we are devoting to work, ministry, and being present at home. Focus our hearts on dividing our attention appropriately between meaningful relationships with family and friends. Lord, will You help us steward our time and equip us to accomplish any pending work? Help us to balance life in a way that honors You and provides our family with stability. May our family and friends admonish us if we are stretching ourselves too thin or encourage us if we should step up and give more energy toward a certain area. Let them be a gong of wisdom to alarm us and help us stay on the right track. We submit our goals and plans to You. We ask You to lead us in the way we should go and in the things we should do, and help us enjoy the process of balancing life along the way. In Jesus's name we pray. Amen.

You therefore, beloved, knowing this
beforehand, take care that you are not carried
away with the error of lawless people and
lose your own stability. **(2 PETER 3:17)**

NO MORE BLAMING

Dear Lord, We confess that it is easy to blame someone else rather than accept fault in ourselves. When our flesh is weak, we can be consumed with figuring out who is to blame for a mess or mistake that stirred up a whole host of emotions. Lord, humble us, especially in intense moments when we want to place blame on one another. Remind us of the grace You have extended to us—how You had the authority to blame us for our sin, yet chose to forgive and wash us white as snow. That is unconditional love! Thank You for taking away our shame and showing us mercy. Lord, instead of blaming one another, we ask You to help us to love unconditionally and extend amazing grace. May we never criticize each other for shortcomings, failures, and sin. Remind us that we are one, that we can bear each other's burdens, and that sometimes we will have similar faults and will desire love and grace in response. Lord, keep us in step with Your Spirit, determining not to point the finger at one another and instead walking with each other in understanding, grace, and mercy. May we lay down our offenses, our opinions, and our opportunity to judge one another so we can experience transforming love. In Jesus's name we pray. Amen.

Therefore you have no excuse, O man, every one of you who judges. For in passing judgment on another you condemn yourself, because you, the judge, practice the very same things. **(ROMANS 2:1)**

ENTERTAINMENT

Dear Lord, Thank You for entertainment, including music, art, television, and social media. Entertainment is not sin, but we know if we aren't careful, it can tempt us to sin. Along with all the good and reputable messages found in entertainment, some messages are in direct opposition to You, God. As we experience the talents of others, please guard our hearts from evil and keep us from sinning. Make us a couple who is aware of what we expose ourselves to and cautious of what we listen to, watch, or engage with. Holy Spirit, help us to consider the forms of entertainment we allow to influence our thoughts and give us boldness to step away from entertainment that isn't pleasing to You. May we stand strong amid temptation, never setting our eyes on anything worthless. Lord, will You help us to be receptive to Your Holy Spirit when He speaks to us, and to each other when we share our concerns? Lord, mature us and give us wisdom in how we use entertainment. In Jesus's name we pray. Amen.

I will ponder the way that is blameless.
Oh when will you come to me?
I will walk with integrity of heart
within my house;
I will not set before my eyes
anything that is worthless.

(PSALM 101:2-3)

FINDING COMFORT

𝒟*ear 𝓛ord,* The promise of eternal life is our ultimate comfort. While we wait our turn to experience eternity, we ask You, Lord, to continually cover us with Your peace. Thank You also that we can comfort one another through physical touch and affirmation. Being married provides a camaraderie in which we can enjoy being known, making a home together, and experiencing life together. We ask You to help us press into our relationship so we can experience a closeness like we never have before. Cultivate an atmosphere of openness and receptivity that allows us to be comforted by each other in beautiful and deep ways. May we seek and find fulfillment in each other's embrace instead of seeking it on our own or in ways that create unhealthy habits. Lord, will You open our eyes to each other's needs and help us to be quick to respond with hearts of selfless serving? In moments that cause stress, chaos, sorrow, or pain, Lord, may we be Your hands and feet, comforting each other to ease the burdens that weigh us down. In Jesus's name we pray. Amen.

This is my comfort in my affliction,
that your promise gives me life.
(PSALM 119:50)

BUSY WORKDAYS

𝒟ear 𝓛ord, Thank You for the work You have given us. Thank You for how busy we have been lately. We appreciate the opportunity, as well as the desire we both have, to work hard. Shape us into a couple who is diligent and efficient in our work. Help us organize our days to make the best use of our time. God, will You show us how to honor You in our places of work, whether that be at home or outside the home? May we never complain about our responsibilities or whom we work alongside. Remove any negative thoughts we have, and train us instead to dwell on all we are grateful for. Fill our cups to the brim with contentment—and enough energy to get any job done well. In whatever we do, we hope to find a sense of purpose. But as much as we may gain from busy workdays, don't let us lose sight of the most important things in life. Lord, don't let our work become an idol. Please help us to keep a good balance with our work schedules so that we can still spend time together to tend to our marriage. Protect us from the temptation of greed and pride. May You be glorified in everything we do. In Jesus's name we pray. Amen.

> *What does man gain by all the toil*
> *at which he toils under the sun?*
> **(ECCLESIASTES 1:3)**

PUTTING OUR
PHONES AWAY

Dear Lord, Excite our hearts to show love to one another today. As we make time simply to be present with each other, we specifically ask You, Lord, to help us put our phones away more regularly. Being on a device, plugged into the world, easily becomes a distraction. We confess that looking at our phones can become all-consuming, and justifying our habits only keeps us from giving each other more affection. Lord, we recognize there is a time and place to use our phones, so we ask You to make us more aware of our usage, revealing to us the moments when we pick up our phones out of habit or boredom, not necessity. Help us to hold hands more than we hold our devices. Help us to look into each other's eyes more than we look at our screens. Please help us to set healthy boundaries and to stick to them. When we get frustrated with the other person's phone usage, encourage us to gently remind each other of the commitments we have made and the values we hold dear. Lord, when there's downtime, train us to check on each other before we check on the news or social media. Make us mindful to put down any distractions so we can give one another our hearts' full attention. In Jesus's name we pray. Amen.

Do not be deceived: God is not mocked, for whatever one sows, that will he also reap. For the one who sows to his own flesh will from the flesh reap corruption, but the one who sows to the Spirit will from the Spirit reap eternal life. **(GALATIANS 6:7-8)**

SHIELD OF FAITH

Dear Lord, Our shield and protector! Thank You for the gift of faith. Thank You for the many different circumstances we have walked through as a couple and the many more we will encounter in the future. Faith is integral to our relationship with You. Without faith we would not understand the power of prayer or how to pray. It is faith that enables us to draw close to You, Lord! We recognize the importance of having a strong foundation in marriage, a relationship established on a bedrock of faith. Lord, we pray You would increase our faithfulness! Anchor our hearts and secure our belief in You so that doubt has nowhere to flourish. In every season and circumstance, remind us to take up the shield of faith to protect our marriage from the flaming arrows of the Enemy. Lord, help us not to let our circumstances dictate how we interact with each other. Ignite a determination in our hearts to walk through life with self-control in our words and actions. We pray in faith, asking You to defend our marriage and make it strong. In Jesus's name we pray. Amen.

*In all circumstances take up the shield of faith,
with which you can extinguish all the flaming
darts of the evil one.* **(EPHESIANS 6:16)**

AGREEMENT IN FINANCES

Dear Lord, We ask You to lead us as we decide how best to manage our accounts. We ask You for wisdom in stewarding our finances as we consider the ways we spend, save, and give. Please unify us in the way we view and address our money. If You desire us to adjust our spending habits, we pray our hearts would be sensitive and malleable to Your correction. Make us considerate of what we can do to prepare for our future while also investing in the legacy we purpose to establish so that generations of our family would benefit from our choices today. Lord, we commit to using our finances to glorify You. We trust You with all that we have because we know it came from You. Keep our lives free from the love of money, and never let it be a source of contention in our marriage. If we feel frustrated over our finances, remind us to bring up our concerns respectfully. Lord, we trust You to always draw us back to the same page and reinforce in our hearts that we are on the same team. In Jesus's name we pray. Amen.

Keep your life free from love of money, and be content with what you have, for he has said, "I will never leave you nor forsake you." **(HEBREWS 13:5)**

STANDING STRONG IN TODAY'S WORLD

Dear Lord, Thank You for imparting Your truth to us. Please help us to abide in Your Word every day and encourage each other to know Your Word intimately. When we feel insecure, may we point each other back to Your truth. Please protect our hearts as we are inundated with news that is overwhelming and out of our control. Our world seems to be enduring an increase of chaos. Shape us into a couple who stands strong in today's world. Though uncertainty seems to be around every corner, please help us to remain firm and stable in our marriage. Lord, will You help us identify any areas of our marriage that are weak or on the verge of being fractured? Will You also help us develop those parts of our relationship? We are confident that we belong to You and that the world lies in the power of the Evil One. May the Evil One and his deeds be dragged into the light and exposed, in Jesus's name! We pray Your truth prevails! Lord, let our marriage be a powerful force in the world to show others Your light. In Jesus's name we pray. Amen.

We know that we are from God, and the whole world lies in the power of the evil one. **(1 JOHN 5:19)**

THE SPIRIT HELPS US

Dear Lord, Your Holy Spirit is a marvelous gift! Thank You that the Holy Spirit directs us to follow You and faithfully reminds us of what Your Word says. We know it is Your Spirit who gives life. Our flesh is no help at all. Because our flesh desires things contrary to Your Spirit, our passions are at war within us. May Your Spirit win us over and help us walk in righteousness. Lord, please help us to control our flesh. Both of us have contributed to hurt in our relationship when we pursued the desires of our flesh. We humbly apologize to You, Lord, and to each other for the destruction we have caused because of our sin. Holy Spirit, thank You for helping us fight against temptation, for providing a way of escape from sin when it knocks at the door of our hearts. Lord, we want to continue to experience growth and victory in our marriage as we surrender our wills to You, our minds to You, and our flesh to You. Please help us keep in step with Your Holy Spirit every day. In Jesus's name we pray. Amen.

*It is the Spirit who gives life; the flesh
is no help at all.* **(JOHN 6:63)**

NO MORE LAZINESS

Dear Lord, Although it seems we have enough to do to keep us busy for a lifetime, sometimes we choose not to do anything important at all. Sometimes we simply choose to be lazy. Lord, will You help us recognize the difference between laziness and prioritizing rest? We don't want to be lazy or apathetic! We trust You to keep molding us to be more like You. Prune any laziness out of us. Transform the parts of us that tend to be lethargic, and reconstruct us to be diligent, resourceful, and wise. Lord, we don't want to be idle in our marriage, relying on the other person to always initiate or do things we don't feel like doing. We want to be a couple who respects each other and acknowledges the demanding work that has to be done to maintain our relationship and our home. Lord, when we feel offended by the other person's laziness, will You help us to calmly communicate how it makes us feel, encouraging one another to step up and contribute? Holy Spirit, strengthen our resolve to resist being slothful. Thank You, God, for being our source of energy and strength! Heavenly Father, we ask You to instill in both of us a desire and resilience to be diligent servants in our marriage, in our jobs, and in our home. In Jesus's name we pray. Amen.

> *Slothfulness casts into a deep sleep,*
> *and an idle person will suffer hunger.*
> **(PROVERBS 19:15)**

PREACHING THE GOSPEL

Dear Lord, Thank You for the power of the gospel and for calling us to share it with others. Lord, will You please make us a couple who is ready in and out of season to preach the Word of truth? Thank You for the conversations in which we have the opportunity to proclaim to others what Your Word says in order to draw them closer to You. Give us the courage to boldly speak the truth in love, and make us a supportive team who shares Your love and light with those around us. May we also never overlook the opportunities we have to preach Your gospel to each other. We need to remind each other of the truth daily! May we know the power of regularly sharing Your testimony with each other. Holy Spirit, bring to mind what we know in Your Word so we can encourage one another with Your wisdom. Lead us to use Scripture to gently reprove and exhort each other in love. May Your testimony be revealed, and the power of Your gospel preached far and wide, as we aim to make it known to the world. In Jesus's name we pray. Amen.

Preach the word; be ready in season and out of season; reprove, rebuke, and exhort, with complete patience and teaching. **(2 TIMOTHY 4:2)**

TAKING CARE OF OUR THINGS

Dear Lord, Thinking about our many possessions is incredible! We never want to overlook giving You thanks for any of it. So we take the time right now to acknowledge the possessions we have accumulated and the experiences we have gained—everything You have allowed us to acquire and consume—and we thank You, Lord, for Your generosity! Help us to value our belongings, even if others don't see any value in them, or if the actual price tag is labeled low cost. Something's value is not just in its monetary worth but also in its perceived necessity or usefulness. May the possessions we keep around bring us joy, as well as some sort of benefit. We invite You to help us evaluate whether any of our possessions have become idols. Help us to also consider whether we struggle with discontentment and buy things unnecessarily. We desire to have a healthy view of earthly, temporary things. Lord, make us a couple who not only takes good care of our things but also holds them loosely, willing to give them away if the need arises. We desire to be generous, using our resources to bless others and giving without expecting anything in return. May we be faithful stewards of what we own. In Jesus's name we pray. Amen.

It is required of stewards that they be found faithful. **(1 CORINTHIANS 4:2)**

SURRENDERING
ANXIOUS THOUGHTS

Dear Lord, When we are weak and experience the churning of anxious thoughts, we ask You to reassure us with Your Word. Please help us to support one another by reminding each other to lay our anxiety at Your feet in prayer. Thank You for giving us Your peace, which surpasses all understanding! We desire to trust You more each day. No matter what circumstances we face or what happens next in this world, help us to hold fast to the Bible. May our faith be unshakable. May our joy be made strong. May our patience be immovable. May our hope be indestructible. Heavenly Father, will You defend us and deflect the temptation to fear? Please suit us up in Your armor—with the helmet of salvation to guard our minds. Combat despair and panic by reminding us to worship You with thanksgiving. We surrender any anxious thoughts we may have right now, in Jesus's name! Holy Spirit, we petition You to cover us with Your peace. When we're cycling through anxious thoughts, please show us how to stop immediately, repent of our worry, and submit to You in prayer. Lord, may we see everything through Your eyes. In Jesus's name we pray. Amen.

Do not be anxious about anything, but in everything by prayer and supplication with thanksgiving let your requests be made known to God. **(PHILIPPIANS 4:6)**

GRATITUDE

Dear Lord, If our gratitude were a well, You could draw from it perpetually and find an infinite supply of appreciation. We are in awe of Your saving grace and unconditional love, by which You've transformed our lives. We pray our hearts would not hold back from sharing our gratitude. We praise You, Lord! Shape our minds to dwell deeply on what we are grateful for about You and what we appreciate in our marriage. Lord, will You develop in us an insatiable desire to tell one another all that we are thankful for in our relationship? Our hearts benefit from hearing the reasons we appreciate marriage, and we know it will bring You glory! Lord, we have much to be thankful for: When one of us randomly leaves an endearing note on the counter. When a day of mundane errands turns into a spontaneous time of connection. When we work together on a project for our home. When a hard day is redeemed with snuggling and our favorite dessert. When one of us prays over our marriage despite thick tension between us. Lord, for all of these moments of marriage, we thank You! We praise You for binding us together and giving us countless opportunities to love each other. May You be glorified as the overflow of our hearts highlight Your goodness. In Jesus's name we pray. Amen.

Let us be grateful for receiving a kingdom that cannot be shaken, and thus let us offer to God acceptable worship, with reverence and awe, for our God is a consuming fire. **(HEBREWS 12:28–29)**

LOVE IS

Dear Lord, Thank You for the way You gently, yet firmly lead us through Scripture to understand the truth about what love is. Thank You for the way Your Word defines love, making it clear exactly how we should love one another. We don't always catch on right away or quickly implementing the truth in our lives—we are creatures of habit—but we are eager to grow, knowing it takes time and conditioning. Let Your truth captivate us and change us. Lord, will You chisel away our selfish ways and enable us to love well? Please help us to be patient with and kind to each other. Remove any envious thoughts or roots of bitterness we have toward each other. God, destroy every part of us that is arrogant and rude. Sanctify us so that we don't insist on our own way! Holy Spirit, please help us to peacefully navigate any decisions we have to make together. When we are irritable with each other, please humble us and remind us to walk in love. Please help us to let go of past hurts and resist holding on to resentment. Lord, we invite You to develop in us the ability to love each other according to Your truth. In Jesus's name we pray. Amen.

Love is patient and kind; love does not envy or boast; it is not arrogant or rude. It does not insist on its own way; it is not irritable or resentful; it does not rejoice at wrongdoing, but rejoices with the truth. **(1 CORINTHIANS 13:4–6)**

BEING UNVEILED

$Dear Lord,$ Thank You for freedom. You have unveiled our hearts and helped us see clearly who You are and what You have done to set us free. You have made Yourself known to us, and we desire to make ourselves known to You. Please help us to remain unveiled before You, humble and transparent in the way we share our hearts with You. Thank You also for the way transparency in marriage can be a catalyst for incredible intimacy. Thank You for the courage to open up to one another, the courage to admit when we are struggling with self-doubt, or the boldness to say we feel weak in our faith. May we never hold back from sharing our hearts with one another. Even when it is challenging to get the words out. Even when our flesh fights against being revealed. Even when it feels like the time is never right. Holy Spirit, activate within us a desire to be known. May we be willing to openly discuss what we feel and think, full of hope for the transformation You are working within us. Please help us drag our hearts into the light and expose what is inside of us. As risk is assumed and fears are laid aside, may our transparency cultivate love, intimacy, and trust with You and with each other. In Jesus's name we pray. Amen.

Now the Lord is the Spirit, and where the Spirit of the Lord is, there is freedom. And we all, with unveiled face, beholding the glory of the Lord, are being transformed into the same image from one degree of glory to another. For this comes from the Lord who is the Spirit. **(2 CORINTHIANS 3:17–18)**

MATURING IN GOD

Dear Lord, Abiding in You has matured us both. Thank You for changing us for the better. May we continue to abide in Your Word daily. May we humbly allow You to mold us as a potter fashions a piece of clay. As we grow in our relationship with You, develop in our character, and flourish in our faith, we know that our marriage benefits. The more we draw near to You, the more we draw near to each other. Thank You for the way our relationships with You impact our relationship with each other. Lord, make us and our marriage into remarkable masterpieces. Expand our faith, anchor our hope, and deepen our love. Increase our desire to read and understand the Bible. As we prioritize reading Scripture, let it comfort us, teach us, and guide us. Lord, help us to lay aside any selfish thoughts or selfish ways, while preserving truth in our hearts so that we continue to experience growth. May we benefit in our marriage as we are sanctified in You. In Jesus's name we pray. Amen.

When I was a child, I spoke like a child, I thought like a child, I reasoned like a child. When I became a man, I gave up childish ways. **(1 CORINTHIANS 13:11)**

WALKING IN VICTORY

Dear Lord, Thank You for redemption! Thank You for setting us free from the bondage of sin and giving us true victory. Sometimes we get discouraged, believing we will never be able to change. Sometimes we sin, causing a great amount of pain in our marriage. Please remove the feelings of failure and shame that plague us, hindering us from maturing. Help us to receive Your forgiveness and be willing to forgive one another when we transgress. When conviction grips us, lead us to repentance so we can walk in victory. We know You provided a way for us to do this when Your Son, Jesus Christ, defeated death and sin on the cross and was resurrected. We believe His power breaks the bondage of sin in our lives so that when we fall short, He reveals our sin to us and gives us everything we need to be reconciled. Lord, help us in our disbelief! Create in us a steadfast faith! Lord, please help us never to doubt the power of the gospel at work in our lives. Renew our minds and destroy the desires that lead us to wrongdoing. May we encourage one another every day to walk in victory, in confidence, and in righteousness. In Jesus's name we pray. Amen.

Thanks be to God, who gives us the victory through our Lord Jesus Christ. **(1 CORINTHIANS 15:57)**

HEALING AFTER CONFLICT

Dear Lord, You are our healer! Like a balm that soothes an open wound, You touch our brokenness and gently restore us. You release us from the clutch of condemnation and shame, covering us in robes of grace. You comfort us. You forgive us. You make us new. Lord, we praise You for the healing we receive from You. Will You show us how to receive healing after conflict in our marriage? Will You teach us how to apply Your wisdom and comfort to one another in tangible ways? Reveal to us the value of confession and being held accountable to each other. Lord, help us to be transparent with one another and to confess what we are wrestling with so that we can support each other through the process of reconciliation. Give us the courage to hold up the shield of faith while praying for one another. When we experience discord, help us seek reconciliation with You and with each other. Our desire is that we would still be willing to be close and intimate after conflict. Lord, will You show us how to embrace each other despite our shortcomings? Help us never to withhold our love or hang on to bitterness. May Your working power transform our lives and our marriage for the better as we chase after You. In Jesus's name we pray. Amen.

Therefore, confess your sins to one another and pray for one another, that you may be healed. The prayer of a righteous person has great power as it is working. **(JAMES 5:16)**

THE ARMOR OF GOD

Dear Lord, Thank You for offering us protection through Your spiritual armor. Thank You for equipping us to stand firm in our faith. The Bible reminds us that we have an Enemy who tries to destroy us. Inspire us to remind each other continually to suit up in Your armor so we are prepared to defend our faith, our marriage, our minds, and our hearts. Train us up to confidently use the sword of the Spirit, which is Your Word. May the power of Scripture break through strong-holds in our lives and destroy the lies of the Enemy. Lord, help us hold up the shield of faith so we aren't pierced by the advances of the Enemy. Please help us to encourage one another in our beliefs. We put on the helmet of salvation to preserve truth in our minds. May we dwell on things above! Fasten the belt of truth around us, and prepare us with the readiness of the gospel of peace so we can share Your testimony with each other and others. Lord, reaffirm in us how putting on the breastplate of righteousness means putting on the righteousness of Christ. May we prepare ourselves for spiritual battle by putting on Your armor, and may we stand firm, ready to defend and protect our marriage every day. In Jesus's name we pray. Amen.

Therefore take up the whole armor of God, that you may be able to withstand in the evil day, and having done all, to stand firm. **(EPHESIANS 6:13)**

WHAT WE WRESTLE WITH

Dear Lord, In this world there are many things we wrestle with and many battles we face. Some of our battles are more obvious, while others are hidden, including those that are spiritual in nature. No matter what situation we experience, we hope to endure it together, steadfast in faith, believing You will win the victory for us. You tell us in Your Word that we do not wrestle against flesh and blood, so please remind us of this truth when we find ourselves in contention. Bring to remembrance that we are one, and assure us who the real enemy is. We are not enemies of each other! We are on the same team. We are wrestling with spiritual forces and need to remain unified and in submission to You to win our battles. Lord, will You help us cultivate a mentality of oneness that supports each other? Help us consider what the other is going through. When challenging times come our way, we pray we would work together and not against each other. Thank You, Lord, for taking away our fear and giving us faith. May we follow as You lead us through every battle. In Jesus's name we pray. Amen.

> *We do not wrestle against flesh and blood,*
> *but against the rulers, against the authorities,*
> *against the cosmic powers over this present*
> *darkness, against the spiritual forces of evil*
> *in the heavenly places.* **(EPHESIANS 6:12)**

NO MORE WITHHOLDING

Dear Lord, Thank You for the amazing way we experience intimacy in marriage. There is no relationship like it! Thank You for the opportunities to spend time together, giving us the chance to cultivate closeness in our relationship. We pray we get more time together! When we prepare our minds and our hearts to be united in physical intimacy, please help us, Lord, not to sabotage our time together. May nothing stop us from being together in the way we intend, in Jesus's name! God, please help us not to let frustrations or selfishness creep up and keep us from being vulnerable with each other. If we're tempted to withhold intimacy from one another, direct our hearts to do what is right. Prompt us to pray when our flesh attempts to push each other away. Help us to embrace each other still. Keep our intimacy alive and passionate. Extinguish any self-centeredness convincing us to withhold until we get what we want. Lord, will You help us to give of ourselves in love? May we satisfy one another's desire for intimacy and connectedness. May our pursuit of one another lead to an extraordinary marriage. In Jesus's name we pray. Amen.

> *I am my beloved's,*
> *and his desire is for me.*
> **(SONG OF SOLOMON 7:10)**

FAITHFULNESS

𝒟ear 𝓛ord, Thank You for being faithful even when we are not. We admire Your steadfastness in fulfilling Your promises. You are trustworthy! We yearn to be faithful to You and each other. Lord, may we seek to live in purity, with self-control over our impulses to indulge in sin. May our thoughts be loyal to one another. Lord, will You show us how to agree on boundaries for our marriage and adhere to them to protect our fidelity? Secure in our hearts the determination to avoid even a hint of immorality. We never want to sever our intimacy with You or with each other. In our ardor for faithfulness, may we find favor and success in Your sight. We hope to maintain our trust and affirm our love by honoring our marriage covenant. Our desire is to cling to one another in pure devotion. Holy Spirit, sustain our loyalty, devotion, and love, and motivate us to persevere in life together while enjoying the splendid journey of marriage. In Jesus's name we pray. Amen.

> *Let not steadfast love and faithfulness*
> *forsake you;*
> *bind them around your neck;*
> *write them on the tablet of your heart.*
> *So you will find favor and good success*
> *in the sight of God and man.*
> **(PROVERBS 3:3-4)**

BEING GENEROUS

𝒟ear ℒord, Generosity reveals the magnitude of benevolence and tender affection in the heart of one who gives without expectation of compensation. You are generous for providing the ultimate gift of salvation for all. May Your generosity inspire us to be gracious givers as well. Lord, will You help us to consider what we have to offer and give without expecting anything in return? In our marriage, will You please motivate us to give lavishly? When we offer physical affection or words of encouragement or lend a hand of support, please show us how to give freely to one another. When we have needs that aren't being met, we ask You, God, to prompt us to approach the conversation warmly, stating what we need. Keep us from withholding what we should give. Our hope is that our marriage would be the place we are satisfied, comforted, and loved intimately. Being a generous couple will enrich our relationship and water our souls. Lord, may You be glorified in the way we love one another. In Jesus's name we pray. Amen.

> *One gives freely, yet grows all the richer;*
> *another withholds what he should*
> *give, and only suffers want.*
> *Whoever brings blessing will be enriched,*
> *and one who waters will himself be*
> *watered.* **(PROVERBS 11:24–25)**

CHOOSING EACH OTHER DAILY

Dear Lord, We praise You for the power of love in our lives. We both have been transformed by Your love and deeply touched by our love for each other. May Your will be done in our marriage! Wake us up every morning ready to choose love. Heavenly Father, ignite a passion in us to be thoughtful in our interactions with each other. With every opportunity we have today, direct us to consider the significance of serving one another. We know that if we do anything without love, it means nothing. Make our intentions pure, in Jesus's name! May we choose each other daily—may we choose each other over worry, over finances, over arguing, and over work. As we balance our lives, may we prioritize our relationship above other relationships, trusting each other to pour more time into our marriage than into family, friendships, ministry partners, and work relationships. When we actively choose each other, we are sending a message to everyone about the importance our marriage has above everything else. Lord, continually show us how our choices impact one another's lives and the condition of our marriage. In Jesus's name we pray. Amen.

If I have prophetic powers, and understand all mysteries and all knowledge, and if I have all faith, so as to remove mountains, but have not love, I am nothing. **(1 CORINTHIANS 13:2)**

BEING HUMBLE

Dear Lord, We are learning that humility is freedom from pride. Without pride governing our hearts, we can have a modest view of ourselves. Pride demands a pedestal position of authority, while humility offers a posture of submission and sacrifice. We confess that pride often comes between us. Lord, will You show us the consequences of pride in contrast to the benefits of humility? In moments when our flesh is tempted with arrogance, will You redirect us to act in meekness instead? Let Christ's example of humility reign in our hearts and minds! Help us to see clearly, and reveal any insight that will contribute to our resolve. May we refuse to fight for what we think is right, but rather, fight for Your truth to prevail. When we desire justice, remind us to bring our case before You, the good judge, in genuine prayer. In Jesus's name we pray. Amen.

> *He has told you, O man, what is good;*
> *and what does the LORD require of you*
> *but to do justice, and to love kindness,*
> *and to walk humbly with your God?*
> **(MICAH 6:8)**

NO MORE COVETING

Dear Lord, We acknowledge the provision You have poured over our marriage, and we are incredibly grateful. Yet there are times our flesh is tempted to covet what others have. Although our souls are satisfied in You and our hearts are satisfied with each other, our flesh never seems to be content. We see the blessings You give to other couples, and we want them. We see the promotions, the possessions, and the peace they have, and envy begins to rise up in us. We see what others are capable of doing, how they dress, the places they travel to on vacation, and the apparent perfect life they live, and we are tempted by the sin of jealousy. We confess there are times when our envy overshadows our sight and we fail to notice the blessings You have given us—consumed with what we want and what we think we need. We repent! We are sorry for letting our flesh control us with its constant desire. Lord, please help us to have self-control over our thoughts. Remove the idols we have allowed in our hearts. Purify us, Lord! Please keep us from comparing our marriage with another or comparing the blessings of others to those we have been given. Bring satisfaction to our flesh, and help us to stop coveting. In Jesus's name we pray. Amen.

You may be sure of this, that everyone who is sexually immoral or impure, or who is covetous (that is, an idolater), has no inheritance in the kingdom of Christ and God. **(EPHESIANS 5:5)**

DEALING WITH TEMPTATION

Dear Lord, We love You and desire to honor You with our lives. We know the truth and strive to walk in righteousness, yet we are still tempted to sin every day. This is hard. We confess that our flesh is weak. We surrender to Your will and know that when we abide in You, we are more sensitive to Your leading. Lord, guard our minds and help us to take our thoughts captive. Please help us combat temptation to sin with the power of Scripture. Just as Jesus responded to the Enemy with Your Word, we pray we would follow His example. Holy Spirit, fight alongside us for purity. Strengthen us so that we deny our flesh. Thank You for never forsaking us. Thank You for always providing a way of escape. Remind us we are never alone because You are with us! May we never be lured away from Your truth. Lord, will You teach us how to keep each other accountable? When we struggle with a specific sin, will You give us the courage to tell one another and then pray for each other? Make us a couple who chooses to live holy and blameless lives. May we stand strong, flee temptation, and endure together. In Jesus's name we pray. Amen.

> *No temptation has overtaken you that is not common to man. God is faithful, and he will not let you be tempted beyond your ability, but with the temptation he will also provide the way of escape, that you may be able to endure it.* **(1 CORINTHIANS 10:13)**

UNTIL DEATH DO US PART

Dear Lord, The covenant of marriage has taught us the gravity and blessing of making and keeping a promise. Marriage is a promise to remain faithful to one another, and we choose to keep that promise every day. Though it seems that long-lasting relationships are rare, our hope is that we would not let passivity tear down our high view of marriage. We desire our marriage to be strong enough to last our lifetime. Lord, will You protect our promise to love each other and help us remain faithful to that promise? Show us how to keep You at the center of our marriage, and bind us together like a three-cord strand that is not quickly broken! May You be glorified for the longevity of our love and our commitment to care for each other. Remind us daily of the vows we declared to each other. Draw us back to the memories of our wedding day and every reason we chose to marry. Our lifetime commitment to one another is intricately woven together with our devotion to You. It is encouraging to know we will experience marriage on earth until death do us part and then experience eternal life with You and the fulfillment of the marriage feast of Christ. While we endure all of life's trials and challenges, please use us to encourage each other to abide in Your love. In Jesus's name we pray. Amen.

But you, beloved, building yourselves up in your most holy faith and praying in the Holy Spirit, keep yourselves in the love of God, waiting for the mercy of our Lord Jesus Christ that leads to eternal life. **(JUDE VV. 20–21)**

CREATIVITY IN MARRIAGE

𝒟*ear* ℒ*ord,* We praise You for the intricate detail You poured into creating us. Thank You forming us with intention and giving us purpose. Like clay kneaded between the hands of a passionate potter, we are the work of Your hands! We desire to be creative as well. Lord, make us an innovative couple. Inspire our hearts to be ingenious with the dates we plan for each other and the projects we aim to do together. May we be inventive in the way we express our love and think outside the box when we serve each other. In our attempts to be clever in building up our relationship, we ask You to also help us receive and appreciate every deed, no matter how eccentric they may be. When others ask us about our passion to love in creative ways, we desire to point them to You! May our vision and enthusiasm to be creative in marriage spur others on to love in extraordinary ways. In Jesus's name we pray. Amen.

> *But now, O LORD, you are our Father;*
> *we are the clay, and you are our*
> *potter;*
> *we are all the work of your hand.*
> **(ISAIAH 64:8)**

BE IMITATORS OF GOD

Dear Lord, May we be imitators of You, laying down our lives for each other in marriage, serving one another in love every day. Lord, help us imitate Christ, being humble and compassionate with one another. Having the desire, motivation, and will to sacrifice for another is a beautiful thing! It is a powerful thing! God, may we experience the richness of love through sacrifice. Please help us to sacrifice our time, our desires, our goals, and anything else that may need to be surrendered for the sake of the other. Show us the importance of prioritizing intimate conversations with each other. Holy Spirit, urge us to put each other's needs above our own. As we strive to imitate You, may Your fruit be produced in our lives and may our marriage reflect Your love story. We yield our souls in humble submission, inviting You to do Your will in our lives. In Jesus's name we pray. Amen.

*Therefore be imitators of God, as beloved
children. And walk in love, as Christ loved us
and gave himself up for us, a fragrant offering
and sacrifice to God.* **(EPHESIANS 5:1–2)**

KINGDOM MINDED

𝒟ear 𝒧ord, Thank You for delivering us out of darkness. Thank You for welcoming us into the kingdom of Christ. Thank You for the opportunity we have today to be a light in this world. May our marriage—the way we communicate, the choices we make, and how we handle ourselves in all the small and big moments—honor You and point others toward You. Give us a heavenly perspective about our marriage, and reveal what it means to be kingdom minded. Unveil the truth that our marriage is for more than just to make us happy. Lord, we ask You to fortify our unity as we aim to carry out Your purpose. Adjust our vision so we may see each other from Your perspective, through the lens of grace and redemption. Lord, we don't want our eyes to be clouded by hurt or offense, but rather may they look upon each other with compassion, knowing You are still miraculously transforming both of our characters for the better. Please help direct our hearts and minds as we pursue You and join You in what You are doing in this world. We give You our marriage and ask You to use us to do Your will. Remind us every day that we are children of light, and help us to encourage one another to walk in the light. In Jesus's name we pray. Amen.

He has delivered us from the domain of darkness and transferred us to the kingdom of his beloved Son, in whom we have redemption, the forgiveness of sins. **(COLOSSIANS 1:13-14)**

SUBMITTING IN LOVE

Dear Lord, You created us to complement one another in marriage. We each have gifts that accompany the other's strengths and weaknesses. Recognizing how different we are from one another allows us the opportunity to consider how our distinctness is a part of Your design. Please help us to appreciate the many ways we complement each other. We also thank You for the way our marriage represents the church and its relationship to Christ. Lord, You have given us this gift of marriage not only to be enjoyed but also to be used as a vessel to show the world the beauty of love and respect. In Your design of marriage, You have given us roles and responsibilities that in turn bless us. Help us embrace and obey Your Word where it addresses and describes our responsibilities to one another. In doing so, we highlight the mystery of the love of Christ and the submission of the church to His divine authority. Teach us how to love sacrificially and submit to each other in honor, fulfilling Your Word. Lord, will You show us how to walk out our roles without grumbling so our partnership can be a sign to the world of whom we follow and serve? Not our wills, but Yours be done, in Jesus's name! Sacrificial love and submission are beautiful and powerful when done for Christ! May our choices honor You. In Jesus's name we pray. Amen.

Wives, submit to your own husbands,
as to the Lord. **(EPHESIANS 5:22)**

LEADING IN LOVE

Dear Lord, Thank You for Your Son, who is a perfect example of a loving and gentle leader. Thank You for Jesus's representation of how to serve one another in humility. Holy Spirit, empower us to do the same. It is Your power that enables us to imitate Him and foster true love. Thank You for the way our marriage becomes a safe place when our hearts are submitted to You. We appreciate that You never force a relationship with us, but instead You pursue us in love and give us time to respond. You are faithful and kind. May we come to You in prayer regularly to reveal ourselves to You. As we make ourselves known to You, will You encourage us to make ourselves known to one another? To be fully known and truly loved is an immeasurable gift, and we long to experience this in our marriage. Please help us to pursue each other in love. May our marriage look unmistakably like You designed it to look so that when outsiders look at us they see sacrificial love and submission. Lord, please lead us to love more every day. In Jesus's name we pray. Amen.

Husbands, love your wives, as Christ loved the church and gave himself up for her. **(EPHESIANS 5:25)**

PREFERENCES
AND OPINIONS

Dear Lord, We acknowledge the significance of beholding unique attributes and opinions. Thank You for animating us with preferences. Our individuality in personality and patterns is the very vibrancy and variance of colorful thread necessary to weave together the tapestry of marriage. We also thank You for the opinions we carry, shaped by our experiences and exposure to powerful influences. May we examine whether the things we consume—such as music, books, movies, and social media—align with Your Word. Holy Spirit, help us to filter our opinions and to have sober judgment for the ones we choose to uphold. Direct us to discuss our preferences and opinions so that we get to know each other even better. Lord, will You keep us from quarreling over opinions? Enable us to communicate about our convictions without creating division. Show us how to value one another's way of processing information, and teach us how to give each other time to navigate hard conversations. For the benefit of our marriage, equip us to understand and reason with each other. Make us agreeable to accommodate our preferences in love. Lord, we ask You to help us maintain our oneness despite any differences. May we lean on and learn from each other so that growth is inevitable. In Jesus's name we pray. Amen.

As for the one who is weak in faith, welcome him,
but not to quarrel over opinions. **(ROMANS 14:1)**

IDOLATRY

Dear Lord, Thank You for speaking against idolatry in Your Word. Has anything in our lives become an idol? Reveal any areas of our marriage we have unknowingly let rule over us. We ask You to open our eyes to see clearly because even honorable intentions can quickly turn into idolatry if we don't examine our hearts. Are we accumulating technology, home décor, or vehicles at the cost of unmanageable debt? Are we chasing success at the cost of sacrificing family time? Are we consumed with our appearances while neglecting our spiritual health? Please train us to regularly check our hearts and our motivations to make sure we are not being deceived into thinking we are doing the right thing, when the reality is that we are creating idols. Sharpen us, Lord, that we may scrutinize our choices and weed out idol worship. Please help us to sound a warning for one another if we see anything that could become an idol. We specifically ask You to eradicate any covetousness in us. This is often where idolatry is rooted! Remove any strong desire to have something that belongs to someone else. Holy Spirit, please guard our minds from dwelling on what others have. Keep our eyes on You! You are our King, and we worship You alone. In Jesus's name we pray. Amen.

Put to death therefore what is earthly in you: sexual immorality, impurity, passion, evil desire, and covetousness, which is idolatry. **(COLOSSIANS 3:5)**

CHEERING FOR EACH OTHER

$\mathcal{D}ear\ \mathcal{L}ord,$ Thank You for every day You give us to tell each other how much we love each other. Inspire us to take time each day to cheer each other on and support each other with verbal affirmation. Our hearts need it! Infuse our words with sweetness so they are easy to digest. May we never give up or slow down in cheering for each other! Lord, make us persistent in encouraging each other to persevere. We pray we would cheer each other on in our work, in our responsibilities at home, in parenting, and in every goal we aim to accomplish. When we face roadblocks, churn with mental hang-ups, or find ourselves in seemingly impossible situations, please show us how to walk side by side, believing in faith that things will work for our good. Let our gestures, such as eye contact, be kind and compassionate. Strip us of any resentment, blame, or "I told you so" attitudes. Use us to comfort one another with our presence, and shape us into steady pillars of strength for each other. Make Your joy complete in us by safeguarding our unity. In Jesus's name we pray. Amen.

If there is any encouragement in Christ, any comfort from love, any participation in the Spirit, any affection and sympathy, complete my joy by being of the same mind, having the same love, being in full accord and of one mind. **(PHILIPPIANS 2:1-2)**

PHYSICAL HEALING

𝒟ear 𝓛ord, Thank You for being our healer and our comforter. Thank You for the miracles shared throughout the Bible. It is wonderful to know You as a miracle worker. You do the impossible! We also thank You for the countless miracles You have granted to us. We are confident You have worked miracles in our lives that we don't even know about. Lord, sharpen our vision so that we see the ways You are working in our lives and in our marriage. We don't want to miss anything You do! As You provide for us, support us, and lead us in the way we should go, we specifically pray for Your guidance with our bodies. Give us wisdom in taking care of our bodies so they are healthy for as long as possible. We ask You, Lord, for miraculous physical healing of the parts of our bodies experiencing pain. Relieve any discomfort. We also ask that You heal any brokenness from emotional pain. Lord, please heal our wounds and restore us. Whether You heal us or not, please direct our hearts to give You glory in everything. In Jesus's name we pray. Amen.

He heals the brokenhearted
and binds up their wounds.
(PSALM 147:3)

COUNT THE COST

Dear Lord, Making decisions together is an important and interesting aspect of marriage. We are grateful for the process of examining our options and applying Your wisdom. Lord, will You please aid us in navigating decisions together? Show us how to communicate respectfully as we share our thoughts. Help us take the time to evaluate every decision and consider how it will affect our marriage and family. Lead us in understanding the benefits as well as the consequences of our choices. Lord, will You instruct us on how to count the cost of our decisions before we confirm them? Whether it is a job opportunity, a choice to improve our home, a season of transition, a move, or any other situation or project set before us, we submit our hearts to You and ask You to reveal Your will. Grant us Your peace over the choices we make together. Holy Spirit, urge us to support and encourage one another as we count the cost in every circumstance. May we get better at surrendering our desires, always willing to submit ourselves to Your will for our lives and marriage. In Jesus's name we pray. Amen.

Which of you, desiring to build a tower, does not first sit down and count the cost, whether he has enough to complete it? **(LUKE 14:28)**

BEARING WITH THE WEAK

Dear Lord, Help us to understand just how much our marriage matters, to grasp the full value of our relationship. Ignite in us a passion to pursue each other daily and to seek peace in our relationship. Show us how to make our relationship a priority by setting aside time for dating one another, having meaningful conversations, and praying together more often. Show us how to build up our relationship and make it strong. In moments when we are weak, when despair cripples us, give us the fortitude to bear with one another in patience. May our weaknesses never irritate one another. Lord, help us to understand that we need to encourage one another through those tough times. May we be a voice that resounds with Your truth when we are bombarded with doubt, insecurity, and anxiety. When we feel physically weak, use us to support one another the best we can until our bodies recuperate and heal. May we be a shoulder to lean on, a nurse to comfort and serve, and a poem to creatively inspire our hearts. Show us how our unity helps us bear each other's weaknesses. We desire to please You as we serve each other. In Jesus's name we pray. Amen.

We who are strong have an obligation to bear with the failings of the weak, and not to please ourselves. Let each of us please his neighbor for his good, to build him up. **(ROMANS 15:1–2)**

HAVING GOOD FRIENDS

Dear Lord, Thank You for the gift of friendship. Thank You for our friendship with each other. As we enjoy each other's company, we ask You to help us find good friends to share life with. Help us seek to cultivate strong relationships with other couples who are also chasing boldly after You. May these friendships be a source of strength and camaraderie. May we sharpen each other like iron sharpens iron. As we spend time together, will You encourage us to share our appreciation for our friends? Will You also lead us to pray for them and direct them to Your Word? Give us the right words to say to stimulate our friends toward new growth. Lord, we ask You to help us support each other in marriage and encourage each other to hold on to hope with each new day. May we be there for one another when the going gets tough, during emergencies, or when we just need company to cheer us up. Please help us to be open, transparent, and quick to listen and to help when needed as we build up our friendships. May these friendships benefit our marriage and family as we all seek to mature in our faith. In Jesus's name we pray. Amen.

He who withholds kindness from a friend
forsakes the fear of the Almighty.
(JOB 6:14)

REFRESH OUR MARRIAGE

Dear Lord, Some days we seem great together in marriage, and other days we feel distant from each other. On the days we struggle to feel close, please draw us closer together. Never let our hearts grow hard or harbor any bitterness. Our desire is to close any gaps in our relationship that have the potential to turn into chasms. Lord, help us to communicate clearly, to be open and honest with each other, and to show affection. Remind us every day why we choose to love each other no matter what—even when it feels hard, even when there is conflict, even when we feel far from each other. May we hold each other tightly as often as we can. Please help us to continue to pursue each other as much as we did before we married. Lord, refresh our souls! Refresh our prayer life! Stir us up to do good to one another, and refresh our marriage. Please give us fresh eyes to see our relationship in a new light, and fill us with hope for our future together. In Jesus's name we pray. Amen.

Repent therefore, and turn back, that your sins may be blotted out, that times of refreshing may come from the presence of the Lord. **(ACTS 3:19–20)**

PURITY IN MARRIAGE

Dear Lord, Thank You for revealing the areas of our lives that are impure. Your Holy Spirit encourages us to do what is right and confronts our desires when we are tempted. We are grateful for the work of Your Spirit in us. We praise You for victory over sin! Please help us to obey Your Word and not sin anymore. We choose to walk in freedom. When we feel the conviction of Your Holy Spirit, please help us to respond immediately by seeking repentance and reconciliation. We want our marriage to be marked by purity. We yearn for our hearts to be pure. We desire our thoughts to be pure. If anything in our lives is hindering us from being blameless, please forgive us. Lord, may our influence in each other's lives be good and beneficial. May we have the courage to speak up when we notice impurity in each other's lives. We acknowledge that living in purity will bless our marriage and protect our relationship from the pain that comes from making poor choices. Choosing purity helps keep our minds focused on You and Your righteousness. Please help us to pursue purity, especially in our marriage. In Jesus's name we pray. Amen.

Blessed are the pure in heart, for they shall see God. **(MATTHEW 5:8)**

SEEKING GODLINESS

Dear Lord, Thank You for calling us to supplement our faith with virtue. Thank You for making it possible to pursue godliness in our lives despite being sinners. Cleanse us from thoughts of shame and condemnation. Wash us as white as snow, and help us to believe that our hearts are truly clean. Thank You for making a way for Your Son, Jesus Christ, to live inside of us and empower us to choose what is right. Shape us into a couple who values virtue and self-control. As we both seek to be self-controlled and godly, we are confident that our ability to love one another well will increase all the more. May others recognize steadfastness in our marriage as we make every effort to pursue holiness. Make us an effective and fruitful couple, and mold our marriage to be a vessel to share Your goodness with the world. In Jesus's name we pray. Amen.

Make every effort to supplement your faith with virtue, and virtue with knowledge, and knowledge with self-control, and self-control with steadfastness, and steadfastness with godliness, and godliness with brotherly affection, and brotherly affection with love. For if these qualities are yours and are increasing, they keep you from being ineffective or unfruitful in the knowledge of our Lord Jesus Christ. **(2 PETER 1:5-8)**

STRENGTH FOR MARRIAGE

Dear Lord,   We praise You for bringing us together. We trust You have a purpose for us, and we pray Your purpose prevails in our marriage. Lord, You are our source of strength! Through Scripture, You have given us courage, hope, and guidance in pursuing all that is good and right. If we tried to live in our own strength, we would fail miserably. You support our marriage, holding us up like the truss of a bridge. Please continue to bear our load, alleviating the compression and tension that builds up over time. Equip us to persevere no matter what pressures we face. Unify and bind us together in perfect harmony so that we can build each other up and experience intimate connection. May true peace radiate throughout our marriage and our home. As we navigate our relationship a little at a time, please make us ready to be patient with each other and patient with You as we wait on You to lead us in the direction You desire us to go! May Your strength be our strength. In Jesus's name we pray. Amen.

Be strong, and let your heart take courage,
all you who wait for the LORD!
(PSALM 31:24)

DO NOT LOVE THE WORLD

Dear Lord, Thank You for revealing the truth to us. Thank You for the caution and command not to love the world or the things of this world. Help us not to admire or desire the world. Increase our inclination to please You, to know You, and to worship only You. When what the world has to offer entices us, please redirect our eyes to stay on You. Guard us from the temptation to seek what is contrary to Your Word. Remind us of the temporal and fleeting nature of this life. When we see one another being drawn into the world, please give us the boldness to say something. May we be watchful, looking out for one another and our marriage. When we're interested in traveling, experiencing new things, or buying things, will You protect us from endlessly craving more or idolizing any of it? We love You, Lord! We pray Your light would fill us so that the darkness flees. In Jesus's name we pray. Amen.

> *Do not love the world or the things in the world. If anyone loves the world, the love of the Father is not in him.* **(1 JOHN 2:15)**

SLOW PROGRESS

Dear Lord,   Thank You for Your faithful work within us. You sanctify us and transform our lives! Although our marriage encounters highs and lows, just like a roller coaster ride, we know You are working in all the details. We have seen the evidence of progress, and we praise You for it! Slow progress is still progress! May we never be discouraged when we fall short. Assure us that You are still working in our lives. We ask You to continue to make us purer and more like Jesus Christ. Help us to see our sin clearly so we can repent of it and turn from our ways. Give us hearts full of patience for each other as we strive to walk in holiness. Lord, reinforce our faith, believing our marriage will continue to grow deeper. Remove the perceptions we have held of each other based on past experiences, and instead give us eyes to see who we are becoming. Lord, we ask You to increase our admiration for each other with each passing year. As we remain determined to better ourselves and develop our character, may we be confident that our relationship is progressing. In Jesus's name we pray. Amen.

We walk by faith, not by sight. **(2 CORINTHIANS 5:7)**

SETTING OUR EYES
ON THINGS ABOVE

Dear Lord, We praise You for Your goodness and grace! Thank You for encouraging us in Scripture and instructing us on what we should think about. Please help us set our minds on You. Consume our thoughts! Lord, adjust our focus, setting our eyes on things above, considering all that is true, honorable, just, pure, lovely, commendable, excellent, and praiseworthy. In moments when we aren't thinking about these things, will You redirect our thoughts? This world tries to steal our attention every second of the day, and the Enemy aims to distract us so that we are tempted to sin. Our flesh even hinders us when it craves things we shouldn't. Lord, we don't want to be distracted or ineffective. Please don't let the world, the Enemy, or our flesh advance. Hold us close to You, and help us hold one another accountable. We praise You, Lord, and we long to be with You. In Jesus's name we pray. Amen.

Whatever is true, whatever is honorable, whatever is just, whatever is pure, whatever is lovely, whatever is commendable, if there is any excellence, if there is anything worthy of praise, think about these things. **(PHILIPPIANS 4:8)**

CREATIVE WAYS TO LOVE

Dear Lord, Thank You for the many ways You have poured out Your love to us and for the many ways we get to pour out our love in marriage. Through our reading of Scripture and our walking with You, You have taught us how to serve one another in meaningful ways. Thank You! We ask You to make us a couple who reflects Your amazing love by how we treat each other. Make us vessels of Your affection, filled to the brim and ready to be poured out on our marriage. Inspire us with creative ways to show our devotion to each other. We invite You to help us plan fun date nights, take time to write love letters and affirming texts, randomly shower each other with our favorite treats, and look intently into each other's eyes when we talk. Intensify our willingness to kiss and hug more often. Help us make the effort to hold each other's hands when we walk side by side. May we tell and show each other how much we love each other every chance we get. We also ask that our hearts be affirmed as our love for each other becomes evident in our countenance. May our marriage reflect Your radiant light as You bind us together in perfect harmony. In Jesus's name we pray. Amen.

And above all these put on love, which binds everything together in perfect harmony. **(COLOSSIANS 3:14)**

LETTING GO OF
PAST OFFENSES

Dear Lord, Thank You for removing our sins as far as the east is from the west! May we never take advantage of Your grace. Holy Spirit, please help us recognize our freedom in Christ and to walk in that freedom every day. We know our trespasses are offensive to You, and we are sorry! Keep us from minimizing or justifying our sin. We pray our wrongdoing would be repulsive to us. Holy Spirit, show us our sin and convict us to repent. Thank You for loving us and covering our offenses. Lord, soften our hearts toward one another, and help us to not be easily offended. Sometimes we irritate each other, and other times we argue to prove who is right. Remove our pride, in Jesus's name! When we choose to reconcile and be unified, please help us to truly let go of past offenses. Loosen our grip so that we don't hang on to offenses when we have already extended forgiveness to each other. In moments of weakness, keep us from reminding each other of our mistakes. Purify our hearts and our minds, and help us to see each other as You see us. In Jesus's name we pray. Amen.

> *Brothers, I do not consider that I have made it my own. But one thing I do: forgetting what lies behind and straining forward to what lies ahead, I press on toward the goal for the prize of the upward call of God in Christ Jesus.* **(PHILIPPIANS 3:13–14)**

APOLOGIZING TO
EACH OTHER

Dear Lord,   When we hurt each other, please help us to humble ourselves and seek forgiveness. May our apologies always be given and received in sincerity. Give us the right words as we explain what happened and what we are sorry for. Guide us to be thorough in addressing our hearts. Please help us never to grow weary in doing good and never to give up. Infuse us with Your strength so that we never tire of apologizing when it is in our power and obligation to reconcile. Our hope is to reap the benefits of walking in humility and truth. We desire connectedness and extraordinary intimacy. Holy Spirit, show us how to rely on Your wisdom when we engage in challenging moments of marriage, and urge us to eagerly participate in the ministry of reconciliation. Draw us close together, and restore our intimacy after conflict. May Your name be magnified as we walk in Your ways. In Jesus's name we pray. Amen.

Let us not grow weary of doing good,
for in due season we will reap, if we
do not give up. **(GALATIANS 6:9)**

OUR CHARACTER

Dear Lord, Thank You for the growth in our marriage. Please continue to shape our character so that our relationship keeps maturing. Refine us and help us walk in grace and compassion. Lead us to understand each other better. Make us a couple who resembles Your good nature. We desire to be faithful, patient, gentle, and generous. Lord, will You show us how to love deeply, walk humbly, and give unselfishly? Lord, shape our temperaments to be honorable, stable, and easy to be around. Impart our souls with integrity and purity. Season our speech with light and hope. May our character lead us to avoid the sting of shame, and may others have only good things to say about us so that You are glorified. We yearn to have a good reputation that honors You. May our character contribute to the health of our relationship, and may our marriage be one that others can admire and be inspired by. In Jesus's name we pray. Amen.

Show yourself in all respects to be a model of good works, and in your teaching show integrity, dignity, and sound speech that cannot be condemned, so that an opponent may be put to shame, having nothing evil to say about us. **(TITUS 2:7–8)**

BLESS OUR MARRIAGE

Dear Lord, Thank You for the good times in marriage and the much harder ones. We know this life is full of different seasons, and we are thankful for the impact of the situations we walk through together. The good times remind us to praise You for Your goodness as we savor the moments that bring us pure joy. The difficult times remind us of the power of prayer and the provision You give us, leaving us feeling utterly grateful. Thank You for never forsaking us. You are always near. You are always working. Lord, right now we ask You to bless our marriage. Lord, bless our communication, bless our intimacy, bless our finances, and bless our work. Help us recognize the blessings You give us and to praise You for each one. Please help us to persevere in our relationship while also enjoying one another. Cover us in love. Lord, we specifically ask You to pour out Your peace over us and guard our hearts and minds. May Your peace protect our minds from dwelling on negative thoughts. Direct our thinking to consider only what is good. Make our hearts content in marriage. God, strengthen our relationship and use it to glorify Your name. In Jesus's name we pray. Amen.

The peace of God, which surpasses all
understanding, will guard your hearts and your
minds in Christ Jesus. **(PHILIPPIANS 4:7)**

SHARING OUR FEELINGS

Dear Lord, Communication in marriage is layered. We know there are thoughts and feelings we must share in order to function as a family, and then there are those we have the privilege to share privately in order to function as an intimate couple. Please help us to determine the appropriate times to share these things. Lord, we ask You to help us value honesty in our relationship. Help us to reveal our hopes and dreams as well as our disappointments and hurts. If we ever feel like hiding our hearts from each other or coping with our feelings in unhealthy ways, will You please convict us and pull us close together? Urge us to carve out time to talk. Lead us to dive deeper beyond surface-level topics. We desire to experience more intimacy than we ever have before. Please help us to be transparent with each other. When we initiate an intimate conversation, please remind us to do so respectfully. Holy Spirit, guide us to engage with grace and understanding. Make us good listeners, quick to tune in and slow to speak. May we create a safe place to discuss important matters with one another. In Jesus's name we pray. Amen.

Know this, my beloved brothers: let
every person be quick to hear, slow to
speak, slow to anger. **(JAMES 1:19)**

UNCONDITIONAL LOVE

Dear Lord, Your unconditional love has radically transformed our lives! Your offer of salvation is a gift we do not deserve. Thank You for lavishing us with mercy, going above and beyond to give us Your peace. In our weakness, may we never doubt Your love for us. We hope to love one another with that same vigor. Make us a couple who loves unconditionally. We know that our love will grow as we increase in our knowledge of You and experience Your love. Please draw us close to You every day and teach us how to love. Help us to continually strive for peace in our relationship. Show us how to affirm our bond of unity and strengthen our oneness. Lord, remind us that our love is not contingent on one another, because love is not transactional. May we be good stewards of this extraordinary gift of marriage You have entrusted to us. May Your purpose be done in us as we choose unconditional love. In Jesus's name we pray. Amen.

Anyone who does not love does not know God, because God is love. **(1 JOHN 4:8)**

SEEING CLEARLY

Dear Lord, Thank You that the Bible directs us to look at our hearts. Thank You for teaching us to humble ourselves. Please give us wisdom in understanding Your Word and how to apply it. Before we ever judge one another, will You make us aware of the sin in our own lives? We don't want to be hypocrites! We don't want to be critical of each other. Lord, if we do address sin in each other's lives, will You lead us to discern in wisdom, share in love, and seek to support each other through the process? Fill us with encouraging words to share with each other, and extinguish the thoughts that scrutinize each other. May we never belittle each other. Lord, just as we would clean our sunglasses to have an unobstructed view, please clean our hearts and wipe away anything that impedes a clear view of ourselves and each other. Please show us how to make reading the Bible a priority, and let the power of Your Holy Spirit refine us. Use us to encourage one another to abide in You daily. In Jesus's name we pray. Amen.

You hypocrite, first take the log out of your own eye, and then you will see clearly to take the speck out of your brother's eye. **(MATTHEW 7:5)**

MARRIAGE UNDER ATTACK

Dear Lord, Thank You for being our protector. Thank You for the warnings You give in Your Word about the Enemy. Make us mindful of the spiritual war that is raging against our marriage. Remind us that Satan is seeking to devour us. Help us to remain strong and steadfast as we abide in You. We cling to Your Word as the sword of the Spirit, to defend ourselves against the Enemy's lies. Lord, help us walk uprightly with confidence, even when the Enemy sends his flaming arrows toward us. Please keep us sober-minded and alert to the Enemy's schemes. Show us how to be watchful over our marriage. Fortify the foundation of our relationship, and strengthen any areas where the Enemy might try to get a foothold. Our marriage may experience the threats of the Enemy, but marriage at large is also under attack. We ask You to guard and protect couples who are bombarded by the Enemy. May our marriage be an example to others of how to stand firm in faith. In Jesus's name we pray. Amen.

Be sober-minded; be watchful. Your adversary
the devil prowls around like a roaring lion,
seeking someone to devour. **(1 PETER 5:8)**

CONTROLLING OUR TONGUES

Dear Lord, May the way we communicate honor You and honor each other. Help us always to control our tongues. When we are tempted to say something harsh or mean, will Your Holy Spirit keep our mouths shut? Make us a couple who chooses our words carefully. Banish bickering from our home, in Jesus's name! Keep us from being snarky, rude, or disrespectful. May our speech be gracious, seasoned with words that are wholesome and helpful. Like the spring showers that soak the ground and provide sustenance for new plant life to flourish, may our words flood one another's hearts and minds with encouragement that feeds our confidence in who we are, as well as affirm our love for each other. Our desire is that we would use every interaction as an opportunity to build one another up in love. In every circumstance, help us exercise self-control over our tongues. Lord, please guide us to speak only what is true and right and holy. In Jesus's name we pray. Amen.

Let your speech always be gracious, seasoned with salt, so that you may know how you ought to answer each person. **(COLOSSIANS 4:6)**

UNDERSTANDING GOD

Dear Lord, We praise You for purifying our hearts and transforming our minds. It is Your truth that sanctifies us and teaches us how to be reconciled to You. It is Your Word that increases our faith, establishes our belief, and renews our hearts. Thank You for the presence and power of Scripture. May we continue to grow in our relationships with You. Fill us full of wisdom and infuse us with understanding. We desire to know You more! We hope to grow in our knowledge of You and Your kingdom, comprehending all that Your Word says, especially about all that is to come. Understanding You helps us understand one another, so we ask You to deepen our grasp of who You are. Help us to chase after You and abide in Your Word. Flood our minds with knowledge of Your will and fill our hearts with peace, that we may align our wills to Yours. Lord, help us to secure our identity in You, and reveal all the ways You are moving in our marriage. Show us how Your Word is changing us. In Jesus's name we pray. Amen.

Sanctify them in the truth; your
word is truth. **(JOHN 17:17)**

OUR PERSONALITIES

$\mathcal{D}ear\ \mathcal{L}ord,$ Thank You for the differences in our personalities. Thank You for the way You created us to think, feel, and behave. May we be a couple who can confidently express ourselves, while also having discernment in what we say and how we say it. May our unique personalities never divide us. Lord, please help us encourage each other to express our thoughts and feelings. Make us a couple who fully embraces each other. Holy Spirit, help us not to allow our differences to irritate or agitate us. We recognize we have distinct roles and responsibilities in our marriage and in the body of Christ. We know You have purposed us specifically to fulfill these functions, and we have confidence that You have equipped us with unique traits in order to do our parts. Thank You for the ways our personalities complement each other and complement the personalities of others in the body of Christ. May our dynamic personalities paint a beautiful picture of married life that impacts others for You. In Jesus's name we pray. Amen.

As in one body we have many members, and the members do not all have the same function, so we, though many, are one body in Christ, and individually members one of another. **(ROMANS 12:4–5)**

MAKING DECISIONS
TOGETHER

Dear Lord, Thank You for the freedom You have given us through Jesus Christ. May we use our freedom to honor You and magnify Your name. Thank You for Your wisdom and truth. Thank You for Your Word, which guides us and teaches us Your ways. Please lead us to be obedient to Your Word. Please shape us into a couple who collaborates and compromises, making decisions according to the wisdom in Your Word. Make us thoughtful and considerate of one another as we navigate decisions together. Please remind us to pray over our decisions and submit them to You. Lord, we ask You to establish all of our steps. Please help us to walk in a manner that is worthy of You. As we make decisions together, we ask You to help us think about legacy living and consider the impact our decisions will have on our family and the generations to follow. When thinking through our options, we ask You to help us yield our wills to Yours, not making selfish decisions. Please fill us with understanding as we seek to honor You in our decisions. In Jesus's name we pray. Amen.

The heart of man plans his way,
but the LORD establishes his steps.
(PROVERBS 16:9)

DAILY ROUTINES

Dear Lord, We know the significance of having good daily routines. We recognize the responsibilities You have given us, and we desire to create healthy habits that make our routines effective and efficient. Holy Spirit, lead us to accomplish the work You have for us while also enjoying the process. Reveal parts of our routine that are functioning well and which ones we should adjust. As we ask one another to evaluate our routines, please soften our hearts toward each other and prepare us for any opinions shared about how to improve our daily routines. Give us ears to receive constructive feedback, suggestions, and encouragement from each other. Lord, make us aware of how our daily routines reflect our trust in You and our desire to please You, such as prioritizing reading the Bible. Make us a couple who is determined yet flexible in our schedules. Impress on our hearts the importance of not allowing our daily work to hinder our marriage relationship. If our family rhythms or our work are ever imbalanced, we invite You to convict us and show us how to recalibrate. May our choices each day contribute to the building up of our family and bring glory to Your name. In Jesus's name we pray. Amen.

> *Let me hear in the morning of your steadfast love,*
> *for in you I trust.*
> *Make me know the way I should go,*
> *for to you I lift up my soul.*
> **(PSALM 143:8)**

GOODNESS

Dear Lord, Thank You for Your goodness. We ask that goodness be a trait others recognize in us and in our marriage. Please produce more goodness in our lives as we abide in You and keep in step with Your Spirit. Motivate us to be good toward each other. Show us how we can support one another. As we aim to do good in this world, we invite Your Holy Spirit to remind us that we are a team purposed to bring You glory. May our love for each other be evident and a testimony of Your love in our lives. In addition to goodness, will You produce all the fruit of the Spirit within us? Cultivate the soil of our hearts so that we flourish in goodness and grace. We desire to be full of love and immense joy. Lord, may patience lead our responses to each other, and let kindness and gentleness be woven into our words. May faithfulness and self-control help us fulfill our vows to each other so Your will is done and Your purpose for our marriage is fulfilled. In Jesus's name we pray. Amen.

The fruit of the Spirit is love, joy, peace, patience, kindness, goodness, faithfulness, gentleness, self-control; against such things there is no law. **(GALATIANS 5:22–23)**

FREEDOM FROM GUILT

Dear Lord, Thank You for sending Your Son, Jesus Christ, to die for our sins. Thank You for creating clean hearts in us. Will You help us recognize the freedom we have in Christ? Remind us that we are no longer slaves to sin. We ask You, Lord, to help us receive freedom from guilt of past sins or decisions that make us feel ashamed. Your Word reminds us that there is no condemnation for us in Christ. Will You please write this truth on our hearts? When guilt burdens our minds, will You lead us to the foot of Your throne to receive grace? We surrender ourselves in humility and ask You to gently restore us. When one of us sins or does something hurtful, please keep us from making each other feel guilty. Our hope is that guilt would draw sin into the light so it can be destroyed. May Your grace and mercy abound in us. In Jesus's name we pray. Amen.

There is therefore now no condemnation for those who are in Christ Jesus. **(ROMANS 8:1)**

LIFE GIVER

Dear Lord, You are the author and giver of life! You spoke and life was created! You put air in our lungs and have abundantly supplied our needs. Thank You! We appreciate the gift of life, and we thank You for uniting us in marriage. Lord, we ask You to help our marriage thrive by the abundant life we give to each other through the power of our words. Our tongues are influential and have the potential to set our whole life on fire! We don't want to destroy what You have brought together. We don't want to allow perverseness in our words. Guard our lips and our hearts, Lord. We ask Your Holy Spirit to teach us how to control our tongues and to use our words to bring peace and life! When we are tempted to hurt, manipulate, or tear each other down, will You please convict us? Remind us that You have made us new creations. We know salt and fresh water can't come from the same fountain, so we ask You to use us to bring the fresh, life-giving water of encouragement, affirmation, and gentleness. Lord, may our gentle words heap blessings on one another, giving refreshment to our souls. Please teach us to speak kindly to each other. In Jesus's name we pray. Amen.

A gentle tongue is a tree of life,
but perverseness in it breaks the spirit.
(PROVERBS 15:4)

OUR BELIEFS

Dear Lord, The power of belief can enable us to do the extraordinary! Yet believing lies or believing the worst about us disables us. Our beliefs are the foundation on which we stand and the motivation for all that we do. Lord, we pray You would solidify Your truth in our hearts and minds, and increase our faith to believe it. Strengthen our foundation of belief. Establish our core beliefs according to Scripture. Whenever we doubt, will You reinforce all that is true? Will You use us to remind one another to stand firm? Lord, we don't want to be swayed by the deception in this world, and we don't want to rebel against You. We confess with our mouths that Jesus is Lord, and we believe in our hearts that You raised Him from the dead. Our allegiance is with You! Remind us that our salvation in You is secure. Lord, stir within us a desire to proclaim Your testimony! Let our belief in You be the light that others see and the interest that draws them toward You. In Jesus's name we pray. Amen.

If you confess with your mouth that Jesus is Lord and believe in your heart that God raised him from the dead, you will be saved. **(ROMANS 10:9)**

EMBRACING OUR ROLES

Dear Lord, We praise You for how You created both of us uniquely. You poured thoughtfulness into the way You made us, giving us different abilities and gifts, which benefits our marriage. Show us how to use our giftings to walk in the roles You have entrusted to us. Teach us to understand and embrace our responsibilities. Help us to work together to bring You glory, each contributing our own part. We know we each have to bear our own load of responsibility, but we also know You gave us to each other so that we can help each other. Make us a couple who is enthusiastically supportive and loving. Remove any envious thoughts regarding one another's gifts. Fill us with an eagerness to learn from one another and grow together. Please smooth out our concerns and show us how to be content in the work right in front of us. Lord, equip us to assist each other to fulfill all that You have called us to do. May our commitment to embracing our roles and fulfilling our responsibilities at home, in work, or in ministry be a testimony to Your power in our lives. In Jesus's name we pray. Amen.

For each will have to bear his own
load. **(GALATIANS 6:5)**

FOR RICHER OR FOR POORER

Dear Lord, We recognize our need for a Savior, and we are grateful for the blood of Jesus. Continue to purify our minds and transform our hearts. Lord, will You show us how to take initiative to affirm our admiration and love for one another? May we express how much we cherish each other. Give us opportunities to experience true joy in our marriage. No matter what circumstances we're facing, whether it is a valley or a mountaintop experience, please help us to remain one. Lord, be our navigator, especially when we are under trial. May we not compare our marriage with other marriages. Whether we have a lack or an abundance of finances, let contentment reign in us. Whether we are rich or poor, keep us humble and happy together. May we trust in You alone. We pray Your will would be done in us and through our marriage. In Jesus's name we pray. Amen.

Blessed is the man who remains steadfast under trial, for when he has stood the test he will receive the crown of life, which God has promised to those who love him. **(JAMES 1:12)**

REJOICING WITH EACH OTHER

Dear Lord, Thank You for the emotion of gladness. We appreciate being able to feel pure joy and happiness. You are our joy, and You are the reason joy is drawn out of our hearts like a bucket of refreshing water from a deep well. May our joy give people hope, encouraging them to consider the reasons they too can rejoice. Thank You for the encouragement Your Holy Spirit gives us through Your Word. Just like Your Holy Spirit affirms us, will You help us to encourage each other every day? Ignite passion inside of us to celebrate our victories and milestones with each other. Lord, make us a couple who delights in You. We rejoice knowing we can trust You. We rejoice considering the change You have brought to our lives. We rejoice for not being alone. We rejoice over our family. Lord, may our rejoicing lead us into profound prayer time with You. And when we receive an answer to prayer, may we never forget to thank You. Our desire is that praying together would cultivate intimacy in our relationship and soften our hearts so that You can bend our wills to Yours as we submit to Your authority. In Jesus's name we pray. Amen.

Rejoice in the Lord always; again I will say, rejoice. **(PHILIPPIANS 4:4)**

INVESTING IN OUR MARRIAGE

Dear Lord, Thank You for working in our lives, even when we don't notice all that You are doing. Your faithfulness is beautiful, and You are trustworthy! As You shape our lives and our marriage, we ask You to show us how to invest in our marriage so that we can intentionally contribute to the shape of it as well. We know our actions significantly impact our relationship, and we desire our marriage to be all that You designed it to be. Lord, we ask You to reveal the motivations and intentions of our hearts and make them pure. Remove selfish ambition far from us. Take away any desire to prioritize the wrong things. Help us pour into our marriage in this next season of life, and make us more deliberate than we have been before. In seeking ways to treasure our marriage and grow closer together, we ask You, Lord, to give us greater intimacy. Help us to set our hearts and minds on loving each other well. In Jesus's name we pray. Amen.

Where your treasure is, there your heart will be also. **(MATTHEW 6:21)**

HOPE

Dear Lord, Thank You for being our blessed hope. Thank You for giving us a reason to live—the hope of eternity. We are grateful to have something extraordinary to look forward to, with eternity on the horizon. Until then, may we live life to the fullest, secure in our hope in You. Lord, grant us incredible amounts of hope for our marriage. Let the desire for our marriage to thrive and the yearning to experience amazing closeness give us a vision for our future together. We trust You with our marriage, and we hope You lead us to work together to impact this world for good. Help us cling to Your promises, especially when difficult days come our way. Give us strength. Give us stamina. Lord, please help us never to give up or give in. May we experience joy in believing in You. By the power of the Holy Spirit, let us abound in hope. In Jesus's name we pray. Amen.

May the God of hope fill you with all joy and peace in believing, so that by the power of the Holy Spirit you may abound in hope. **(ROMANS 15:13)**

OVERCOMING FEAR
AND WORRY

Dear Lord,   Thank You for being our God! Thank You for being our deliverer! We aren't always quick to recognize Your power in our lives. Sometimes worry blinds us. When anxious thoughts rush over us, please compel us to trust in You. Holy Spirit, remind us that You are near. When doubt and insecurity bombard our minds, please hold us up and encourage us with Your truth. We ask You to deliver us from fear and to lay to rest the thoughts that weigh us down. Whatever the reasons for our anxiety, help us to find a solution to those circumstances. Lord, when dread grips us, aid us in exercising control over our emotions—may our negative emotions not unleash harsh words or actions toward each other. When we are overwhelmed with angst, will You show us how to support each other by sharing a specific Scripture? Please put encouraging words on the tips of our tongues, and help us to be quick to seek You in prayer. Lord, may Your will be done in us so that the fact that our marriage is still standing proclaims Your purpose for marriage to the world. In Jesus's name we pray. Amen.

> *I sought the LORD, and he answered me*
> *and delivered me from all my fears.*
> **(PSALM 34:4)**

INCREDIBLE SEX

Dear Lord, Thank You for the gift of sex. Thank You for the extraordinary way You designed two to become one flesh in marriage. Thank You for the extreme closeness we get to experience. We ask that our intimate experiences would become increasingly more enjoyable. Allow us to feel comfortable with each other, and make our hearts tender toward each other during sex. Please help us pay attention to the way sex makes us feel, and enable us to be flexible in our expectations. Mature us in this area of our marriage. Please help us to be willing to learn each other's preferences. Lord, show us how to fulfill one another in love by serving each other according to our preferences so that we can fully embrace and engage in sexual intimacy. Give us the courage to go out of our way to make each other feel loved and cherished. Show us the different ways we can express our desire for each other. Awaken us to the privilege of participating in marriage and building up our relationship in this way. May our sex affirm in our minds the adoration we carry for each other in our hearts. In Jesus's name we pray. Amen.

> *Awake, O north wind,*
> *and come, O south wind!*
> *Blow upon my garden,*
> *let its spices flow.*
> *Let my beloved come to his garden,*
> *and eat its choicest fruits.*
> **(SONG OF SOLOMON 4:16-17)**

SUPPORTING EACH OTHER'S GOALS

Dear Lord, You have planted dreams, desires, and goals in our hearts. We are grateful for the way You have infused us with interests and passions to pursue and pray for wisdom in navigating how to do that together. Thank You for the goals we have already accomplished together and for the ones we have yet to set. Lord, please help us support each other in what we decide to pursue. Will Your Holy Spirit lead us in discerning which goals are from You and which ones are not? We don't want to waste our time pursuing things that are not Your will. Remove anything that distracts us from pursuing Your purpose for our marriage. When we communicate our hopes and dreams, may we support one another and not argue for our own way. Make our speech be sweet like honey so we can communicate our vision for the future with respect and kindness. We surrender our wills and ask You to lead us in the goals You want us to accomplish. Lord, we commit to You our endeavors. More than chasing our pursuits, may we boldly chase after You! Establish our steps and show us the way we should go. In Jesus's name we pray. Amen.

Commit your work to the Lord,
and your plans will be established.
(PROVERBS 16:3)

MAKING THE MOST
OF TODAY

Dear Lord,   Thank You for the opportunities we have today to serve You and to love one another. Open our eyes to see how special today is—simply because we can choose to make it so! Lord, show us all the wonderful ways You are moving in our lives and in this world. Show us how we can join in the good work You are already doing. We look forward to the day when Your work in us is complete! We ask You also to show us how we can make the most of today, specifically in loving one another. Keep us from being selfish when we make plans, inviting each other to share opinions of how we can best use our time today. Will You help us take into account both of our desires and to collaborate in deciding what we will do? Help us to resist disagreeing with one another. May we walk in the fruit of Your Spirit, with hearts full of joy. Throughout the day, will You inspire us to make each other feel special? Thought of? Cherished? Lord, remind us of the stark reality that neither one of us is guaranteed tomorrow. Life is but a vapor, incredibly fragile and brief. May we love each other intently in the time that we have. Be glorified in our marriage today as our love draws both of us even closer to You. In Jesus's name we pray. Amen.

I am sure of this, that he who began a good work in you will bring it to completion at the day of Jesus Christ. **(PHILIPPIANS 1:6)**

FELLOWSHIP WITH OTHERS

𝒟ear 𝐿ord, Thank You for the body of Christ, Your bride, the church. May we seek to participate in the body of Christ, confident that we have a purpose to fulfill within it. Lord, reinforce the truth that fellowshipping with believers need not be constrained to Sundays, but rather it can happen all throughout the week. Every interaction we have with Your body is an opportunity to honor You and support others. Help us embrace hospitality, inviting others into our home so we can get to know them. Guard our thoughts from insecurity, fear, or anything else that gets in the way of fellowshipping with others. Holy Spirit, we invite You to help us to prioritize spending regular quality time with other believers. We specifically pray for our church right now. You know our church's history and future, You know our role in the church, and You know the dynamics of interpersonal relationships within our church. We ask that our church would experience new growth. Let this church be a blessing to our marriage, and let our marriage be a blessing to this church. As we engage with others, will You give us the courage to be transparent with them? Will You use us to rally everyone to operate in their giftings? Lord, we ask You to purify us and prepare us as Your bride for the day we meet You in eternity! May Your name be magnified as the body works as You designed it to. In Jesus's name we pray. Amen.

If we walk in the light, as he is in the light, we have fellowship with one another, and the blood of Jesus his Son cleanses us from all sin. **(1 JOHN 1:7)**

TRANSFORM US

𝒟ear 𝒧ord, Thank You for the way Your Word transforms us. Thank You for renewing our minds. Thank You for helping us discern Your good and perfect will for our marriage. We trust You! Sanctify us by stripping away the parts of us that don't reflect Your holy character. We hope to be more like You with each new day. Remove our harshness and make us gentle. Turn our pride into humility. Shift our perspectives from critical to caring. Alter our words to reflect respect. Convert our irritation into joy and our discontent into gratitude. Lord, may any testing prove our hearts' desire to please You and please each other. The world constantly tempts us to conform to patterns of thinking that don't align with Your ways and do not please You. We petition You to conform us to Your ways and guide us away from temptation. May we refuse to give in to the patterns of this world, in Jesus's name! Our desire is to follow You. Whenever the pressures of this world increase, may our faith increase even more. Holy Spirit, draw us in to abide in Scripture every day. As You mature our character, we pray our marriage is transformed as well. In Jesus's name we pray. Amen.

Do not be conformed to this world, but be transformed by the renewal of your mind, that by testing you may discern what is the will of God, what is good and acceptable and perfect. **(ROMANS 12:2)**

SHARING WHAT WE HAVE

$Dear Lord,$ Thank You for filling our lives and our home with treasures. You have blessed us, and we are grateful for what we have. Please keep us from hoarding our belongings. Shape us into a generous couple who is willing to share from our abundance. Lead us to be joyful givers, especially to each other. Please help us never to neglect to do good in our marriage. We pray our marriage would be the first relationship that is blessed by our willingness to share. May our countenance be generous, sharing with one another our smiles, our kind eyes, our hands to hold, our bed, our home, and even the centers of our cinnamon rolls. Please help us find joy in making more memories by experiencing our favorite movies, our favorite foods, and our favorite places together. May we share in laughter at our favorite jokes. We pray we would express our worries and our dreams of the future so that we can pray with each other. May our hearts be filled up by the way we share with one another. We ask You to also make us quick to share what we have with others, including our family, friends, neighbors, and even strangers. Please use what we have to be a blessing in the lives of those around us. In Jesus's name we pray. Amen.

Do not neglect to do good and to share
what you have, for such sacrifices are
pleasing to God. **(HEBREWS 13:16)**

TEMPORARY THINGS

𝒟*ear* ℒ*ord,* Thank You for the constant reminders that this life is temporary, delicate, and incredibly brief. Make us a couple who approaches every day with gratitude—simply happy to be alive. Our time is fleeting. Lord, help us make the most of today. Sometimes we allow busyness to consume us, forgetting that we can't stop time or get it back. Help us to spend it in a way we won't regret. Holy Spirit, show us how to use every moment of every day to fulfill Your purposes, to do good, and to love greatly. Lord, admonish us to take every opportunity to tell each other, "I love you." When tension erupts in our relationship, remind us that whatever we are arguing about is also temporary. May we be courageous and humble enough to throw down our pride, embrace one another, and pray to You. Equip us, Lord, to climb over the hard things together, crawl through the mud of impossible, and get up again to run the race set before us. Then, in the moment You have already appointed, may we enter Your eternal kingdom and experience true rest. In Jesus's name we pray. Amen.

Since all these things are thus to be dissolved,
what sort of people ought you to be in lives
of holiness and godliness. **(2 PETER 3:11)**

OUR RESPONSIBILITIES

Dear Lord, You have entrusted to us many responsibilities in life and in marriage. Make us dependable and capable people who are ready and willing to do all that You call us to do. May we strive to do our work to the best of our ability, without complaint. Lord, we ask You to help us take our duties seriously and to tend to them joyfully. Whether we are cleaning the house, fixing the car, preparing our meals, or going through our finances with a fine-tooth comb, remind us to work as though we are doing it for You. If job tasks, church commitments, or extended family obligations start to wear us down, please infuse our souls with stamina. When stress stirs up agitation, show us how to adapt without treating each other unkindly. Grow our capacity so that we can receive the work You have for us as well as offer assistance to each other, working together to fulfill Your purpose. When we feel stretched, strengthen us so we can carry the weight of our responsibilities. When we put our hands to work, we ask that gladness would flow from our hearts, knowing we are working for You, Lord. May our determination to serve You magnify Your gospel. In Jesus's name we pray. Amen.

Whatever you do, work heartily, as for the Lord and not for men, knowing that from the Lord you will receive the inheritance as your reward. You are serving the Lord Christ. **(COLOSSIANS 3:23–24)**

STANDING FOR BIBLICAL TRUTH

Dear Lord, Thank You for the gift of the Bible. Thank You for giving us Your truth as a foundation to stand on. Thank You for the way the truth sets us free. We desire to use our freedom to proclaim the truth to others and to each other. Give us the courage to stand boldly in today's culture. The world's messages look very different from Your message. While the world's messages preach self-centeredness, Your message encourages selflessness. While the world affirms happiness at any cost, You proclaim the significance of humility and sacrifice. While the world promotes promiscuity, You oppose sexual immorality. May we stand up for biblical truth regardless of what the world tells us we should think or feel. May we never be tempted to drift away or sway from the truth. We invite Your Holy Spirit to walk with us and to help us not be afraid or ashamed to share Your testimony. When we struggle to know what is right or when doubt invades our minds, will You remind us of all that is true? Impart Your wisdom and show us how to apply Your Word so we can be comforted and encouraged through the trials we experience. Help us immerse ourselves in Scripture daily. May Your truth be preserved forever. In Jesus's name we pray. Amen.

You will know the truth, and the truth will set you free. **(JOHN 8:32)**

EXPECTATIONS

Dear Lord, We appreciate that we can tell each other how we feel. We know how important it is to honestly share our hearts with each other regularly. Please mature our communication skills. Being able to walk in understanding with one another requires us to communicate our emotions and expectations. Teach us to respectfully discuss these things. We ask You to make us flexible, willing to change our expectations when necessary. Lord, please help us meet each other's expectations in marriage. And when we fall short, we ask You to bring us close together and restore us from any disappointment. Please keep us from the hurt of unmet expectations. Please set us up to carefully talk through the things that matter to us so that we avoid arguing with or offending one another. Enable us to be good listeners. With our hearts turned toward each other, please help us to navigate our emotions and all that is tied to them. Resolve unmet expectations in us so that they never get in the way of how we love each other. In Jesus's name we pray. Amen.

Now to him who is able to do far more abundantly than all that we ask or think, according to the power at work within us. **(EPHESIANS 3:20)**

HOSPITALITY

Dear Lord, Please help us to be hospitable toward others. We ask You to give us a desire to bless others, especially those in need. If we are unhealthily attached to our belongings or our finances, others might not feel welcome in our home. So shape us into a generous couple by helping us live openhandedly. Show us how easy it can be to invite people to our table, to feed them, and to get to know them. May we never hesitate to share the gospel with our guests. Please flood our minds with interesting topics to discuss. Grant us an extra dose of boldness to pray with them. Our hope is that our willingness to show hospitality would be the beginning of beautiful friendships. Lord, will You help us never to grumble or complain about having people in our home or using our resources to bless others? Put us on the same page about the gift of hospitality and how we can work together to expand Your kingdom. Get us out of our comfort zone, teach us to build relationships with others, and prepare our hearts for the next time we have people over. May our willingness to grow in hospitality bring You glory and draw other people closer to You. In Jesus's name we pray. Amen.

Show hospitality to one another
without grumbling. **(1 PETER 4:9)**

THINKING OF OTHERS

Dear Lord, Will You continue to strengthen our relationship and use us to be a blessing in this world? May we never be so preoccupied with each other that we don't see the needs of others. We long to be a couple who seeks to build friendships. Lord, help us make ourselves available to support others, send them encouragement, and plan fun outings together. May Your love flow out of us and pour into the lives of those around us. Lord, we ask that our family, our friends, our neighbors, and even strangers would recognize Your power and presence in our lives. Holy Spirit, nudge us to consider the many ways we can use our talents and resources to bless others. As we spend time with people we care about, we pray that Your truth pours out of us. Give us words to share Your testimony, and inspire us to tell of all the ways You have worked in our marriage. Lord, help us to think fondly of others and value their presence in our lives. God, may Your love abide in us as we abide in You. In Jesus's name we pray. Amen.

If anyone has the world's goods and sees his brother in need, yet closes his heart against him, how does God's love abide in him? **(1 JOHN 3:17)**

WAITING ON GOD

Dear Lord, You are patient! Thank You for being good to us. Lord, help us to be patient with each other, just like You are with us. We also pray we would be patient as we wait on You to move in our marriage. We rely on You and trust You to lead us in every area of our lives. We desire to follow You and pursue what You want us to do. Please keep us from rushing into anything that is not of You. As we make decisions together, we ask You for wisdom and clarity. Direct our every step. Heavenly Father, we surrender our lives to You, humbly admitting that we need You. Save our marriage from the wake of the hurtful choices we've made, from our mistakes, from the destruction resulting from lies we have believed, and from our unhealthy habits and unchecked poor attitudes. As we wait on You to answer our prayers, to comfort us in despair, to speak to us when we need guidance, and to provide in times of desperation, we pray our souls will trust in You. Help us to wait for You to make a way for us, just like the Israelites waited for and watched the miracle of the Red Sea parting before their eyes. We have tasted Your goodness, and we trust in Your promises. As we wait on You, may we remember that You are the author of life and that You are still writing our story. May we have the assurance and fortitude to wait patiently on You and seek after You daily. In Jesus's name we pray. Amen.

The Lord is good to those who wait for him,
to the soul who seeks him.
(LAMENTATIONS 3:25)

THANKFUL FOR WORK

Dear Lord, We declare Your steadfast love and faithfulness. Thank You for always making a way for us to be supported and supplied! Thank You for the work You have provided for us. We praise Your name! We submit our jobs and responsibilities to You, asking You to help us do them well. Whether we stay in our current work or move on to something else, will You give us confidence in the choices we make and the work we say yes to? Please give us wisdom as we make decisions about the direction and viability of our jobs. Show us how to count the cost of how our jobs affect our marriage. May our positions and workload never negatively impact our marriage, and if they do, help us examine whether a change is necessary. Make us a diligent couple who values hard work. When our work is challenging, remind us to work for You and not just the business providing our position. Our hearts' desire is to fulfill Your purpose for our life together, and we know part of that is through our jobs and responsibilities. May we experience Your peace when we wake up to get ready for the day and when we lay down to rest in order to do it all again. In Jesus's name we pray. Amen.

> *It is good to give thanks to the LORD,*
> *to sing praises to your name, O*
> *Most High;*
> *to declare your steadfast love in the morning,*
> *and your faithfulness by night.*
> **(PSALM 92:1–2)**

NO MORE BITTERNESS

𝒟*ear Lord,* Thank You for encouraging us to drag sin into the light. Shine Your light into the depths of our hearts, and expose anything rooted there that shouldn't be. Show us if there is any bitterness or anger so we can repent immediately. Reveal any lingering resentment toward one another that we have stored up in our hearts. Purify us. Cleanse us from all unrighteousness. We know the works of darkness don't produce any good, and we don't want our marriage to suffer because of what is inside of us. Please uncover any areas of our lives we have not submitted to You. We surrender them right now, in Jesus's name! We specifically pray over anything in our hearts that we buried because of past experiences. Unveil any bitterness toward each other so that we can take the next right step of repentance and reconciliation. We know this won't be easy or comfortable. Yet we know we need to clean the slate with one another and be emotionally reunited in our marriage. Please give us a refreshing perspective of our relationship and where You are taking us. As we pursue holiness in our lives and in our marriage, we pray Your name is magnified. In Jesus's name we pray. Amen.

Let all bitterness and wrath and anger and
clamor and slander be put away from you,
along with all malice. **(EPHESIANS 4:31)**

PERSEVERANCE

Dear Lord, Thank You for Jesus Christ being the ultimate example of how to live. Please keep our gaze on Christ as we look to Him and imitate Him in our responses toward each other, toward others, and toward our circumstances. Give us hearts of perseverance, and help us rely on You to endure hard things. When our minds convince us we can't take anymore, when our bodies feel like failing, and when life's hurdles look daunting, may Your peace engulf us and Your strength help us stand uprightly. Reassure our weary souls. Quiet the negative thoughts swirling inside us so that we have a chance to persevere together. Everything we go through and every milestone we meet forges hope deep within us. Thank You for the way Your Holy Spirit guides us to live according to Scripture. Where would we be without life's manual? When we feel the crushing weight of despair pressing in around us, encourage us to put our arms around each other in genuine embrace. Use our presence as a wave of peace to protect our minds from fear. Let us lock eyes, sending a message of determination that we will get through this and that we will be okay! May we never lose hope to stand side by side encouraging one another through the journey of marriage. In Jesus's name we pray. Amen.

We rejoice in our sufferings, knowing that suffering produces endurance, and endurance produces character, and character produces hope, and hope does not put us to shame, because God's love has been poured into our hearts through the Holy Spirit who has been given to us. **(ROMANS 5:3–5)**

PEACEMAKERS

Dear Lord, Your peace is incomparable! Thank You for the relief You give us in the midst of chaos. Instead of us experiencing a constant barrage of frustration, worry, or despair, Your peace covers us like a warm fleece blanket. When emotions bombard us, You help us move from one state of mind to another, from frantic to reassured. We are grateful for the power of Your peace in our lives. Although this world and the challenging circumstances we go through try to steal our peace, we know we can find it again when we abide in You and in Your Word. We are confident that You will continue to supply us with Your peace, but that we must be willing to receive it. Please remind us to draw near to You and to trust You in everything. Help us to be peacemakers, especially in our marriage. As far as it depends on us, may peace rest in our relationship and in our home. Make us peaceful in our countenance, in our speech, in our actions, and in our approach to each other. Lord, show us how to be at peace with You, with each other, and with others, living peaceably with all. In Jesus's name we pray. Amen.

If possible, so far as it depends on you, live peaceably with all. **(ROMANS 12:18)**

LET GENTLENESS ABOUND

Dear Lord, Thank You for Your gentleness. Thank You for the patience You have toward us. Thank You for loving us by showing us our sin and firmly leading us away from it. Please continue to refine us. We specifically ask right now that You fill us with an extraordinary measure of gentleness. Our desire is to be gentler with one another. May we be gentle in talking to each other, in pointing out sin in each other's lives, and in showing physical affirmation. Will You help us grow in gentleness, making sure our words are kind and that our every action is done in tenderness? We ask, Lord, that our willingness to be softer and kinder would be a blessing to each other. Please help us to be humble toward each other. Lord, may Your wisdom lead us to be peaceable in our interactions. Make us open to reason and full of mercy and good fruit. Lord, make us impartial and sincere. Let gentleness be a mark in our marriage that reflects Your good nature so that You are glorified through us. In Jesus's name we pray. Amen.

The wisdom from above is first pure, then peaceable, gentle, open to reason, full of mercy and good fruits, impartial and sincere. **(JAMES 3:17)**

EMOTIONAL INTIMACY

Dear Lord, Thank You that You designed us to feel a variety of emotions. Thank You that marriage supplies immeasurable opportunity to experience emotional connectedness and intimacy. We appreciate feeling close to one another. We also confess we don't always take advantage of the opportunities to engage in emotional intimacy. Change this in us, God! We yearn to grow in this area of our relationship. Please keep apathy, as well as fear, far from our hearts. When we feel too timid to talk about what is weighing us down, challenging us, or causing sorrow within us, please embolden us to initiate that conversation anyway. Help us to be aware of and also to describe where we are emotionally. Lord, grant us discernment in reading each other's faces, reading between the lines, and asking direct questions. Teach us to show compassion, to be thoughtful in our responses, and to find solutions that are encouraging and helpful. As we endeavor to be good communicators, please bless us with moments of connection. May our interactions help us learn more about each other so that we contribute to each other's emotional health. In Jesus's name we pray. Amen.

> *A glad heart makes a cheerful face,*
> *but by sorrow of heart the spirit is*
> *crushed.*
> *The heart of him who has understanding seeks*
> *knowledge,*
> *but the mouths of fools feed on folly.*
> **(PROVERBS 15:13–14)**

FEELING CONNECTED

Dear Lord, Thank You for the power of the cross. Thank You for all that You bore to reconcile us to Yourself. Lord, please help us to feel deeply connected to You. May our relationships with You flourish. When we go days without actively reading Scripture, we feel distant from You. We know this is because of choices we have made and not because You have pulled away from us. Please help us to engage with You and to feel connected once again. Our intimacy in marriage seems to increase when we spend quality time with You. Thank You for the way our connectedness to You influences our marriage. We ask, Lord, that You inspire us to draw close to each other today. Feeling connected involves understanding where the other person is emotionally. Please help us recognize each other's emotional state so that we can respond appropriately. If one of us is celebrating something exciting, may we join in with genuine joy. If one of us is suffering or full of sorrow, may we be willing to understand the depths of that pain and turmoil. Holy Spirit, make it apparent how we should connect with each other. Will You make us brave to initiate intimacy today? May our marriage reflect the closeness that can be gained in a relationship with You. In Jesus's name we pray. Amen.

Rejoice with those who rejoice, weep with those who weep. **(ROMANS 12:15)**

ENDURING TRIALS TOGETHER

Dear Lord, Thank You for the many trials we have endured together and the countless trials ahead of us. Although our flesh cringes at the discomfort of challenges, Your Word encourages us to count it all joy. We believe what You say—that the testing of our faith produces steadfastness. We desire our marriage to be faithful and steadfast. We hope to be perfect, lacking in nothing. When trials come our way, please bring Scripture to the surface of our hearts so that we can patiently endure those trials. Lord, will You remind us to be supportive of one another during these trials? Please help us to find words to acknowledge and affirm the growth we see in each other. Heavenly Father, please help us not to blame each other for the challenges we face. Show us how to embrace hardships, fall to our knees in prayer over every one, and implement Your wisdom when navigating through them. Our desire is that others would see us persevere and know we can do so only because we believe in You. In Jesus's name we pray. Amen.

Count it all joy, my brothers, when you meet trials of various kinds, for you know that the testing of your faith produces steadfastness. And let steadfastness have its full effect, that you may be perfect and complete, lacking in nothing. **(JAMES 1:2-4)**

GROWING OUR FRIENDSHIP

Dear Lord, Thank You for the friendship we have cultivated. We are intensely grateful to have companionship. We are thankful for what we have in our relationship, but we know there will always be room to grow. Lord, please continue to mature us. May we make time to support each other as we recognize the unique needs we have. Inspire us to give good gifts to one another that affirm our friendship. Help us to create an atmosphere in our home that is happy and fun. With the sweetness of friendship blossoming in our marriage, will You help us share and receive earnest counsel from one another? Will You help us to confide in each other? We yearn to share wise advice with each other in whatever situation we are going through. We also desire to make date nights a priority as we find fun activities to do together. Heavenly Father, show us how to relax with each other, how to laugh more and play more. Sometimes we take each other too seriously or we let past hurts define how we interact. Please break down any barriers that keep us closed off, and rebuild our relationship to be an adventurous one. May our friendship in marriage be one that glorifies You. In Jesus's name we pray. Amen.

> *Oil and perfume make the heart glad,*
> *and the sweetness of a friend comes*
> *from his earnest counsel.* **(PROVERBS 27:9)**

OVERCOMING DEPRESSION

Dear Lord, Thank You for never abandoning us. Thank You for walking us through challenging circumstances. Hard seasons of life stir up a variety of emotions, some of which linger well after the hardship has passed. Sometimes depression has felt like diving in the deepest parts of the ocean while the oxygen tank is running out of air. The darkness, the heaviness, and the suffocating feeling of depression affect marriage too. Experiencing unwanted seasons of depression, whether brief or prolonged, is devastating. Yet You have never left us to endure it alone. You are near! And in marriage, we have each other! Thank You for letting us help each other through those challenging times. Thank You for using us to be a tangible source of comfort. May we always overcome depression, in Jesus's name! No matter what type of darkness or valley we enter, we pray we would not fear! Will You send Your body of believers to surround us and support us with Your Word? We lift up our future together and ask that depression not be the end of our story. May victory in this area of emotions and mental health be evidence of Your power in our lives. In Jesus's name we pray. Amen.

> *Even though I walk through the valley of the*
> *shadow of death,*
> *I will fear no evil,*
> *for you are with me;*
> *your rod and your staff,*
> *they comfort me.* **(PSALM 23:4)**

CONFESSING OUR SINS

Dear Lord, Thank You for the accountability we experience in marriage and for the oneness that is unique to marriage. We know intimacy and communication are ways we can experience closeness in our relationship. We ask You, Lord, to help us be open and transparent with each other. Increase our willingness to share what we're wrestling with so that we can keep each other accountable and encouraged. We also pray we would confess our sins to each other, especially those that impact our marriage. Please make us quick to repent, turning from those ways, never to go back to them again. Lord, will You lead us in being reconciled and restored through the power of forgiveness and mercy? When we are tempted to conceal our sin, please help us in our weakness. Give us boldness to step over the hurdle of embarrassment and share anyway. Help us obey Your Word and expose our sin so that the Enemy does not have a foothold in our lives. May our honesty and forthrightness cultivate a bond of trust that helps us prosper. In Jesus's name we pray. Amen.

> *Whoever conceals his transgressions will not prosper,*
> *but he who confesses and forsakes them will obtain mercy.* **(PROVERBS 28:13)**

COMMUNICATION

Dear Lord, Thank You for the beautiful art of communication, which gives us the capacity to share our thoughts and feelings with each other through speech and body language. We often overlook the importance of how we communicate with one another because we have done it for so long. Please give us a fresh sense of good communication in marriage. We ask Your Holy Spirit to quickly correct us when we are communicating disrespectfully. May no corrupt talk come out of our mouths. Please give us self-control, considering what to say before we say it. Lord, will You help us to love one another like You love us by speaking in love and in truth? We also pray You would make us into incredible listeners. The moment one of us starts to speak, help us to tune in to hear not just what they are saying but also the message behind what they are saying. Give us an intuitive understanding of each other that would bless us and help us in our communication. Lord, inspire us to share clearly and calmly the stirrings of our hearts. May our communication build one another up. In Jesus's name we pray. Amen.

Let no corrupting talk come out of your mouths, but only such as is good for building up, as fits the occasion, that it may give grace to those who hear. **(EPHESIANS 4:29)**

DEALING WITH TRAUMA

Dear Lord, We specifically pray today for any trauma that has happened in our lives. Whether it is a current situation or trauma from our past that is still affecting us, we ask You to help us lay it all at Your feet. We ask You to guide us as we process our feelings and deal with them in a healthy way. Please keep us from getting hung up and consumed with the "why" of what happened. Instead, walk us through the impact it had on us, and show us how our perspectives of it have settled in our hearts and minds. Although we are eager to know why something traumatic has happened to us, we also desire to trust You even when we don't know why things happen. May trauma never hinder us from drawing close to You or to each other. We also pray we never let trauma or difficult situations be the reason we treat each other poorly. Lord, we ask for healing from our trauma. Please show us how to cast all our anxieties on You, knowing that You care for us. May we refuse to blame You or be bitter toward You for allowing us to walk through hard things. May our ability to honor Your sovereignty in our lives bring You glory. In Jesus's name we pray. Amen.

Humble yourselves . . . casting all your anxieties on him, because he cares for you. **(1 PETER 5:6–7)**

KEEPING WATCH

Dear Lord, Marriage provides support, giving us the ability to look after each other and keep each other accountable to living holy lives. There is solace in knowing we are not alone. We appreciate the privilege of having someone special close by to experience life with. Lord, will You allow us to experience happiness, pleasure, and success in our marriage? Will You also show us that uncomfortable experiences can also produce benefits, such as calling out sin in order to get rid of it? Lord, may we be a couple who is willing to keep watch over one another. If we catch each other in the midst of sin, please help us not to be personally offended, but rather to bring up what we witnessed in a loving way in hopes of restoring each other in gentleness. May we also keep watch over ourselves so that we aren't tempted to sin. Lord, please teach us how to keep each other accountable. May our marriage refine us as we keep watch and refuse to let sin rule in us. In Jesus's name we pray. Amen.

Brothers, if anyone is caught in any transgression,
you who are spiritual should restore him in a
spirit of gentleness. Keep watch on yourself,
lest you too be tempted. **(GALATIANS 6:1)**

SETTING BOUNDARIES

Dear Lord, Thank You for the simple instruction in Your Word to be believable and dependable in what we say. It is important for us to realize the weight of our words. Our words and our commitments impact the lives of others, most significantly in marriage. Lord, when we say yes or no to something, please help us to follow through, doing what we said we would. Actions aligning with words is a crucial part of keeping boundaries in relationships. May we be a couple who makes clear relational rules that benefit and protect each other's hearts. Lord, direct us in communicating and creating the types of boundaries we need. Give us the fortitude to stick to these principles. Help us agree on boundaries in areas of our marriage such as social media usage, finances, friend time, self-care time, relationships with parents, and any other area that stirs up contention, insecurity, doubt, and worry. With these perimeters set, we hope to better serve each other by fulfilling our promises. When we break trust because we fail to adhere to these protective measures, will You help us address it in love with hopes of restoring trust? May we honor each other and You, Lord, when we carry out our marriage vows, as well as embrace the boundaries we establish together. In Jesus's name we pray. Amen.

Let what you say be simply "Yes" or "No"; anything more than this comes from evil. **(MATTHEW 5:37)**

BEING GOOD LISTENERS

$Dear$ $Lord,$ We are grateful for the areas of our marriage that are flourishing. We are also grateful for the parts of our relationship that need repair, because the challenges remind us to rely on You. Grow and stretch us so that we support each other well, making our marriage even more pleasurable. We specifically pray right now that You would transform us into better listeners. Lord, the moment one of us starts to talk, will You nudge us to give all of our attention to the conversation?. Will You help us hear what is said, as well as any messages that might remain unsaid? If we have a phone in our hands, will You encourage us to put it away? Make us quick to discern the seriousness of the discussion and our part in it. We ask You to grant us insight to see clearly what might be a burden or cause for stress so that we can attempt to alleviate it in love. As we become good listeners, we also ask You, God, to guide us in sharing an understanding response. Please inspire us to love each other through listening. In Jesus's name we pray. Amen.

Let the wise hear and increase in learning,
and the one who understands obtain
guidance. **(PROVERBS 1:5)**

YIELDING TO THE HOLY SPIRIT

Dear Lord, We praise You for being our God! Thank You for wrapping us in Your never-ending love. May we continue to keep in step with Your Spirit as You lead us through life and marriage. Make us sensitive to the ways You speak to our hearts through Your Word. When You correct us, we deeply desire to respond to Your authority with obedience. Lord, we repent of our sin and petition You to restore us. Make us new again. We yield to Your Holy Spirit. May we never disregard the voice of Your Holy Spirit leading us to walk in righteousness. Keep us tuned in to the conviction of Your Holy Spirit. Lord, we ask You to help us receive Your Spirit and never to push away Your warnings and rebukes. Our desire is to be quick to respond in humility, with a willingness to repent and be reconciled to You. Lord, will You urge us to encourage one another to walk in this way, knowing it will benefit our marriage? We desire to honor You as we submit to all Your ways. In Jesus's name we pray. Amen.

Do not quench the Spirit. **(1 THESSALONIANS 5:19)**

THE STRESS OF LIFE

Dear Lord, Thank You for being immovable, for being sturdy and strong. You are an amazing comforter, a good Father, and our hero! Thank You for letting us cast our burdens on You. Thank You for sustaining us. There are many circumstances that stir up stress for both of us. In those situations, we sometimes resort to unhealthy habits or indulgences to cope with stress. Instead, show us ways of managing our stress that are healthy and beneficial for our marriage. We ask Your Holy Spirit to shepherd us through Your Word, letting Scripture ease the weight of our burdens by giving us hope. Lord, retrain our minds to deal with stress by relying on and trusting You. When panic swirls inside or when the strain of a situation keeps us occupied, inspire us to encourage one another. Help us not to add to the intensity by responding with uncontrolled emotions. Correct us if we ever mistreat each other in the chaos. Lord, make us a couple who stops and prays over our hearts as soon as we recognize tension. May You uphold us, lead us, and keep us from being moved. In Jesus's name we pray. Amen.

Cast your burden on the Lord,
and he will sustain you;
he will never permit
the righteous to be moved.
(PSALM 55:22)

WHAT WE SEEK

𝒟ear 𝓛ord, Thank You for the many memories we have made together. Thank You for the goals we have pursued and for the vision for our future we have cast. We believe there is value in seeking the things above, where Christ is, so that we don't get distracted with the ways of the world. Lord, keep our eyes on You and on Your will. We ask You to help us chase after Your purpose for our life together. If we get off course or make goals that only satisfy our flesh, will You redirect us? Convict our hearts about what we strive for, what we desire to gain, and the choices we make to satisfy ourselves. Purify our intentions. Lord, we ask You to plant desires in our hearts for Your will for our lives and for our marriage. Lead us to build up our relationship in unique ways. May we have a greater desire to read the Bible together, to talk about the things we are learning about You, to pray together, and to be willing to do ministry together. As those seeds take root and grow, may our marriage flourish. In Jesus's name we pray. Amen.

If then you have been raised with Christ, seek the things that are above, where Christ is, seated at the right hand of God. **(COLOSSIANS 3:1)**

RESOLVING CONFLICT

Dear Lord,   Thank You for teaching us how to walk humbly with each other. Thank You for revealing in Scripture how to apologize and how to forgive. We yearn to mature in how we resolve conflict. During conflict, Lord, impress our hearts to pray immediately. Remind us to invite You into the mess we have made. We ask You to lead us to find a resolution. Will You remind us that the passions at war within us are the cause of our fights? We know this is true, and we have experienced the destruction our selfishness has caused. Make our hearts quick to recognize when we are wrong or have hurt each other. Show us how to kill our pride and the determination to be right so we can sincerely seek peace and resolution. When we offend each other, give us the fortitude to forgive and be reconciled again. Lord, chisel away our selfish perspectives of our conflict, and remove the thoughts that keep us divided. May we choose to walk in wisdom and refuse to let the Enemy gain a foothold in our marriage. In Jesus's name we pray. Amen.

What causes quarrels and what causes fights
among you? Is it not this, that your passions
are at war within you? **(JAMES 4:1)**

WHEN TIREDNESS STRIKES

Dear Lord, We have experienced the discomfort of being tired, run-down, and drained. Whether tiredness strikes because of our workload, relationship strain, or the constant demand of daily routines, it affects us and our marriage. Lord, no matter the reason for our exhaustion, please compel us to recuperate. We desire to pace ourselves better, attending to our needs to avoid the weariness that turns into agitation. When tiredness overcomes our bodies, will You guide us to find good rest by intentionally slowing down? Show us how to come to You for rest when we feel the heavy weight of our work or the emotional toll of relationships we care about. May we also be a couple who chooses to rest in You by keeping the Sabbath holy each week. You created our bodies to need downtime, so we ask You to help us not to overextend ourselves and encourage one another to rest often. We honor You for being our source of energy and strength. In Jesus's name we pray. Amen.

> *My flesh and my heart may fail,*
> *but God is the strength of my heart and*
> *my portion forever.* **(PSALM 73:26)**

HEAVY BURDENS

Dear Lord,   Regardless of what heavy burdens overwhelm us, Your Word reminds us not to worry or fear. Teach us to run to You sooner and trust in You more. Show us what it looks like to lay our burdens at Your feet. Lord, please bring to mind past experiences where You faithfully provided for us. May those memories bolster our faith. When we are weak, please hold us up. We praise You for keeping us firmly in Your grip! Thank You for comforting our hearts when we feel out of control. When it is difficult to share our struggles with each other, will You give us the words to express our emotions? When our hearts are heavy, may we turn not only to You but also to each other so we can encourage and support one another. If there are any burdens we have not laid at Your feet, we lay them down right now. We surrender how these burdens make us feel, and we ask You to give us true rest. In Jesus's name we pray. Amen.

Come to me, all who labor and are heavy laden,
and I will give you rest. **(MATTHEW 11:28)**

SEEING EACH OTHER
AS A GIFT FROM GOD

Dear Lord, Thank You for the gift of companionship. Thank You for the gift of marriage and friendship. Give us eyes to see one another as a gift from You. Lord, help us receive one another wholeheartedly. We ask You to show us how to embrace one another every day. Encourage us to consider the good and perfect gift of marriage. Flood our minds with thoughts of gratitude for our relationship. May we be a couple who takes care of each other and tends to one another's needs. May we also cherish one another daily. Lord, please show us how to unwrap this gift of marriage so that we continually discover new things about each other. Will You also help us to receive the wonderful gift of intimacy in marriage? Inspire us with creative ideas to show how much we love each other. Soften our hearts toward each other, and help us to communicate tenderly. As we receive one another as a gift from You, may we appreciate the sanctity of marriage and recognize the unique bond we share. In Jesus's name we pray. Amen.

> *Every good gift and every perfect gift is from above, coming down from the Father of lights, with whom there is no variation or shadow due to change.* **(JAMES 1:17)**

POSITIVE AFFIRMATION

Dear Lord, Thank You for the power of words. Thank You for the ability to pick our words and decide how we will deliver them. Thank You for the freedom to use our words to influence and encourage one another. Lord, please infuse us with positive affirmation for each other. May our words be gracious, warming our souls like a cup of soup on a cold day. Guide us in speaking truth to one another. Give us insight to describe the wonderful ways we see each other growing. May we be bold enough to say hard things in love, and may our words stimulate new growth in each other's lives. When we are tempted to say something negative or hurtful, we ask You to give us self-control. May we never use our words to manipulate or control each other. God, please protect us from saying anything that might cripple our confidence in each other or stir up doubt about our love for one another. Help us to refuse the urge to bring up past sins to shame each other. Instead, we want to be respectful, giving grace just like You do for us. May every word that leaves our lips be a sweet encouragement, bringing health to our souls. In Jesus's name we pray. Amen.

Gracious words are like a honeycomb,
sweetness to the soul and health to the
body. **(PROVERBS 16:24)**

GIVE US WISDOM

Dear Lord, Thank You for Your Holy Word, which guides us and gives us wisdom. Your Scripture illuminates our path and shows us the way we should walk. Wisdom is implemented knowledge. With all the knowledge and understanding we gain, we ask You to show us how and when to implement it. Please help us to remain obedient to Your Word. Train us to abide in it every day. Lord, please help us to remember Your words so that our hearts and minds are led by Your wisdom. Scripture warns us about the influences of others, sin's power to corrupt our character, and the consequences of our actions. Please help us take these truths to heart. We also pray we would cling to the wisdom that choosing righteousness leads to long life and peace. Please grant us understanding of Your ways. Give us more wisdom, especially when it comes to marriage, so that we are equipped to build our home and family according to Your Word. We desire to be a wise couple as we make decisions together. We desire to honor You and each other as we live prudently. Please help us in areas where we are foolish, and mature us in our thinking. In Jesus's name we pray. Amen.

By wisdom a house is built,
and by understanding it is established;
by knowledge the rooms are filled
with all precious and pleasant riches.
(PROVERBS 24:3-4)

DELIVER US

Dear Lord, You care for us in our brokenness and provide a way for us to be saved. We praise You for being our Father! Thank You for delivering us! Thank You for drawing our hearts out of the wilderness and giving us everlasting water. You satisfy our hunger and thirst for righteousness. Lord, will You continue to rescue us in times of need? Sometimes we need to be delivered from anxiety. Sometimes we need to be delivered from our circumstances. Sometimes we need to be rescued from contention in marriage. Sometimes we need healing from past brokenness. Sometimes we feel troubled but we can't gather the words to explain everything we are feeling and thinking. All this to say, we need You! We will always need You. Lord, You are our portion and our delight. We rest in You because we know we would not survive without You. We lift up the current state of our marriage to You and ask that You continue to mature us in our relationship. Lord, we surrender our lives and our wills. We ask You to continue to deliver us for the sake of Your steadfast love. In Jesus's name we pray. Amen.

Be gracious to me, O Lord, for I am languishing . . .

Turn, O Lord, deliver my life; save me for the sake of your steadfast love. **(PSALM 6:2, 4)**

MINISTRY OF RECONCILIATION

Dear Lord, We acknowledge the sacrifice of Christ on the cross and that the power of His resurrection has saved us from the consequence of sin. You forgave our trespasses and washed us white as snow. Our hearts are deeply thankful for all that You have done for us and for the truth that You aren't done with us yet. You continue to sanctify us. You continue to shape us into the people You created us to be. When hurt hardens our hearts, You soften us and remind us of all You have forgiven us. We must not compare the weight of our sins and try to judge which are more condemnable than others. All sin is wrong. Jesus Christ gave up His life to cover all sin. Lord, we know You hate sin. Please help us to hate it too. May we never justify our sin. You have given us the ministry of reconciliation, and we hope to spread this goodness in the world. When others wonder why we have joy and strength and hope, we want to point their hearts to You. May our love, forgiveness, and grace be an example of how to experience true reconciliation. In Jesus's name we pray. Amen.

All this is from God, who through Christ reconciled us to himself and gave us the ministry of reconciliation. **(2 CORINTHIANS 5:18)**

CREATED FOR GOOD WORKS

Dear Lord, Thank You for bringing us together in marriage, unifying us, and making us one. Our hearts' desire is that You would use our marriage for good. Make us as a couple who testifies about who You are, all You have done, what You are doing, and what You will do. We acknowledge Your workmanship in creating us for good works, and we pray we would walk in them. Holy Spirit, keep selfishness from getting in the way of us fulfilling Your will. We invite You to lead us, to convict us when we are wrong, and to comfort us when we need restoration. May we not fight against each other, but instead fight together for our marriage and to protect our unity. Lord, will You teach us to walk humbly with You and with each other? Help us to preach Your Word, especially through our actions and the way we love one another. Use us to carry out Your purpose, whether in great big bold ways or in simple and hidden ways. We are Yours and our marriage is Yours. In Jesus's name we pray. Amen.

> *We are his workmanship, created in Christ Jesus*
> *for good works, which God prepared beforehand,*
> *that we should walk in them.* **(EPHESIANS 2:10)**

BUILDING A HOME

Dear Lord, Thank You for providing us a place to call home. Thank You for the opportunity to build a life together. We understand this life is temporary, along with all the things we fill our house with. Yet we enjoy adding our unique touch to our home. Lord, may we never become consumed with thoughts of building or filling a home, but rather consider using our home to be a blessing, a place where we feel safe and others feel welcomed. Will You protect us from making an idol out of our home? Lord, please help us to stay on the same page when it comes to decorating and upgrading our home, refusing to let those things become a source of contention between us. Heavenly Father, mold us into a couple who never neglects the habits of being built up spiritually in You, conscious of the truth that we are like living stones that make up a spiritual house. Inspire us to be an encouragement to each other, acknowledging the ways You are spiritually maturing us. May we remain humble and steadfast, ready and willing to offer spiritual sacrifices that are acceptable to You. Lord, will You bless our home and make us ready to use it to do Your will? In Jesus's name we pray. Amen.

You yourselves like living stones are being built up as a spiritual house, to be a holy priesthood, to offer spiritual sacrifices acceptable to God through Jesus Christ. **(1 PETER 2:5)**

HELPING EACH OTHER

Dear Lord, Thank You for sending Your Holy Spirit to aid us in understanding Your Word and for helping us to obey it. We praise You for being our helper! Thank You for the special way marriage provides opportunities to help one another. Please aid us in recognizing when one of us needs assistance. Equip us to step in and support each other with an extra hand, a word of affirmation, or an outpouring of knowledge. May we complement one another in the way we help each other, and may we never take each other's help for granted. Lord, keep us from misusing each other, such as expecting the other person to do hard work around the house while refusing to chip in. Direct us in marriage so that we experience balance in the way we work together, taking turns in maintaining our home, initiating in our relationship, managing our schedules, and sharing any other responsibility that we both can and should participate in. Will You help both of us to embrace the tasks in front of us and to ask for help when we truly need it? As we become diligent in our work, may we also have eyes to see and know each other's interests in work and in play. May we be selfless in the time we give one another to pursue those interests. Lord, keep us from being selfish. Help us not to be lazy. May Your power working in us bring peace and pleasure to our marriage. In Jesus's name we pray. Amen.

*Let each of you look not only to his own interests,
but also to the interests of others.* **(PHILIPPIANS 2:4)**

EXPERIENCING GOD

Dear Lord, Thank You for the amazing experience of knowing You. Thank You for leading us through Scripture and helping us understand it. May we continue to gain insight into Your Word. Thank You for the gift of Your Holy Spirit. We ask Your Holy Spirit to impart wisdom to us and teach us all that You desire us to know. Thank You for the history of Your testimony recorded in the Old and New Testaments. It is a blessing to be able to see a glimpse of the miracles You have done in the lives of others as we read about their experiences with You. It is important to get to know Your awesome power as we study Scripture and learn about Joseph, Moses, Daniel, the disciples, Paul, Stephen, and many more. As we experience You in powerful ways through Your Word and in our lives, we pray we would effectively carry out Your will on earth. As we abide in You and seek You in prayer, may our experiences affirm our belief in Your truth. Please show us how our marriage can leave a legacy for others as we trust in You. In Jesus's name we pray. Amen.

Now we have received not the spirit of the world, but the Spirit who is from God, that we might understand the things freely given us by God. And we impart this in words not taught by human wisdom but taught by the Spirit, interpreting spiritual truths to those who are spiritual. **(1 CORINTHIANS 2:12–13)**

FEELING REFRESHED

Dear Lord,   You lead us beside still waters and You restore our souls. Thank You, Lord! Please help us prioritize a beneficial bedtime routine so that we can rest and recuperate before each new day. Our desire is to wake up in the morning feeling refreshed and ready to fulfill Your will. With each new day, may our heart posture be one of gratitude for all You have done and determination to please You in everything we do. Lord, we lift up our marriage and ask You to guide us to interact in ways that leave us both feeling refreshed. If there is any tension between us, we ask You to release it. May strife cease, in Jesus's name! Holy Spirit, please cover us in Your peace and put to rest any anxious thoughts we may be wrestling with. As we go to bed tonight with the intention of affirming our love for each other, we pray we would build confidence and hope in the future of our marriage. Lord, we ask You for wisdom and insight in how to refresh our love for each other, especially on days when we feel stagnant in our relationship. May we refuse to be idle or lazy in loving each other well. Please motivate us to continue on the path of righteousness. In Jesus's name we pray. Amen.

The LORD is my shepherd; I shall not want.
He makes me lie down in green
pastures.
He leads me beside still waters.
He restores my soul.
He leads me in paths of righteousness
for his name's sake. **(PSALM 23:1–3)**

FINDING EACH OTHER WORTHY

𝒟ear ℒord, Thank You for the special way You designed human beings. Nothing else on earth thinks, feels, and operates like we do. You considered us worthy of being made in Your image. Then You sent Your perfect Son to be the propitiation for our sin, making us worthy of heaven and eternal life. You have shown us in Your Word that we have value. Please give us the ability to see each other's value. May we regard one another as special. Help us to find one another worthy as a spouse, not because of what we are capable of, but rather because of the covenant we have made together. Lord, please help us to acknowledge the value we hold in each other's lives and to verbally affirm our appreciation for one another. May Your Spirit help us never to put other people and other relationships on a pedestal. Lord, we ask You to help us hold each other's hearts closely. May our love lift one another up and help us be the people we were created to be. In Jesus's name we pray. Amen.

Look at the birds of the air: they neither sow nor reap nor gather into barns, and yet your heavenly Father feeds them. Are you not of more value than they? **(MATTHEW 6:26)**

MATURE THINKING

Dear Lord, We value the ability to think. We love logic. Thank You for the amazing power of thought. Lord, You are awesome in the way You created our minds to process our experiences and emotions. We are captivated by You! We pray over our thoughts right now. Lord, we ask You to purify our thoughts. Refine our minds so that we always honor You. We don't want to be childlike in our thinking. Rather, we desire to be mature in our thinking. As we abide in You, grow in Your wisdom, and gain understanding, will You polish our thoughts and cultivate in us a habit of healthy meditation? May we think positively about one another as we dwell on each other's good traits. May we think highly of each other. Lord, please protect our thoughts from the Enemy. Please keep the Enemy from having a foothold in our minds. Give us discernment to recognize temptation. And when we're tempted, please help us consider the consequences so we can flee from sin. Equip our minds to fight temptation and keep our flesh under control. When we disagree, please help us to contemplate the impact of our words. Lord, will You guide us in choosing our words wisely? As we strive to be mature in our thinking, please give us peace of mind. In Jesus's name we pray. Amen.

Do not be children in your thinking. Be infants in evil, but in your thinking be mature. **(1 CORINTHIANS 14:20)**

HANDLING BOREDOM

Dear Lord, Thank You for the new opportunities we have every day to praise and serve You. May our lives and our marriage be abundantly full of extraordinary experiences. Our hope is to bring You joy while also enjoying one another in marriage. When we encounter boredom, please shift our minds to see the creative ways we can enjoy the moment. Encourage us to view a moment of slowness in our schedules as an opportunity to rest. Show us how to utilize boredom as a catalyst for creativity. The Enemy would want us to believe that being bored is a bad thing or means we don't have purpose. Guard us from believing such lies, in Jesus's name! Will You fill our hearts and minds with peace so lies cannot seep in to destroy the moment? Lord, increase our capacity to embrace slow days. May we be willing to accept Your will for us, even if that includes the moments we think are dull. In Jesus's name we pray. Amen.

The thief comes only to steal and kill and destroy. I came that they may have life and have it abundantly. **(JOHN 10:10)**

SOCIAL MEDIA

Dear Lord, Thank You for the advancement of technology and the many systems we use to stay connected. We have tools that make communication easier and more accessible than any generation has had before. With the increase of social media and apps that help connect people, will You give us wisdom in using these technologies? Make us a couple who easily commits to social media boundaries in an effort to protect our marriage. Convict our hearts when we are tempted to sidestep those boundaries. Help us never to hide our online interactions from one another. To keep each other accountable, may we be quick to give each other access to our devices. Lord, keep us from being foolish in how we use social media or the internet. Make us keenly aware of how it all influences our minds and our behaviors. Do not let our flesh fool us into pursuing sin, for our flesh will never be satisfied. We ask You, Lord, to give us wisdom in whom we connect with online. We know that bad company corrupts good morals. Our desire is to protect ourselves so that we are not deceived or corrupted. May we use social media to further glorify Your name. In Jesus's name we pray. Amen.

Do not be deceived: "Bad company ruins good morals." **(1 CORINTHIANS 15:33)**

SOWING GRATITUDE

Dear Lord, Thank You for giving us hearts with the capacity to experience deep gratitude. We are grateful for our marriage and how it has impacted our lives. May we sing Your praises every day! Lord, teach us to sow gratitude in our marriage by regularly sharing with one another the reasons why we appreciate each other. If anything tempts us to think negatively about one another or our circumstances, will You please guard us from it? Protect our minds and our mouths from complaining. If we do complain, will You gently correct us and show us a different perspective, one that gives us hope? Inspire us to see the joy of what today brings. Lord, we are grateful for Your steadfast love. Help us to have steadfast love in marriage. Our desire is that our love for one another would endure forever. As we sow gratitude, expressing our adoration and thankfulness, may we reap the blessing of contentment in our relationship. May others around us be encouraged to consider why they are grateful for their marriage as well. In Jesus's name we pray. Amen.

Give thanks to the LORD, for he is good,
for his steadfast love endures forever.
(PSALM 136:1)

KNOWING GOD'S WORD

Dear Lord, Thank You for the power of Scripture. Thank You for the gift of the Bible and the written account of all the wonderful things You have done and will do in the future. We believe Your Word, and we know the importance of reading it daily. As we read the Bible, please help us to memorize it. Impress on our minds Scriptures that will lead us through the circumstances we are facing today. Encourage us to discuss Your Word and help each other to gain a better understanding of it. Lord, write Your Word on our hearts! May Scripture transform our lives as it reveals who we are in Christ—new creations, free from our old lives of sin and bondage. As a sharp sword pierces its target, may Your Word cut to our hearts and expose anything that we need to drag into the light. As we grow to know Scripture better, we ask You to help us use Your Word to encourage one another to live righteously. We praise You Lord, and we thank You that the Bible is a lamp for our feet, guiding us through this life and showing us the way You want us to go. In Jesus's name we pray. Amen.

The word of God is living and active, sharper than any two-edged sword, piercing to the division of soul and of spirit, of joints and of marrow, and discerning the thoughts and intentions of the heart. **(HEBREWS 4:12)**

REASSURING EACH OTHER

Dear Lord, We are grateful that You sent Your Son to die to save us. Even though we have received salvation, we still struggle with sin. But You love us and gently draw us back to You. Your love is amazing, and we are deeply grateful for the ways You have changed our lives. Yet despite Your power in our lives, we confess moments of weakness when we are uncertain about what we believe and struggle with doubt. When we doubt Your love for us, we ask Your Holy Spirit to affirm us and increase our faith. Help us to remain steadfast and faithful in our belief of the truth. When fear causes us to doubt the love we have for one another, we pray You would use us to encourage and remind each other of all that is true. Doubt stirs up tension in our hearts, and when we don't feel confident in our love for each other, our marriage suffers. Please graciously walk us through how best to reassure each other of our adoration and affection. Lord, flood our minds with memories of the good times we've shared, and wash away our insecurities. Inspire us to express our love for each other regularly, leaving no room for doubt. Lord, may love abound in our relationship, and may You be glorified as our marriage flourishes. In Jesus's name we pray. Amen.

God shows his love for us in that while we were still sinners, Christ died for us. **(ROMANS 5:8)**

CULTIVATING AN EMOTIONALLY SAFE ATMOSPHERE

Dear Lord, Thank You for being our sanctuary and shelter. Thank You for being our source of safety. Lord, will You help us to be a safe place for one another? Will You remind us of our need to embrace one another as often as possible? Make us a source of comfort for each other, and help us to give one another a sense of security. Please help us to cultivate an emotionally safe atmosphere in which we can run to each other when we need refuge, when we need support, and when we need to share how we are feeling. Please let Your light shine brightly through us as we seek to be Your hands and feet, working in our marriage to serve in love. Lord, teach us how to create a space for sharing the things that matter to our hearts. Please help us to be good listeners so that we truly hear the pain or stress in one another's lives. Holy Spirit, please work in us to encourage one another through that pain and stress. Just as You never let us down, may we never let one another down. Keep us from neglecting one another, and keep us from avoiding conversations about the condition of our hearts. In Jesus's name we pray. Amen.

He who dwells in the shelter of the Most High will abide in the shadow of the Almighty. **(PSALM 91:1)**

OUR LOVE

Dear Lord, Thank You for teaching us what true love is. Thank You for the commandment to love and respect each other. Lord, will You help us to see each other as You see us? Please remove the tinted lenses covering our eyes that have painted each other in a poor light. Show us who we are becoming as we mature in You. May we refuse to define each other by past sins or failures. We petition You for pure eyes. Give us fresh eyes, in Jesus's name! Grant us a heavenly perspective of each other and our marriage. Our desire is that our love would outweigh any frustration or discontentment we may wrestle with. We pray grace would abound in our relationship. Please fill us with patience, gentleness, faithfulness, and goodness so that we walk in a way that honors each other. Lord, will You help us recognize our relationship as extraordinary, not ordinary? We know You have brought us together for a purpose. Lord, may You be pleased as we chase boldly after Your purpose for our life together. In Jesus's name we pray. Amen.

This is love, that we walk according to his commandments; this is the commandment, just as you have heard from the beginning, so that you should walk in it. **(2 JOHN 1:6)**

DIVINE COURAGE

𝒟ear Lord, Thank You for watching over us as a good Father. Thank You for shielding us from the powers of darkness. We praise You and pray that Your will continues to prevail in our marriage. Lord, give us insight that will help us navigate all that we are going through. May we see from Your point of view as we watch it all unfold. We also pray we would respond to our circumstances with confidence as we trust in You. Heavenly Father, increase our ability to wait on You for wisdom regarding our situations. Please give us divine courage right now, and remind us to walk in Your Spirit. May we always have the courage in life and in marriage to do what is right. Lord, grant us boldness and steadfastness in our faith. We ask that You would give us strength when we face pain, grief, and discomfort. May our hearts take courage as You move in us and in our marriage. You are our leader, our counselor, and our commander, so we will wait for You to tell us what comes next as we yield ourselves to Your authority. May Your name be magnified as we defer to You. In Jesus's name we pray. Amen.

> *Wait for the Lord;*
> *be strong, and let your heart take*
> *courage;*
> *wait for the Lord!* **(PSALM 27:14)**

FACING CRISIS

Dear Lord, Thank You for being our tower of refuge and our help in time of need. Thank You for overcoming this world and for being our fountain of peace. When the world seems unsteady and trials come our way, we know we can trust in You with all our hearts. Please keep us from leaning on our own understanding. May we not be consumed by this world and the troubles that are ever present in this life. When the reality of crisis sets in, please remind us that our hope is in You. Whether we are facing crisis on a large scale in the world or on a more personal one in our marriage, we ask You to sustain us and keep us from feeling troubled. May we find rest and security in You. Lord, remind us to run to You in prayer and lay our anxious thoughts down at the foot of Your throne. Please show us how to always direct each other to draw closer to You. Keep fear and worry away from us so that we aren't trapped in hopelessness. May Your peace that passes all understanding guard our hearts and minds. In Jesus's name we pray. Amen.

I have said these things to you, that in me you may have peace. In the world you will have tribulation. But take heart; I have overcome the world. **(JOHN 16:33)**

GIVING GOD GLORY

Dear Lord, Thank You for being our light in the darkness. Thank You for being the way, the truth, and the life. Thank You for guiding us and for all the ways You help us navigate decisions, continually propelling us forward toward new growth in Christ. Help us to remain in submission to You as You lead us and teach us. As we draw closer to You each day, we ask You to encourage us to also draw closer to each other. We pray You would bless our marriage, and we ask You to grant us deeper intimacy and deeper communion with one another. For these blessings and many more, we give You glory! We give You glory for holding us in the palm of Your hand and for the joy we experience in marriage. We give You glory for the talents You have given us and allow us to use for ministry work. We give You glory for helping us through hard times. We give You glory for letting Your light shine in us. We give You glory for our home and the life we have built together. As we live and work together, may others see You in us and the good You have done in our marriage. In Jesus's name we pray. Amen.

Let your light shine before others, so that they may see your good works and give glory to your Father who is in heaven. **(MATTHEW 5:16)**

UNITY IN MARRIAGE

Dear Lord, Thank You for the bond we have. Thank You for being our strong foundation and for Your Word, which shows us how to walk in unity with one another. Thank You for healing us and for giving us the ministry of reconciliation in our marriage. Please help us to choose reconciliation every time there is conflict between us. We ask You, Lord, to protect our marriage, specifically our unity. Help us remain strong and steadfast in Christ. Lord, keep us united and keep us close. If anything jeopardizes our unity or threatens to break our bond, we ask You to remove it far from our home and hearts. Remind us daily that our marriage represents Christ and His love for the church. May our unity be a testimony of Your love and power in our lives. We cannot have unity in our own strength, so we ask for Your strength to equip us. Lord, please teach us to have sympathy, love, tender hearts, and humble minds toward each other. Give us peace as we strive to be on the same page about how we operate as a couple. May You be glorified as Your fruit is produced in us. In Jesus's name we pray. Amen.

Finally, all of you, have unity of mind, sympathy, brotherly love, a tender heart, and a humble mind. **(1 PETER 3:8)**

THE POSTURE OF
OUR HEARTS

Dear Lord, Thank You for the gift of another day to live a life of worship, praising You with our actions and our words. Will You direct our eyes to notice all the moments You give us today to make right our posture before You and before each other? Holy Spirit, will You work in our hearts, making them pleasing and honoring to You? May the posture of our hearts be humble and sincere. Lord, remove any pride and self-ishness that creeps up in us. Give us deep consideration for one another, being thoughtful to check in with each other. Make us a couple who listens with pure compassion and grace. Help us seek to benefit one another in any way we can. Lord, we ask for a supernatural understanding of each other. Give us the gift of being keen on how each other is doing so that we may know each other well and bless each other. If we are in conversation and hear something that stirs up anger, encourage us to eval-uate the posture of our hearts. May we address our emotions and work them out with self-control. Lord, please help us to walk righteously and humbly, trusting You in all Your ways. In Jesus's name we pray. Amen.

Trust in the LORD with all your heart,
and do not lean on your own
understanding. **(PROVERBS 3:5)**

GENUINE LOVE

Dear Lord, We know we are not promised tomorrow, making every day a beautiful gift from You. With the breath in our lungs, we worship You! Thank You for today! Lord, may our fervor for life be evident in our expressions of joy today. Thank You for loving us more than we could ever understand. It is because of Your heart toward us that we surrender to You. We also recognize that our love for one another is only possible because of Your perfect love in us. May our love for one another be genuine and pure. Lord, will You allow us to experience an incredible moment of intimacy today? Whether we are able to discuss an important matter, connect through physical touch, or a combination of both, please help us to make time to spend together. Knowing that we are asking for a special moment together, we also ask You to help us avoid sabotaging this moment. Protect this moment by helping us not be easily offended. Cover our minds and keep insecurities far from us. Lord, help us to lay aside our selfishness and to love each other with a Christlike, unconditional love. May Your name be magnified as we hold fast to what is good. In Jesus's name we pray. Amen.

> *Let love be genuine. Abhor what is evil; hold fast to what is good.* **(ROMANS 12:9)**

LOVING OUR NEIGHBORS

Dear Lord, Thank You for defining what love is for us in Your Word. Thank You for emphasizing the importance of serving others, as well as giving us the examples of Christ that show us how to serve others. Thank You for teaching us the significance of loving our neighbors. We recognize that our neighbors can be our literal neighbor or anyone near us. Scripture describes the fondness and care we should have for all. May we serve You today by intentionally loving others. Give us time to work together to come up with creative ways to bless our neighbors. And grant us an encounter today that allows us to put one of those random act of kindness into practice. Lord, shape us into a couple who is generous, kind, and considerate. Lord, please help us to be thoughtful of others and the ways You can use our marriage to be a blessing in their lives. As we pursue serving others in love, may we also never neglect to serve each other in love. Use us as a team for Your glory, to speak truth in love and to serve our neighbors. In Jesus's name we pray. Amen.

Love does no wrong to a neighbor; therefore love is the fulfilling of the law. **(ROMANS 13:10)**

NO MORE SICKNESS

Dear Lord, Thank You for being our healer. Thank You for being our refuge, our rock, and our redeemer. We praise You for Your many blessings. We praise You for taking our challenging circumstances and using them for good. Thank You for helping us overcome hardship. Thank You for equipping us to endure through life regardless of what comes our way. We have not always reacted righteously to hard circumstances, such as sickness or financial changes. We are sorry for our lack of faith. Please help us to trust You more. Grant us the ability to always respond with gratitude, believing You will work through every situation to do Your will. We specifically ask You to remove the hardship of sickness from our home. When sickness does come, we ask for quick healing and a strong recovery. No matter how much we struggle or what type of sickness we encounter, we pray we would maintain a positive attitude. May peace and joy remain in our hearts as You sustain us. Restore us to full health, in Jesus's name! As illness comes and goes, may the unity of our marriage never be destroyed. In Jesus's name we pray. Amen.

The LORD sustains him on his sickbed;
in his illness you restore him to full
health. **(PSALM 41:3)**

HONORING EACH OTHER

Dear Lord, Thank You for the power of submission and the beautiful example of meekness found in Christ. Thank You for the humility Christ exemplified in lowering Himself to earth, serving others, and especially laying down His life in love. Thank You for Christ's heart of compassion. Lord, make us more like Jesus Christ every day! Show us how to love deeply and respect one another. May meekness be a mark of our character. We ask that You help us endure this life with patience and humility. Holy Spirit, enable us to interact with one another in gentleness and kindness. Our desire is that we would lead every conversation with a posture of compassion. As we abide in You and remain faithful in marriage, may we delight in abundant peace as we honor each other through our actions. May our hearts find peace from turmoil. May our minds find peace from anxiety. May our home be filled with Your extraordinary peace. Lord, please help us to submit to Your Word and Your authority every day. In Jesus's name we pray. Amen.

The meek shall inherit the land
and delight themselves in abundant
peace. **(PSALM 37:11)**

NO MORE MANIPULATION

Dear Lord, Thank You for our intellect. Thank You for the gift of intelligence and communication. It is an incredible joy to be able to communicate with each other and use that gift to accomplish great things, such as hitting goals we set, parenting, building better habits, and loving each other well. May we resolve never to use this gift of communication and intelligence in manipulative ways. Lord, help us to avoid exploiting what we know about each other to try to get what we want. Please keep us from being controlling. May Your Holy Spirit reveal to us if our communication is influencing each other in negative ways, causing shame or stirring up feelings of inadequacy. We ask You to transform the parts of our character that are not beneficial, are dangerous, or are sinful. Teach us to speak to each other respectfully. May our words come from a place of true love for one another. Lord, we also pray we would have eyes to see and hearts to discern the intentions of others. Make us aware if someone is using their position of authority to manipulate us. Help us to guard our marriage by being alert, grant us courage to confront manipulators we encounter, and help us fight for what is right. In Jesus's name we pray. Amen.

Beware of false prophets, who come to you in sheep's clothing but inwardly are ravenous wolves. **(MATTHEW 7:15)**

RECONNECTING WITH
EACH OTHER

𝒟ear 𝓛ord, We desire to take advantage of every moment we have together to share what is on our hearts and minds. Please guide us in exploring through conversation all that You have for our marriage, including the goals we should aim for and the work we should strive to do together. May we feel reconnected as we spend time talking and dreaming together. We also ask You to help us reconnect through physical touch. Whether it has been a long while or just a short time since we experienced physical intimacy, we ask You to give us the confidence and desire to draw close to one another. Please protect our marriage, and help us to create a safe and secure atmosphere to be together. We know marriage goes through seasons of good times and challenging times, and we are grateful that our marriage has withstood all of them. May the season we are currently in be one in which we are intentional to do everything in love, with the hope of feeling a close connection. In Jesus's name we pray. Amen.

Let all that you do be done in love.
(1 CORINTHIANS 16:14)

OUR TALENTS

Dear Lord, Thank You for the beautiful design of our bodies and the purposes You have created us for. Thank You for the thoughtfulness You poured into our characters and personalities. Thank You for the talents You have given us. We also praise You for the way our talents complement one another! We appreciate You using all that we have to do good in our marriage and in this world. Please make known to us what our talents are, as well as the potential we have to grow in new ones. Show us our strengths and abilities. Help us receive and embrace the giftings You have given us, so that we put them to use in full confidence. Holy Spirit, enable us to share our talents to bless others in every opportunity You offer us. Our desire is to always have a posture of submission toward You. Lord, we ask that using our talents to serve one another in love would benefit our marriage and bring You glory. As we strive to be good stewards of Your grace, will You refine our talents and giftings? Will You increase our knowledge and ability? Please help us to use all that we have to build each other up. In Jesus's name we pray. Amen.

As each has received a gift, use it to serve one another, as good stewards of God's varied grace. **(1 PETER 4:10)**

WALKING A STRAIGHT PATH

𝒟ear 𝓛ord, Thank You for revealing Yourself through Scripture, as well as through our personal experiences with You. Thank You for Your goodness. Lord, please help us to keep You as the top priority in our lives. Help us to put You first and not let anything else take Your place, becoming an idol. Give us words to encourage one another to read the Bible and pray every day. Will You help us to trust You when You change our course or direction? Will You make us flexible, welcoming interruptions from You? Please guide our steps and help us lay aside what we think might be the best thing for our marriage so we can walk in Your will for us. Lord, make straight our path as we walk in all Your ways. Inspire us to seek Your face, to worship You, and to possess a confident faith. Please help us not to be distracted from spending time in Your Word or prayer. Please help us to be keenly aware of what is absorbing our time so that we can be disciplined in the way we spend it. May You be glorified through us as we acknowledge You. In Jesus's name we pray. Amen.

In all your ways acknowledge him,
and he will make straight your paths.
(PROVERBS 3:6)

BE PATIENT AND PRAY

Dear Lord, Thank You for using our marriage to grow our patience with ourselves and with each other. Thank You for the way our love matures as we practice patience. Thank You for our friendship, which deepens as a result of showing each other grace. Lord, we desire to be unwavering, faithful, and calm during the tribulations and trials we face. Help us to remember to pray through those trials and to ask You to give us endurance and strength. When we long for our plans to come to fruition or yearn for a struggle to pass, point us to the hope we have in Christ, that we may rejoice instead of growing weary. May our rejoicing in hope also train us to be steadfast in You. Please use our marriage and our circumstances to guide us toward patience. We love You Lord and praise You for the patience You have shown us. Though we may fall, You do not forsake us! Though we may sin, Your forgiveness and grace abound. Your patience and kindness are what lead us to repentance. May You also lead us to be more like You in showing patience toward one another. In Jesus's name we pray. Amen.

Rejoice in hope, be patient in tribulation,
be constant in prayer. **(ROMANS 12:12)**

LOVE AND RESPECT

Dear Lord, You teach us in Your Word why You created marriage and how marriage works best. Please enrich our understanding of the purpose of marriage. May we never stop learning how to be good spouses and may we never stop sharing our hearts with each other. Fill us with respect for each other, even when we are dealing with conflict or sin. Give us eyes to see one another through the lens of grace, mercy, and love. Please help us to remain close. Help us refuse to see each other as an enemy, instead seeing each other as a team. We ask You to help us choose to love, honor, and respect each other every day, moment by moment. May our high esteem for one another be a testament to others of Your gospel and powerful presence in our lives. Lord, we know You desire us to treat each other with deep love and admiration because You want us to represent what You created marriage to symbolize, which is the mystery of the union of Christ and the church. In Jesus's name we pray. Amen.

*However, let each one of you love his wife
as himself, and let the wife see that she
respects her husband.* **(EPHESIANS 5:33)**

NO REVENGE

Dear Lord, Thank You for saving us from Your wrath. Despite what we deserve because of our sin, You save us and lavish us with Your grace. Thank You for loving us. Holy Spirit, thank You for comforting us and teaching us all Your ways. Lord, sometimes we feel hurt or angry in marriage, which leads us to want to retaliate. Lord, forgive us for thinking this way! Please keep us from seeking revenge in our relationship. We also ask You to help us forgive one another. Lord, show us how to let go of our hurts and surrender our emotions to You. Teach us how to trust You as our vindicator and our avenger. Guard our minds from dwelling on thoughts of revenge toward each other or toward others. When we feel the need to teach someone a lesson, will You remind us that Your Holy Spirit is already at work? Will You help us walk in humility and self-control? May we be quick to have mercy on the person who offended us, bringing them to You in prayer instead of seeking revenge. May we have hope in and love toward others as we choose to forgive. In Jesus's name we pray. Amen.

Beloved, never avenge yourselves, but leave it to the wrath of God, for it is written, "Vengeance is mine, I will repay, says the Lord." **(ROMANS 12:19)**

HAVING SELF-CONTROL

Dear Lord, Thank You for convicting our hearts about sin and leading us to live lives of righteousness. Thank You for the fruit of the Spirit, which is produced in us when we abide in You. We specifically pray You would help us to have self-control in all things. Without self-control, we know we cause destruction in our lives and in our marriage. Our desire is to protect ourselves from destruction and sabotage. Please help us to have self-control in our emotions, respectfully sharing how we feel but not justifying our lashing out at each other because of our feelings. Give us self-control in our eating so that we are able to enjoy the variety of flavors and types of food that nourish our bodies without experiencing shame from overeating. Shape us to be self-controlled in our desires, experiencing certain pleasures in life but denying our flesh when it comes to sin. Please help us to have self-control in our speech, resolved never to use our words to shame or belittle each other. May we glorify You as we live in self-control. In Jesus's name we pray. Amen.

> *A man without self-control*
> *is like a city broken into and left without*
> *walls.* **(PROVERBS 25:28)**

FIGHTING FOR OUR MARRIAGE

Dear Lord, You have established marriage as a sacred covenant. We love and appreciate Your design of marriage and the purposes You have created it for. We are deeply grateful for our relationship. We implore You to remind us daily of the vows we committed to before You. Lord, as valuable as marriage is to us, we know we have a real Enemy who hates marriage. We ask You to defend us from the innumerable threats from the Enemy, who aims to damage our relationship. Please aid us to do everything in our power to protect our marriage against anything that would hurt our marriage. Give us the tenacity to fight for our marriage with strength and dignity. Keep us resolute to deny our flesh so that we do not become a threat that is capable of unraveling our relationship. We believe You have joined us together, we believe our marriage is important, and we believe You will help us thrive in marriage. Lord, we ask You to fight for us, in Jesus's name! When we are weak, when we are tempted to sin, when the stress of life wears us down, please hold up a shield of faith for us. Please watch over us when we fail to watch over ourselves so that nothing separates us. May Your purpose for our marriage prevail. In Jesus's name we pray. Amen.

What therefore God has joined together,
let not man separate. **(MARK 10:9)**

MAKING OURSELVES KNOWN

Dear Lord, Thank You for the courage to make ourselves known to one another in marriage. Thank You for every moment we have shared together and the many more still to come. We have been blessed to spend intimate time together, which helps us cultivate a healthy marriage. Thank You for giving us opportunities to be known in a more profound way. We invite You to help us unveil ourselves to one another through deep conversation. If there is anything we need to share with each other, please draw it up out of us like a waterwheel fetches water repeatedly. Make us brave enough to open up, to be truthful, and to be vulnerable. Keep pride out of our hearts. Heavenly Father, we ask You to create in us a desire to constantly learn more about each other. And may we use that information when we are planning dates, buying gifts, or considering ways of serving each other. Our desire is to bless one another as we consider each other's needs and attempt to fulfill them. In revealing ourselves to each other, may the foundation of our marriage be strengthened. In Jesus's name we pray. Amen.

I can do all things through him who strengthens me. **(PHILIPPIANS 4:13)**

INITIATING INTIMACY

Dear Lord, We acknowledge the extraordinary and exclusive way we get to love each other in marriage. Thank You for the gift of intimacy. We are deeply grateful for being truly known and loved by one another. Thank You for pursuing us and showing us that we are valued by You. We desire to value each other as You value us. Make us a couple who pursues each other with great passion. As we share our hearts and bodies with one another, we ask You to help us to wholly embrace each other. Prompt us to initiate intimacy, both emotionally and physically, even when there is tension in our relationship or when circumstances are difficult. Will You help us to be a romantic couple? Will You urge us to consider the desires both of us have for intimacy and do what we can to fulfill those desires? Lord, help us prioritize our marriage and protect our time together so that we don't neglect our relationship. May we always be there for each other, ready to affirm our love for each other in tender ways. Please bless our marriage as we seek to bless each other. In Jesus's name we pray. Amen.

As you wish that others would do to
you, do so to them. **(LUKE 6:31)**

GIVING GOOD GIFTS

Dear Lord, Thank You for Your perfect provision. Thank You for all the good gifts You have given us. We are grateful for the ways You have lavished us with Your love. Will You make us good gift givers like You? Lord, we desire to be thoughtful in the gifts we give as well as in how we serve one another. When we give each other treasures, we ask You to help us find meaning in the gifts we present. Please inspire us with creative gift ideas, especially for special holidays or our anniversary. Flood us with interesting gift ideas, some that are extravagant and others that are simple, such as cooking breakfast in bed, planning a surprise getaway, or letting the other person control the TV remote. May we never feel obligated to produce gifts for one another. Rather, we ask You, Lord, to prepare our hearts with tender expectation and joy so we look forward to blessing each other. Remove any pressure of giving or receiving in our relationship. Lord, please help us embrace the love we have for each other and to express it through giving good gifts. May our thoughtfulness in every offering prove our steadfast love and faithfulness in marriage. In Jesus's name we pray. Amen.

In all things I have shown you that by working hard in this way we must help the weak and remember the words of the Lord Jesus, how he himself said, "It is more blessed to give than to receive." **(ACTS 20:35)**

KNIT US TOGETHER

Dear Lord, Thank You for the unity of oneness in marriage. You have taken us from being two individuals to being one in wholeness. Thank You for designing marriage as a way to experience camaraderie of friendship and the intricacy of intimacy. Marriage is layered with ways of connecting that knit us together. Thank You for the blessing our marriage has been to us. Please help us maintain our relationship, tending to each other's needs and keeping our unity a high priority. Will You knit us even tighter together? Lord, we petition You to help us feel incredibly close to each other. We ask You to keep us together—us plus You—in an unbreakable, threefold cord of harmony. May we seek You with sincerity, putting You at the center of our marriage. Heavenly Father, show us how to surrender our worries and our unnecessary desires for the sake of protecting our oneness. Make us knitted so tightly together that we may not be quickly broken. In Jesus's name we pray. Amen.

> *Though a man might prevail against one who is alone, two will withstand him—a threefold cord is not quickly broken.* **(ECCLESIASTES 4:12)**

RECEIVING FROM THE LORD

Dear Lord, We thank You for the parables and metaphors You share in Scripture, which teach us more about You. Thank You for the books of Psalms and Proverbs, which increase our faith and wisdom. We praise You for filling us with wisdom! As we abide in Your Word, will You please write Your wisdom on our hearts? Open our ears so that we may hear Your advice, warnings, and instructions, becoming familiar with Your voice. Make us diligent to implement all the ways the Bible directs us to walk uprightly. As we read the Bible, we ask You to keep our hearts soft so that we can receive from You rebuke and correction, encouragement and comfort. May Your words transform our lives and shape who we are becoming. Mature us and sanctify us, making us more like You. Lord, make us into a couple who receives from You with gratitude and joy, whether this life is easy or difficult. Please help our hearts to trust You. In Jesus's name we pray. Amen.

Listen to advice and accept instruction,
that you may gain wisdom in the future.
(PROVERBS 19:20)

NURTURING OUR MARRIAGE

Dear Lord, Thank You for the unique way we get to nurture each other in marriage. Thank You for teaching us how to encourage one another and spur each other on to do good works. Please continue to develop our character. Refine the way we talk, the way we view circumstances, and the way we serve one another. We invite You to use challenging situations to put us to the test. May steadfast faith secure us and hold us up. Grant us knowledge and discernment so that we can be blameless before You. We dedicate our hearts to pursuing godliness. As we grow in our faith and integrity, we hope to experience exponential growth in our marriage. Please show us how to nurture our marriage relationship. Help us identify areas of our relationship that need to be mended, reconciled, or fixed. Humble us and give us courage to address the parts of us that still need to mature. We ask You to direct us as we seek to bless each other in speaking words of encouragement, in achieving goals together, in supporting one another, and in tenderly showing our affection for each other. May Your love abound in our marriage more and more. In Jesus's name we pray. Amen.

It is my prayer that your love may abound more and more, with knowledge and all discernment, so that you may approve what is excellent, and so be pure and blameless for the day of Christ. **(PHILIPPIANS 1:9-10)**

MOVING FORWARD

$Dear\ Lord,$ Thank You for providing a way forward. Despite our sin, weakness, and failures, You don't leave us to wallow in self-pity. You pick us up out of miry clay with gentle yet firm encouragement. You shine Your light in the direction we need to go. You are faithful, even when we are not. Thank You for Your faithfulness! No matter what circumstances we face today, help our hearts to remain steadfast in our trust in and love for You. Protect our thoughts from using our pasts to define us. Keep us from letting shame, guilt, or embarrassment hold us back from trying to do what is right. Please give us the courage to take the next right step in our relationship. As we persevere in our faith in You, please help us gain forward momentum so we can experience a thriving marriage. May we see victory in areas where we have struggled and find strength to keep pressing on. Lord, please give us encouraging words to express to each other, cheering each other on. When we feel the burden of despair, use us to remind one another of who we are in Christ. Lord, remind us that we are a new creation. May Your faithfulness carry us when we feel too weak to do even the simplest of things. May Your strength bolster our faith and keep us going. In Jesus's name we pray. Amen.

If we are faithless, he remains faithful—for he cannot deny himself. **(2 TIMOTHY 2:13)**

STRENGTHEN US

Dear Lord, Thank You for being our source of strength. We recognize our weaknesses and rely on You for security, energy, and wisdom. When we feel confused, You guide us to a place of understanding. When we are insecure, You steady our feet, planting them firmly on the Rock. When we feel overwhelmed, You make us lay down by still waters. When we are discouraged, You send us affirmation. When we feel anxious, You give us Your transcending peace. You are faithful and thoughtful in the ways You support us. Thank You for doing so much for us! Thank You for using us to encourage each other, especially in tough times. We are grateful to have each other. Will You strengthen us today so that we can endure together? We pray You would increase our gratitude for leading us and carrying us through life. Please equip us with everything we need, as each day presents new challenges. Help us remain humble as we rely on You for everything. In Jesus's name we pray. Amen.

The LORD is my strength and my song,
and he has become my salvation;
this is my God, and I will praise him,
my father's God, and I will exalt him.
(EXODUS 15:2)

SPREADING JOY

Dear Lord, Thank You for the assurance of salvation. Thank You for making a way to be with You for eternity. Thank You for the gift of joy. We know it is Your joy that is in us. We are grateful to experience the richness of joy and the treasure of happiness. May we be vessels who carry Your joy with us wherever we go, pouring Your joy onto others. Lord, please let gladness be evident on our faces, in our eyes, and in our countenances. Our hope is that we would be conduits of Your joy, leading others to seek You. We desire others to ask us about our joy so that we can tell them about You and all You have done for us. We ask that the contentment and elation evident in our marriage would be a catalyst to share Your testimony with the world. May the joy dwelling deep in our hearts anchor feelings of security between us. Please make Your joy full and complete in us. In Jesus's name we pray. Amen.

These things I have spoken to you, that my joy may be in you, and that your joy may be full. **(JOHN 15:11)**

IRON SHARPENS IRON

Dear Lord, You offer perfect wisdom through Your Word. Thank You that Your wisdom has sharpened our character. Thank You for the delight we feel when we spur each other on toward growth. Please make us a couple who is known for making wise choices. Use us to sharpen one another just as iron is used to sharpen iron. May we never be afraid of friction in our relationship, confident that those interactions will force us to confront how we behave, including our attitudes, our words, and our actions. In seasons of irritation, instead of feeling discouraged, we ask You to help us look for the good that these seasons can produce in us. Like a piece of sandpaper is used to sand down the rough edges of a piece of wood, please sand down our rough edges. Smooth out our roughness. Refine us. Polish us. Lord, we trust You to use our marriage for our benefit, to mature us. May we truly appreciate hard situations we encounter and submit them to You in prayer, expressing our desire for good to come out of them. Please help us to stimulate growth in each other and draw one another closer to You. May You be glorified as we pursue living according to Your truth and wisdom. In Jesus's name we pray. Amen.

> *Iron sharpens iron,*
> *and one man sharpens another.*
> **(PROVERBS 27:17)**

SHARING OUR HOBBIES

Dear Lord, Although we recognize our oneness in marriage, we know You made us distinct individuals. You creatively and thoughtfully designed our strengths, abilities, and passions. Exploring one another has been an interesting journey. As we grow to know each other deeply, study likes and dislikes, and gain understanding in how You have created us, we humbly ask You to help us appreciate our likenesses and differences. One of the areas we have learned about each other is the hobbies we are interested in. Will You please help us find ways of inviting each other to join in and enjoy our individual hobbies of interest? Motivate our curiosity to learn more about our hobbies, and allow us to mutually savor the time we invest in them. Let our experiences bring us closer as we do things together that we love. Help us to take pleasure in each other's interests, even if we never desired to do them before. Lord, teach us to keep our hobbies under control and not allow them to consume us or take over all our free time. Show us how to encourage one another to find balance so that our hobbies take their proper place in our hearts and home. In Jesus's name we pray. Amen.

> *You make known to me the path of life;*
> *in your presence there is fullness*
> *of joy;*
> *at your right hand are pleasures*
> *forevermore.* **(PSALM 16:11)**

HELP US NOW

Dear Lord, Thank You for always helping us in times of need. You know every detail of our lives and what we are going through. You know exactly what we need before we even pray about it. Thank You for providing for us, for giving us wisdom, and for giving us Your peace. We praise You for being our helper! We petition You to help us right now. We need Your guidance. Holy Spirit, will You remind us of the wisdom in Your Word and show us how to implement it in the situation we are experiencing? Direct our minds and our hearts to pursue reconciliation and restoration with each other. When we feel particularly vulnerable, protect our marriage from any threats of the Enemy. In the face of hardship, please hold us firmly so that we are not shaken. Keep us from feeling afraid of or troubled by our present circumstances. Inspire us to encourage each other to trust You and to rest in Your peace. Lord, we ask You to help us understand all that is happening right now. Give us insight. Grant us discernment. Please reveal how this circumstance is impacting one another, and aid us in walking through it with compassion. In Jesus's name we pray. Amen.

Peace I leave with you; my peace I give to you. Not as the world gives do I give to you. Let not your hearts be troubled, neither let them be afraid. **(JOHN 14:27)**

A STRONG FOUNDATION

Dear Lord, Thank You for Your strong arm. Thank You for revealing truth to the world. Thank You for helping us build a strong foundation of belief and love in our marriage. We are building our foundation on You according to Your Word. You are our Rock! May our marriage foundation be well built. Lord, help fulfill our good intentions to make our marriage unbreakable. When flood waters rise, when challenging situations come flowing our way, make our marriage capable of withstanding the pressure. Make us immovable in our faith and in our love for one another. Lord, make our hearts tender toward one another no matter how much force is being pushed against us. If any parts of our relationship need to be torn down to be built back up stronger, will You gently lead us through that process of reconstruction? We desire to have an incredible marriage foundation so that You can use us as a light in the lives of others and be a blessing in this world. In Jesus's name we pray. Amen.

> *He is like a man building a house, who dug*
> *deep and laid the foundation on the rock.*
> *And when a flood arose, the stream broke*
> *against that house and could not shake it,*
> *because it had been well built.* **(LUKE 6:48)**

SHOW US OUR SIN

Dear Lord, We praise You, for You are good! Thank You for being our rescuer and our redeemer. We humbly come before You to ask that You show us our sin so that we can repent. We don't want any unrighteousness in our lives. Sometimes we don't see how we have been tempted to sin or how we have chosen to sin. If there is anything we are doing or have done that we have not acknowledged, please reveal it to us. Open our eyes so that we are not deceived. We desire to walk in purity in our marriage. We know sin affects our relationship with You and with each other, so please Lord, sanctify us. Please give us the courage to be honest with ourselves, with You, and with each other. Help us to repent of sin and choose reconciliation so that we can find mercy and healing. Please help us not to fail to do what is right. In Jesus's name we pray. Amen.

Whoever knows the right thing to do and fails to do it, for him it is sin. **(JAMES 4:17)**

REPLENISH OUR MARRIAGE

Dear Lord, Thank You for all the sweet ways You lead us to live devoted to one another. We specifically want to share our gratitude for the innumerable opportunities You have given us to step into our roles as a married couple and to love one another through serving one another. Lord, may we never grow weary of doing good to one another. When we do feel worn out, please sustain us with Your energy. When we are confronted with weakness, please let Your strength be evident in our lives, lifting us up and equipping us to carry on. Replenish our marriage with peace, joy, playfulness, and endurance. Renew us as we express our love to each other. When we have downtime, will You inspire us to write a letter of affirmation to or be silly with one another? May we pursue each other affectionately and feel emboldened to plan a spontaneous date. Inspire us also to find joy in resting together. May our love never dwindle or be dull. In moments of insecurity or doubt, when our souls feel weary, we ask You to replenish us. Fill us with Your strength so that our souls never languish. In Jesus's name we pray. Amen.

I will satisfy the weary soul, and every languishing soul I will replenish. **(JEREMIAH 31:25)**

EMBRACING EACH OTHER

Dear Lord, We praise You for the extraordinary way marriage provides closeness and intimacy. Thank You for the opportunity You have given us to embrace each other. We submit to You our desires right now, including the desire to grow our intimacy. Please encourage us to be willing to serve one another and meet those desires. Please help us never to deprive one another, especially as a means of control. If we need to take time to devote ourselves to prayer, fill us with understanding so our hearts feel secure in truth. Lord, help us lay aside any selfish ways that hinder us from loving well. Lead us to give abundantly when our flesh feels like withholding affection. Lead us to appreciate each other when we desire to be recognized. Lead us to be thoughtful when we want to be thought of. Lead us to be understanding when our hearts yearn to be understood. May we always be quick to hold each other closely and our expectations of each other loosely! If any conflict or tension is keeping us divided or emotionally distant, may Your powerful love transform our hurt into hope. Lord, please help us experience closeness with each other and with You. In Jesus's name we pray. Amen.

Do not deprive one another, except perhaps by agreement for a limited time, that you may devote yourselves to prayer; but then come together again, so that Satan may not tempt you because of your lack of self-control. **(1 CORINTHIANS 7:5)**

SPIRITUAL MATURITY

Dear Lord,   Thank You for the preeminence of Your Holy Spirit in our lives. Thank You for convicting our hearts when we are choosing to walk in the flesh, and thank You for the ministry of reconciliation. We praise You for shaping us like clay in the potter's hands! Mold us into something marvelous! We desire the work of Your hands to be evident in our lives and in our marriage. Lord, may we pursue loving You by reading the Bible and submitting to You in prayer every day. As a potter uses tools to contour a delicate work of art, we ask You to shape our marriage. We long to grow in spiritual maturity. We are confident that our character refinement—becoming strong in our thinking and stable in our emotions—will positively impact our relationship. The more deeply rooted we are in You, the more sensitive we will be to the leading of Your Spirit. Please show us how to keep in step with Your Spirit, resolved to please You and deny our flesh. May our spiritual maturity bless our marriage and magnify Your name. In Jesus's name we pray. Amen.

Walk by the Spirit, and you will not gratify
the desires of the flesh. **(GALATIANS 5:16)**

BUILDING UP KNOWLEDGE

Dear Lord, Thank You for designing us with the ability to learn. Our brains are so incredible! Our capacity to gain knowledge is great! We ask You to fill us with wisdom and increase our intelligence. Lord, make us a couple who pursues learning with curiosity and an open heart. Show us how to explore a subject in greater depth, as well as examine how You relate to it. May we use the knowledge we acquire to build up our lives through wisdom, and make our marriage more interesting as we share information with each other. As we invest in learning, we ask You to show us how to use what we know to engage one another's minds in a deeper way. Inspire us to develop how we think and process information. May our knowledge help us in making choices that improve our way of living. We also ask You to soften our hearts so that we receive teaching from each other. Keep us humble, even as our knowledge increases. May our diligence to learn, grow, and walk in wisdom bring glory to You. In Jesus's name we pray. Amen.

An intelligent heart acquires knowledge,
and the ear of the wise seeks knowledge.
(PROVERBS 18:15)

INVESTING IN OUR FUTURE

Dear Lord, Thank You for our future and the precious time we have left to spend together. Thank You for our legacy and the impact our marriage will have in this world. Thank You for the wisdom You have imparted through Your Holy Word and for teaching us the power of investing. Lord, will You make us mindful of how our current choices will affect our future? Please lead us in the best ways to invest in our future. We ask You for financial wisdom. Lord, please help us to agree on how we devote our time, money, and resources. Teach us to consider potential circumstances and how we can best prepare for the worst. Lord, we ask You to inspire us in the ways we can support our marriage and family in the long term. Most of all, we pray our legacy would reveal the investment of sowing Your truth and yield a bountiful return. May generations of family that come after us see our faithfulness and know You walked alongside us to show us the way. Lord, help us choose obedience to Your Word and let our obedience be fruitful. Keep us from worrying about tomorrow and boasting about what we have. We submit each day to You and humbly trust Your will. In Jesus's name we pray. Amen.

You do not know what tomorrow will bring.
What is your life? For you are a mist that
appears for a little time and then vanishes.
Instead you ought to say, "If the Lord wills, we
will live and do this or that." **(JAMES 4:14–15)**

PURSUING EACH OTHER

Dear Lord, You are the way, the truth, and the life, and we desire to cling to You! We praise You for being our everlasting hope! Thank You for pursuing us and loving us. You have never stopped loving us, even in our despair and pain. You have sought after our hearts and have cared for our well-being. Thank You for providing the present of marriage. May we never stop pursuing each other. Give us the courage to say why we love each other, to ask how we are doing, and to pray for each other, especially when we need it most. Encourage us to plan date nights, to do activities that build our friendship, and to support each other in stressful situations. Please help us to feel confident initiating physical intimacy. Please keep pride from getting in the way of embracing and enjoying each other. Help us to seek each other and You wholeheartedly every day. May You be blessed as we bless each other. In Jesus's name we pray. Amen.

> *With my whole heart I seek you;*
> *let me not wander from your*
> *commandments!* **(PSALM 119:10)**

A GREATER DESIRE

Dear Lord, Our relationships with You and with each other are significant to us. We hold them in high esteem. We want to cherish these relationships and cultivate them. Thank You for having a relationship with us. Thank You for the gift of prayer and how easy it is to come to You. Lord, we ask You to give us a greater desire to know Your Word well and to read it more consistently. Show us how to delight ourselves in You, especially when we pray. Lord, we invite You to align our hearts to Yours so that Your desires become our desires. May our souls be satisfied in You. Please give us a deeper yearning to spend time at the foot of Your throne. We also pray for an even greater desire for one another. Give us a craving for more intimacy and connectedness, and fill us with a longing to spend quality time together. Lord, may our desires motivate us toward unity and oneness. In Jesus's name we pray. Amen.

Delight yourself in the L*ORD*,
and he will give you the desires of
your heart. **(PSALM 37:4)**

EXTENDING GRACE

Dear Lord, Thank You for Your amazing grace and Your steadfast faithfulness! Thank You for Your wonderful and powerful love. Lord, please give us the ability to show radical grace in our marriage. Teach us to be slow to become angry with one another, refusing to be easily offended. Please help us seek forgiveness when we do not walk uprightly and then to truly forgive one another as needed. Lord, train us to lay our offenses at the cross before we let them dig a root of bitterness in our hearts. Please help us to reconcile quickly to protect our bond of unity. May our love be powerful, our faithfulness be steadfast, and our grace extended be amazing. Lord, will You guide our communication, that we may speak humbly and respectfully? When a conversation turns into a conflict, will You remind us that we are one, called by You to walk in love? May we not consider our own lives more important or valuable than the other's. Lord, help us to walk in a worthy manner, and let Your name be a testimony to others because of the grace we share in marriage. In Jesus's name we pray. Amen.

I do not account my life of any value nor as precious to myself, if only I may finish my course and the ministry that I received from the Lord Jesus, to testify to the gospel of the grace of God. **(ACTS 20:24)**

TRUSTING EACH OTHER

Dear Lord, We have been blessed by the support, encouragement, love, and trust we have experienced in marriage. We also appreciate the accountability we have with each other. We are responsible to one another, and we don't take that lightly. Lord, please reveal the best ways to keep each other accountable, making sure we are walking in Your ways, acting with integrity, and being trustworthy. Please continue to show us how to build up trust in our marriage. Remove any doubt from our hearts that tempts us not to trust each other. May we be a couple who insists on living with honesty and virtue. Lord, help us to be who we say we are, even when no one else is around. We also pray for any area of our marriage where trust has been broken, and we ask You to restore it. We ask You to help us rebuild trust in our relationship and to keep us from breaking it again. May we walk securely and confidently as we let integrity lead our hearts. As we trust in You, may Your light shine brightly in us. In Jesus's name we pray. Amen.

> *Whoever walks in integrity walks securely,*
> *but he who makes his ways crooked will*
> *be found out.* **(PROVERBS 10:9)**

ENDURANCE

Dear Lord, Thank You for encouraging us and equipping us to endure together. Many challenges in life tempt us to be frustrated or even to give up. We are confident our endurance in life and marriage comes from You. We praise You for being our source of energy and strength! We praise You for sustaining us with Your power! Please help us to carry on, especially in the tough times. May our resolve to remain united in marriage set us apart from this world, giving others the opportunity to see Your light at work in us. May they discover that our hope is in You! Lord, will You help us find encouragement in the Bible? When the needs of the family push us to our limits, when the demands of work chip away at our time, when guilt makes us feel unworthy, or when insecurities about the future stir up anxiety, we pray You would step in and make Your presence known. When we feel weak, will Your Holy Spirit remind us of Scripture to reinforce our reliance on You? Lord, please use us to urge one another to press into You. Affirm our hearts with hope, and strengthen our minds to persevere in marriage and in every circumstance we encounter. In Jesus's name we pray. Amen.

> *Whatever was written in former days was written for our instruction, that through endurance and through the encouragement of the Scriptures we might have hope.* **(ROMANS 15:4)**

292

TRANSFORM OUR HABITS

Dear Lord, Your Word convicts our hearts and gently leads us through a process of sanctification. Thank You for the transformation You have done in us already. We ask You to complete Your work in us. We pray specifically over our daily habits and choices. There are many things we can choose to do, but we know not all things are beneficial. We ask You to help us do what is right. Lord, give us discernment in taking the next step to change our habits. Reveal what we should pursue and what we should stop doing. Please help us listen to each other and examine how our choices can negatively impact our marriage. When we share suggestions for change, please help us communicate them respectfully. And Holy Spirit, please keep our hearts tender toward each other so that we can graciously receive those suggestions that have the power to help shape us for the better. Lord, destroy any unhealthy habits we have! Remind us every day that we are not enslaved by anything. Will You also build up good habits in us and give us the stamina to follow through with the changes we are making, even when it feels hard? We pray for an abundance of self-control as we work on building helpful habits. We submit our wills to You and ask that Your will be done in us. In Jesus's name we pray. Amen.

"All things are lawful for me," but not all things are helpful. "All things are lawful for me," but I will not be dominated by anything. **(1 CORINTHIANS 6:12)**

A FRESH NEW DAY

Dear Lord, Thank You for another day to worship You, to love You, and to love each other. We praise You for a fresh new day! We praise You and rejoice for all that today will bring! With the gift of the present, please help us unwrap today with a heart of gratitude. May our minds dwell richly on the characteristics we love about You and on all that You have done in our marriage. May we also dwell on the characteristics we love about each other and the memories we have made together. Lord, help us to approach this day slowly, considerate of how we can bless You and bless each other. We ask You to lead us to fulfill the purpose You have for us today. Open our eyes to clearly see how we can use this day to serve our marriage. Any remnant from yesterday—any leftover friction or any unresolved situation—please help us to overcome. Dissolve any tension or conflict. Lord, settle our hearts and fill us with gladness. We ask that You teach us to operate in marriage according to Your wisdom. Make us feel secure in You and in our marriage as we seek to enjoy today. In Jesus's name we pray. Amen.

This is the day that the LORD has made;
let us rejoice and be glad in it.
(PSALM 118:24)

HELPING OTHER MARRIAGES

Dear Lord, We have traveled countless hills and valleys together. Thank You for transforming our hearts and minds to be aligned with Yours. Thank You for growing our love for one another. Thank You for keeping our unity intact when it has been under attack. You are the only reason our marriage is still standing. Thank You for helping our marriage survive! Lord, will You use our experiences to encourage other marriages? Just as You have given us an abundance of strength to persevere and hope to carry on, we desire to share that strength and hope with others. Marriage can be a strenuous relationship. Every day brings opportunities for conflict or overwhelm. We specifically lift up couples who are struggling right now. Lord, will You use us to support and encourage them, reminding them that they are not alone? Speak through us to affirm that better days are ahead. Please hold these marriages in Your hand, protecting them from the threats of the Enemy. Lord, please keep these couples' unity intact! Just as You sent faithful couples to encourage us in times of need, please use us to encourage other couples to put their trust in You. In Jesus's name we pray. Amen.

Give, and it will be given to you. Good measure, pressed down, shaken together, running over, will be put into your lap. For with the measure you use it will be measured back to you. **(LUKE 6:38)**

OVERCOMING INTIMACY FEARS

Dear Lord, It is wild to consider how You made us one in marriage. Thank You for the gift of intimacy and for the way this gift keeps on giving. Lord, help us never to rely on the other person to initiate, but instead make us bold to initiate without contingency. Motivate us to do what is right and to fulfill our roles in marriage, even if the other person doesn't. May our love for each other never be transactional. Remind us to love freely and deeply. Keep us from holding on to resentment or anything that could get in the way of us experiencing intimacy. As we engage romantically with each other, will You extinguish any intimacy fears or insecurities we may have? Please help us to trust one another with our bodies. We pray we would experience extraordinary closeness, fully able to enjoy being with one another. Increase our confidence, especially when we feel vulnerable. Embolden us to embrace each other passionately and keep our love alive. In Jesus's name we pray. Amen.

God gave us a spirit not of fear but of power and love and self-control. **(2 TIMOTHY 1:7)**

ADMIRING EACH OTHER

Dear Lord, As difficult as it may be to face trials in marriage, we trust You through them. We expectantly trust You to help us remain strong through every storm or challenging circumstance. When we feel overwhelmed, may we never lose sight of who we are to each other. Keep our eyes set on things above, in Jesus's name! No matter what we face, please remind us of the significance of our marriage and help us to see the good in each other, especially when we are tempted to see only the things that stir up frustration. When stress comes our way, strengthen our bond of unity. Lord, stir up admiration in our hearts and minds for one another. Teach us how to regularly share our approval and our appreciation of each other so that our confidence is built up in love. Give us the forethought to inquire about each other's needs and consider how we can meet those needs. Inspire us to outdo one another in random acts of kindness and in honoring each other. Make us a couple who is quick to affirm our love through physical affection. Lord, will You help us to pursue one another even when we don't feel like it? May Your love pour out of us and fill up our marriage. In Jesus's name we pray. Amen.

Love one another with brotherly affection. Outdo one another in showing honor. **(ROMANS 12:10)**

CONTROLLING OUR ANGER

Dear Lord, You designed us to feel deeply and intensely, yet You teach us the importance of self-control. Thank You for creating us with emotions. We ask Your Holy Spirit to help us exercise self-control with every emotion we experience. We specifically ask You to help us to control our anger. Transform our character so that we are slow to become angry. May we also be slow to get offended. Instill in us the fortitude to hold our composure and our tongues when we feel anger well up inside. Please help us to control our emotions, instead of our emotions controlling us. In our anger, please keep us from sinning. May our anger never motivate us to say words we will regret, and may we never allow our hurt feelings to cause us to hurt each other. Our desire is that Your righteousness would be evident in our lives. If we sin in our anger, we cannot produce Your fruit. We ask You to keep us humble so we can deal with our anger in a righteous way. Please help us to walk in Your Spirit with every response we give to each other and others. In Jesus's name we pray. Amen.

The anger of man does not produce the righteousness of God. **(JAMES 1:20)**

LIVE IN FREEDOM

Dear Lord, Thank You for providing a way to walk in freedom from sin. May we refuse to use our freedom as an opportunity to sin. Please help us to be above reproach. Equip us with the power of Your Word so we can resist temptation. Lord, may we experience victory over sin as we walk in righteousness. Inspire us to encourage one another to choose righteousness over sin. When temptation knocks, when stress is a burden, or when mistakes are made, we pray for resolve to speak words that are encouraging, not critical. May our marriage benefit from us choosing to live in freedom. If there are areas of our lives that are still in bondage to sin, will You reveal them so we can repent? Will You give us the strength to deny our flesh? Lord, make us brave enough to remind the Tempter that we have been set free from sin by the blood of Christ. We never want to be a source of temptation for one another. Holy Spirit, please help us consider what we are inviting into our lives and into our marriage. Convict us to strive to be pure and holy. May we use our freedom to serve one another in love. As we deny our flesh and live in the freedom of Christ, may Your testimony spread far and wide. In Jesus's name we pray. Amen.

You were called to freedom, brothers. Only do not use your freedom as an opportunity for the flesh, but through love serve one another. **(GALATIANS 5:13)**

DENYING OUR FLESH

Dear Lord, Thank You for encouraging us to take up our cross daily to follow You. Denying our flesh what it craves is not easy, yet we know it pleases You. Thank You for renewing our minds. Thank You for transforming our lives and teaching us how to be pure. When we are tempted to sin, You give us a way of escape. Lord, make us sensitive to Your leading so that we can take advantage of that way of escape and resist temptation. Lord, help us exercise self-control in all things. When we encounter unbelief and doubt, will You protect us from drifting away from Your truth? Instead, we ask You to make us secure in You and increase our faith. Enable us to believe that the strongholds in our lives have been broken and that we can walk in victory, in Jesus's name! When our flesh is weak, craving more and more, we ask You to help us to say no. Teach us to count the cost of our choices and to consider the consequences of sin in our lives and in our marriage. May the weight of those consequences, and the weight of what Jesus did on the cross, motivate us to deny our flesh. We ask for an outpouring of wisdom to fill us up and enable us to obey Your Word. May our faith be an encouragement to one another, and may You be glorified in our marriage. In Jesus's name we pray. Amen.

> *He said to all, "If anyone would come after me, let him deny himself and take up his cross daily and follow me. For whoever would save his life will lose it, but whoever loses his life for my sake will save it."* **(LUKE 9:23-24)**

BEING TRANSPARENT

Dear Lord, You search our hearts, You see our thoughts, and You know our intentions. Thank You for knowing us and loving us still. Thank You for Your compassion. We feel loved and cared for by You! Lord, we ask You to continue to search us and know us. If there is any grievous way in us, we ask You to change us. Lead us in Your will and in Your way everlasting. Although You already know us, may we continually offer You our hearts by sharing with You what we are going through. Lord, help us to be transparent in our relationship with You. Help us to run to You in prayer and express our feelings to You. We ask You to embolden us to communicate our struggles and our victories. May our trust in You lead us to be more and more transparent and open. We know that by freely sharing ourselves with You, our relationships with You and with each other will grow. Thank You for comforting us in prayer and through Your Word. May we also be a comfort to one another as we share Scripture pertaining to our circumstances. Please keep our hearts open toward each other. Give us the courage to honestly share how we are doing. May our transparency lead to deeper intimacy and more trust. In Jesus's name we pray. Amen.

Search me, O God, and know my heart!
Try me and know my thoughts!
And see if there be any grievous way in me,
and lead me in the way everlasting!
(PSALM 139:23–24)

GIVING TO OTHERS

𝒟ear 𝓛ord, We feel abundantly blessed! Thank You for everything You have given us. Our desire is to be considerate of all we have and to be good stewards of it. Lord, shape us into a couple who is known for being generous. We ask You to keep our hearts open and our hands loose so that we are prepared to give to others as You see fit. Use our marriage to be a blessing to others, just as You have been a blessing to us. As we sow generosity, may we reap joy, knowing we were able to give only because of all that You have given to us. Please help us to give wholeheartedly, without obligation or expectation. We also ask You to take away any insecure thoughts surrounding giving. May we be eager, not reluctant, to give. If one of us struggles to be generous, use the other person to encourage generosity. Heavenly Father, make us cheerful givers, whether we're giving encouragement, money, or tangible things. Please move through our marriage, using it to show others Your goodness. In Jesus's name we pray. Amen.

Each one must give as he has decided in his heart, not reluctantly or under compulsion, for God loves a cheerful giver. **(2 CORINTHIANS 9:7)**

OVERCOMING INSECURITIES

𝒟ear 𝒧ord, Thank You that Your Word leads our hearts in truth. Thank You for showing us how to be people of integrity. Please build the foundation of our marriage on Your truth. Equip us to stand courageously and firmly on Scripture. Thank You for Your wonderful works, including us! We know we are fearfully and wonderfully made. When insecurities flood our minds—such as not liking the way our bodies look, feeling inadequate to be used spiritually, wrestling with thoughts of failure, or even feeling too insecure to pray—please reiterate Your truth to combat any and all lies. If we ever catch ourselves listening to and being impacted by a voice of condemnation that tempts us to hate ourselves, please extinguish that voice immediately. Help us to be grateful for who we are and who we are becoming through sanctification. May we refuse to let our insecurities influence the way we treat each other. We also ask You to keep us from feeling defeated when insecurities flare up. Please transform and renew our minds so that we do not let negative thoughts hinder us from fulfilling our purpose. We ask You to continually increase our faith in You and our confidence in our marriage. In Jesus's name we pray. Amen.

I praise you, for I am fearfully and
wonderfully made.
Wonderful are your works;
my soul knows it very well.
(PSALM 139:14)

EXPERIENCING GRIEF

Dear Lord, You care for our well-being and our mental health. You help us carry our concerns and handle our emotions. Thank You for the ability to feel deeply. Thank You for meeting us where we are and gently leading us through it all. We trust that You are with us, supplying our every need. Lord, grief is an unimaginable pain. Loss is difficult to comprehend. The questions of why we experience loss make it challenging to to move forward. Yet when the pain of grief strikes us to our core, You are near. When profound sadness clutches our hearts, You are near. When our knees hit the floor in distress and we don't know how to comfort each other, You are near. In the midst of our weeping, You are near. You are the God who sees us. Please help us to receive Your comfort. When we experience grief, will You please give us insight in how to comfort and encourage one another? Will You help us find the courage to keep moving forward despite the grief we carry? We pray Your comfort would be a unifying experience that strengthens our marriage and supplies us hope. In Jesus's name we pray. Amen.

Blessed are those who mourn, for they
shall be comforted. **(MATTHEW 5:4)**

COMPLEMENTING EACH OTHER

Dear Lord, Thank You for the way we complement each other in marriage. Our unity completes us. Just like two puzzle pieces, we are two very different individuals who fit together side by side. Help us to embrace every aspect of each other more than we ever have before. We are beyond grateful that You've brought us together. May Your perfect love exist in our marriage, and may it be reflected in us so the world can see You. Lord, please help us to accept and appreciate one another's giftings. Give us words to encourage each other to use our giftings for Your glory. Help us to insert ourselves in situations where we know we can use our strengths to accomplish something good. We know two are better than one because we have double the energy, double the insight, double the help to get a job done well. Help us to eagerly work together to meet goals and experience joy in our relationship. We ask You to inspire us to also compliment each other in public through admiration and appreciation. Our hope is that others would be encouraged to see our love for one another as we cherish each other. Holy Spirit, bless our marriage today as we use our hands and our hearts to serve together. As we mutually embrace the way we complement each other, may we be encouraged by one another's faith and belief in what we can accomplish together. In Jesus's name we pray. Amen.

That is, that we may be mutually encouraged by each other's faith, both yours and mine. **(ROMANS 1:12)**

OUR MONEY

Dear Lord, Thank You for being our provider. Thank You for the money You've given us to use for our marriage and family. Please help us operate as a team as we learn how to use our money to care for ourselves. Lord, will You please grant us insight and wisdom in money management? Will You also keep the love of money from entering our hearts? We pray we would never hoard wealth or gain it at the cost of pushing aside other significant responsibilities such as our marriage or family time. We yearn to use our income wisely and, if possible, invest for the benefit of future generations of family. We don't want to chase money and wealth in vain. We desire to have balance in our lives and in our marriage. Lord, we submit our finances to You and ask You to lead us in how we spend, how we save, and how we give. Give us resolute minds to refuse to let money become a divisive conflict in our relationship. Please help us to understand one another's perspectives about money and boundaries. May You put us on the same page and teach us how to be in agreement with our financial decisions. When it is in our power to help others, inspire us to be generous givers. May You be honored in our hearts' attitude toward money. In Jesus's name we pray. Amen.

> *He who loves money will not be satisfied with money, nor he who loves wealth with his income; this also is vanity.* **(ECCLESIASTES 5:10)**

FLEEING TEMPTATION

Dear Lord, Thank You for the victory we have in Jesus. Thank You for setting us free from sin. Thank You for telling us the truth over and over again. When we are lured by temptation, please help us to be quick to flee. Holy Spirit, direct us right in that moment literally to stand up and do something completely different. Please aid us in shifting our thoughts so that we don't sin. May we never give in to our flesh's sinful cravings. The reality is that our flesh will never be satisfied because it constantly craves more. Lord, help us to have self-control over our desires and thoughts. Lord, we ask You to give us strong minds that combat temptation with the power of Scripture. When we are weak, help us to reach out to tell one another so that we can pray together. Please enable us to pursue righteousness, faith, love, and peace with pure hearts. As we run from sin and chase boldly after You, may we be quick to encourage each other and direct one another's hearts to remain steadfast in You. In Jesus's name we pray. Amen.

Flee youthful passions and pursue righteousness, faith, love, and peace, along with those who call on the Lord from a pure heart. **(2 TIMOTHY 2:22)**

ROMANCE

Dear Lord, You have given us countless ways to love one another. We praise You for Your extraordinary design of intimacy and connectedness! Please show us how to cultivate romance in our marriage, stimulating our minds with new ideas that would bless each other—including flirting with each other more regularly, perhaps taking dancing lessons, or making the effort to light candles for a romantic atmosphere. Develop a strong desire in us to be affectionate toward each other. As we pursue each other, may our quality time together become increasingly more enjoyable. Inspire us to spend time each day considering how we can affirm each other emotionally. We also ask You to teach us how to improve at initiating physical intimacy. When we initiate sex, we pray we would be mindful of each other's needs, including simple things such as being aware of what time it is and how that can impact one another the next day. Lord, keep us from justifying why we can't initiate intimacy. Sometimes we feel insecure about our bodies. Sometimes we are afraid of rejection. Sometimes we are lazy. Sometimes we are too busy or waste time on other things. Give us confidence to take the next right step to be close to each other. When we are together, may we be satisfied by each other. Lord, help us embrace romance and adventure. We pray You would give us innumerable opportunities to delight in our life together. In Jesus's name we pray. Amen.

How beautiful and pleasant you are,
O loved one, with all your delights!
(SONG OF SOLOMON 7:6)

STEADFAST LOVE

Dear Lord, Your steadfast love is a great comfort! Thank You for loving us! May our marriage honor You! In everything we say and do, we pray that our respect for You is evident. Lord, help us make every moment count, even if they seem mundane or inconsequential. Tune our hearts to be concerned about the details of each other's lives. Inspire us to ask how each other is doing and if there is anything we can do to help make life easier. Please make us good listeners. Lord, thank You for being slow to anger. We know that even when we sin, You are patient with us. You are abounding in steadfast love and faithfulness. Will You make us steadfast in our love? Heavenly Father, we ask You to help us be loyal to one another. Help us to be merciful and gracious with each other. Make our hearts resolute to serve one another in love. Lord, please fill us with an unwavering faithfulness that protects our covenant of marriage. May we make the most of our time together and bless each other as we love like You love. In Jesus's name we pray. Amen.

You, O Lord, are a God merciful and gracious,
slow to anger and abounding
in steadfast love and faithfulness.
(PSALM 86:15)

SURRENDER

Dear Lord, Thank You for showing us what sacrificial love looks like. As we choose to love each other unconditionally, we ask that our marriage be refined. Please show us how to willingly sacrifice our time, our desires, our goals, our pride, and our routines for the sake of oneness. May we even be willing to lay down our lives for each other if the opportunity ever arose. Lord, our hope is that our love would run so deep that we would be willing to give up everything to make sure our marriage thrives. We also pray for the ability to surrender everything to You. We lay aside our worries, we surrender our thoughts, we submit our decisions, and we lay everything at Your feet. Give us a greater understanding of spiritual worship and how we can live to please You. Help us to listen to Your Spirit as You guide us to live according to Scripture. Please help us not to act selfishly. Rather, may You be glorified as we surrender to You and walk in Your ways. In Jesus's name we pray. Amen.

I appeal to you therefore, brothers, by the mercies of God, to present your bodies as a living sacrifice, holy and acceptable to God, which is your spiritual worship. **(ROMANS 12:1)**

310

PRESSURES OF THE WORLD

Dear Lord, Thank You that Your Word always remains relevant and powerful. Thank You that it is living and active in our lives. Scripture leads us, teaches us, and comforts us no matter what is going on in this world. You are constant, never changing, and reliable. As the pressures of the world seem to grow, we ask You to secure our foundation. Lord, we ask that our marriage would never be shaken. Please help us to surrender any anxieties we have about current news. Teach us how to process what we see and hear by talking with one another, being quick to remind each other that You are on the throne! Thank You for being our peace! Don't allow the world to pull us away from You or the way You want us to live. If we're acting worldly in any way, will You help us address it right away? Show us how to test everything according to Your Word. Lord, we ask You to let Your Word shape our thoughts and actions. We know You are on our side and desire our marriage to succeed. Encourage us to call on You whenever we are distressed. May Scripture counsel us, and may we receive from You a peace beyond understanding. In Jesus's name we pray. Amen.

Out of my distress I called on the LORD;
the LORD answered me and set
me free.
The LORD is on my side; I will not fear.
What can man do to me?

(PSALM 118:5-6)

NO MORE LYING

$Dear Lord,$ Thank You for the light of the truth. Keep us in Your truth, and help us abide in Your Word so that we have no doubt about what the truth is. It seems this world has turned upside down on itself. Today's culture is redefining everything under the sun. Please show us how to support what is true and how to get rid of anything that is contrary to the truth. Holy Spirit, we invite You to impart Your wisdom and fill us with knowledge. Keep us from boasting about what we know, and instead show us how to share it in truth. Make us truth tellers. Transform us to have the utmost integrity in our character. Please help us to have self-control with our tongues. Holy Spirit, show us how to resist lying. We know You hate lying! Please keep us from saying even a small white lie. Renew our minds and keep us far from sin. If we are ever tempted to lie, please help us to tell the truth, no matter how difficult it may be. If we lie, we invite You to convict our hearts so that we may repent. May we abide in Your truth every day, that it may affirm what we believe. We ask You to help us obey Your Word. Lord, we desire to live reconciled to You, pure and steadfast in our faith. We need Your help to be people of light. In Jesus's name we pray. Amen.

> *Lying lips are an abomination to the LORD,*
> *but those who act faithfully are his*
> *delight.* **(PROVERBS 12:22)**

ENCOURAGEMENT OF OTHERS

Dear Lord,　Thank You for the plethora of marriage resources that can help us to learn more about marriage. Thank You for using other couples to encourage us through their love stories, as well as their challenging experiences. Thank You for couples who passionately share their expertise on marriage topics. We are grateful for the many couples who recognize their purpose in bringing hope to others through the power of encouragement. May we take advantage of marriage resources so they can benefit and bless our marriage. Please help us invest in our relationship by devoting time and energy to reading and implementing relationship advice that can direct us and give us insight. We ask You to bless those couples who have allowed You to use their marriage experience to produce something good in this world. May the boldness of others embolden our hearts to also be used by You to encourage other married couples. As we share the testimony of You working in our marriage, please remind us to be strong and courageous. In Jesus's name we pray. Amen.

Have I not commanded you? Be strong and courageous. Do not be frightened, and do not be dismayed, for the LORD your God is with you wherever you go. **(JOSHUA 1:9)**

USE OUR MARRIAGE

$Dear Lord,$ We are growing in our understanding of how marriage represents a picture of Your redeeming love and amazing grace. Our relationship with You and with each other has transformed our lives for the better. Although we sometimes walk through hard situations, You never leave us. In fact, You take the hard things and use them for good. When You call us to persevere and we make it through trials together, we know our bond of unity is being strengthened. We ask You to continue knitting us together and fortifying our foundation so that we can continue to stand firm. Please take hold of our marriage to do good in this world. No matter what the good turns out to be, our hope is that we would surrender to You and allow You to use our love story to encourage others. Our desire is to give others the same hope we have needed when hard times press in. Hope for better days. Hope for true love to flourish. Lord, use us as Your hands and feet to do Your will here on earth. Please use our marriage to carry out Your will, and help us to work together as a team for Your glory. In Jesus's name we pray. Amen.

This is the will of God, that by doing good
you should put to silence the ignorance
of foolish people. **(1 PETER 2:15)**

MAKING MORE TIME
FOR TALKING

Dear Lord, Thank You for the wisdom in Scripture that warns us about the impact of our words. Thank You for sharing Your thoughts about how we should consider and evaluate what our tongues speak. Our desire is that we would use our tongue with self-control. We appreciate the ability to communicate, and we want to honor You in our word choices as well as the delivery of those words. It is beautiful to think about how we can understand the meaning of words and then string them together in a way that someone else can understand. We are grateful for the times we can share our hearts with each other. We love to dream together, debate with each other, and discuss things we are learning with one another. Please remind us daily of the gift of being able to verbalize how we feel. Make us confident communicators. Please help us to create a safe environment where trust and love are present. When we talk with each other, may our words never be rash. Instead, may our words bring healing, in Jesus's name! Please help us to be clear and kind in our communication and to make more time for talking together. May You be glorified in the way we speak to each other. In Jesus's name we pray. Amen.

There is one whose rash words are like
   sword thrusts,
      but the tongue of the wise brings
healing. **(PROVERBS 12:18)**

COMFORTING EACH OTHER

Dear Lord, Your Holy Spirit comforts us and brings to mind all that You have said in Your Word. We are grateful for the gift of the Holy Spirit in our lives. Lord, will You make our hearts sensitive to the leading of Your Holy Spirit? When we sin and shame sits heavy on our hearts, we ask You to comfort us. May we be quick to respond to Your Holy Spirit, to turn away from sin, and to repent. We love You, Lord! In the current circumstance we're facing, we ask You to comfort us. Wrap Your arms around us and cover our marriage with Your peace. We also ask You to send others to encourage us and remind us that there is hope in You, for You work to bring good out of all things. Lord, please give us insight into how this circumstance is stirring up anxious thoughts and how we can surrender those thoughts to You. Equip us to know how to interact with each other, especially knowing how best to comfort each other. Teach us how to be good comforters as we try to walk in understanding and compassion. Lord, make us quick to console each other and provide support, just as Your Holy Spirit does for us. In our efforts to comfort each other, may our hearts and minds be affirmed and encouraged to carry on. In Jesus's name we pray. Amen.

Blessed be the God and Father of our Lord Jesus Christ, the Father of mercies and God of all comfort, who comforts us in all our affliction, so that we may be able to comfort those who are in any affliction, with the comfort with which we ourselves are comforted by God. **(2 CORINTHIANS 1:3-4)**

PURSUING GOD

Dear Lord, Thank You for pursuing us. Thank You for Your still, small voice speaking truth to us and reminding us that You are near. Thank You for the encouragement we receive through the text of a friend, a Scripture shared, an invitation to fellowship at church, or a phone call from a loved one just checking in. Thank You for the ways You are revealing Yourself to us. Thank You for showing us Your artistry through things like the beauty of nature or the colors of a vibrant sunset. Thank You for the nudges You give us to pray for each other and the prompts to share words of encouragement with one another. Lord, may our hearts pursue You all the days of our lives. Enable us to find true rest in Your Word. Show us what it looks like to be dedicated to prayer. Please give us courage to invite each other to chase boldly after You together. As we seek You wholeheartedly, we ask You to draw us ever closer to You. In Jesus's name we pray. Amen.

You will seek me and find me, when you seek me with all your heart. **(JEREMIAH 29:13)**

FAMILY BIBLE TIME

Dear Lord, You lead us with strength and might. Thank You for loving us perfectly. Lord, help our hearts submit to You and trust in You more. Will You help us commit to daily family Bible time? We know it is important to make Bible reading a priority in our home. We love that reading Your Word together stimulates conversation, and we are confident that reading and discussing Scripture together cultivates spiritual maturity. Our desire is to experience more maturity and understanding in our relationship with You and one another. Please help us to make time to study Scripture. Please use us to help one another grasp Your Word in a deeper way. May our discussion of Your Word help us identify and weed out any lies we have been believing. We pray that our family would be known by our love and devotion to You! Lord, encourage us to obey Your Word and live it out courageously. In Jesus's name we pray. Amen.

These words that I command you today shall be on your heart. You shall teach them diligently to your children, and shall talk of them when you sit in your house, and when you walk by the way, and when you lie down, and when you rise. **(DEUTERONOMY 6:6-7)**

WHEN DISAPPOINTMENT HITS OUR HEARTS

Dear Lord,   Thank You for Your goodness. Thank You for fulfilling Your promises. Thank You for faith, for helping us believe even when we cannot see. Will You increase our faith? We petition You for growth in our relationships with You and with one another. The things in our marriage that cause us pain need to be pruned and thrown away. Please remove the parts of our character that are unreliable and untrustworthy. Please cut out our desires that lead to sin. We hate that we hurt one another's feelings in marriage! We hate that we are sometimes the source of disappointment in each other's lives! Heavenly Father, please help us navigate our emotions when disappointment hits our hearts. Enable us to see the truth, but also give us eyes to look ahead in faith at what our marriage can be as we follow You. When we disappoint one another, fail one another, or hurt each other's feelings, we ask You to help us reconcile and restore our relationship. Keep our eyes focused on You, and fill our hearts with hope. In Jesus's name we pray. Amen.

> *I lift up my eyes to the hills.*
> *From where does my help come?*
> *My help comes from the LORD,*
> *who made heaven and earth.*
>
> **(PSALM 121:1–2)**

GROWING SPIRITUALLY TOGETHER

Dear Lord, We know You are refining us and making us new in Christ! Thank You for transforming our lives and our marriage. Please continue to grow us up spiritually. Teach us to dig into resources that will challenge us to go to the next step in our relationship with You. Lord, search our hearts and reveal anything that is not of You. We humble ourselves and ask You to purify us. We know that when we ask this of You, testing of our faith will come. Lord, please prepare us to endure any test or trial You allow us to endure. May the testing of our faith produce every good thing. Lord, will You show us how to be prayer warriors? Will You inspire and encourage us to pray daily for each other? Lord, remind us to get down on our knees, plant our faces to the floor, and cry out to You. We plead and petition You to move in our marriage and in the lives of people we love dearly. Please set our minds and our hearts on spiritual things so that the things of this world never entice us. Lord, we desire to abide in You and bear good fruit in every good work we pursue. In Jesus's name we pray. Amen.

Walk in a manner worthy of the Lord, fully pleasing to him: bearing fruit in every good work and increasing in the knowledge of God. **(COLOSSIANS 1:10)**

NO PORNOGRAPHY

𝒟*ear* ℒ*ord,*   Thank You for the transparency we have in our marriage. Thank You for honesty and truth. We praise You for helping us navigate hard situations and always encouraging us to pursue reconciliation. Thank You for commanding us to walk in purity. We know our marriage will benefit from us choosing to be pure in our thoughts, pure in our desires, pure in our intentions, and pure in our actions. Holy Spirit, please convict us when anything impure is present, and lead us to repentance. Please help us to be people of our word. Help us to have integrity. We ask You to build us up to be trustworthy as we daily choose to do what is right. We pray against the temptation to be impure. We pray against the temptation of pornography, in Jesus's name! In this world that idolizes pornography, please supernaturally guard our hearts and minds from seeing it. Lord, please help us resist pornography in Your strength. Help us to hold our marriage in honor and keep our marriage bed undefiled. May we never be ensnared by sexual sin. Lord, please remove any lust in our hearts, and enable us to keep our lives pure. In Jesus's name we pray. Amen.

Let marriage be held in honor among all, and let the marriage bed be undefiled, for God will judge the sexually immoral and adulterous. **(HEBREWS 13:4)**

LAUGHING MORE

𝒟ear ℒord, We love each other so much! Thank You for the gift of friendship in marriage. We appreciate the adventure and fun we get to experience together. Thank You for the moments of pleasure and joy we have spent together. We know friendship is an important aspect of our relationship. We believe our marriage is strong when our friendship is strong. May we continue to grow to like each other more and more. As we grow old together, we ask You to strengthen our attraction to one another. Lord, let our countenance express excitement to be around each other. Amid the regular routine of life and work, please help us not to neglect playing together. Please help us to find humor in the ordinary. Lord, will You inspire us to laugh more? Instead of being serious all the time, we want to allow ourselves room to be silly together. Break the mold in our minds of what's expected so we can embrace the surprise and thrill of the unexpected. Please show us creative ways we can enjoy our relationship, even in our simple interactions throughout each day. May we be a light in each other's lives. In Jesus's name we pray. Amen.

A joyful heart is good medicine,
but a crushed spirit dries up the bones.
(PROVERBS 17:22)

322

PROTECTION OF
OUR MARRIAGE

Dear Lord, We praise You, for Your kindness has impacted our lives! Thank You for caring about every little detail. Thank You for Your provision for and Your protection of our marriage—we cherish it. We are grateful for every day we get to spend together. Lord, will You continue to protect us against unforeseen threats? Will You prepare us for the storms that lay ahead? We ask You to destroy any flaming arrows of the Enemy and ask You to hinder any of the Enemy's schemes to harm our relationship. Please mature us so that we ourselves don't bring any ruin or destruction to our marriage. Continually sanctify us so that sin has no room to thrive in us. We fear You and You alone! We know You are always working in our lives. We know there are things You have provided for us and protected us from that we aren't aware of. We praise You and we thank You for all of it! Lord, will You also protect us from getting hurt or sick? Please watch over us and keep us healthy and whole. No matter what, we trust in You. In Jesus's name we pray. Amen.

The fear of the Lord leads to life,
and whoever has it rests satisfied;
he will not be visited by harm.
(PROVERBS 19:23)

TRULY FORGIVING
EACH OTHER

Dear Lord, Thank You for Your mercy and grace. Thank You for the gift of forgiveness. Lord, make us a couple who truly forgives each other. Please help us to stop feeling angry with each other. If there are any lingering feelings of resentment between us, will You please dissolve them? Please help us to reconcile our hearts and minds so that we remain strong as one. God, we ask You for a season of rest and relief from emotional pain and turmoil. Teach us how to cover each other in unconditional love. May we never be easily offended. Open our eyes to see the good in each other. When we are tempted to think negatively of each other, we ask for Your Holy Spirit to radically redirect our thoughts. Lord, please help us pay attention to how we interact with each other so that we can repent of any grievous ways. When we see sin in each other's lives, show us how to gently rebuke each other and also forgive. May Your love be made evident in our marriage through the way we treat each other and walk humbly in oneness. In Jesus's name we pray. Amen.

Pay attention to yourselves! If your brother sins, rebuke him, and if he repents, forgive him, and if he sins against you seven times in the day, and turns to you seven times, saying, "I repent," you must forgive him. **(LUKE 17:3-4)**

WHEN HARD DAYS PERSIST

Dear Lord, Although hard days are challenging, we believe they test our faith and can produce good in us if we remain self-controlled, relying on Your strength to get us through. So we praise You for the difficult situations we face. We praise You for being our very present help in trouble. When we're walking through burdensome days, please help us have an appreciation for the good days. Holy Spirit, remind us that tough days are inevitable. May we feel encouraged knowing we aren't enduring them alone, for we have You and we have each other. Teach us to be content in every circumstance. Anchor our souls in joy and peace, and give us the stamina to serve and support each other always. When hard days persist, may we be quick to encourage each other in truth and to alleviate the pressure each day brings. Please help us to be considerate of and compassionate toward each other as we process hard days differently. Please give us the strength to endure through anything and to do it in unity. In Jesus's name we pray. Amen.

God is our refuge and strength,
a very present help in trouble.
(PSALM 46:1)

CONFRONTING OUR ISSUES

Dear Lord, Thank You for never failing us. We praise You for Your faithfulness! Thank You for creating us with the ability to feel deeply and think through the circumstances we encounter. Thank You for the partnership marriage provides so that we have someone to endure alongside. Lord, open our hearts and show us how to honestly share what we are going through and how it makes us feel. Please help us to speak up when we're frustrated. We ask You to show us our marriage from Your perspective. Correct us if we are looking at something the wrong way. As we confront issues in our lives and in our relationship, we invite You to lead us in understanding them and resolving them with grace. Help us not to be led so much by our emotions, but more so led according to Your wisdom. As we address any concerns, we ask You to help us do so in confidence, vocalizing and affirming our love for each other. Lord, remind us that the reason we are motivated to confront our issues is because we love each other and desire a successful marriage. In Jesus's name we pray. Amen.

Better is open rebuke
than hidden love. **(PROVERBS 27:5)**

GOD'S DESIGN OF
MARRIAGE

Dear Lord, Thank You for Your design of marriage. Thank You for the creative way You made it possible for two to become one. God, please help us recognize and understand the power of our unity in marriage. We acknowledge the many ways You created us different and how those differences benefit our marriage. May we never let our differences keep us from feeling unified. Even more, we ask You to help us grasp the truth that our differences complement one another for a perfect purpose—similar to the way butter complements a dinner roll. Lord, please show us how to walk confidently in our roles and responsibilities in marriage. Encourage us to embrace the work You have for us to do in our marriage with gratitude. As we complement one another, affirming the talents You have given us to complete the good work You have established for us, we ask You to radiate Your light through us. May our relationship be an example to others of how to love greatly. Our desire is that others would witness the way we conduct ourselves and know without a doubt that our love is from You. May You be glorified in our marriage. In Jesus's name we pray. Amen.

We love because he first loved us. (1 JOHN 4:19)

NO MORE SHAME

𝒟ear 𝓛ord, Your mercies are new every morning! We praise You for Your amazing grace! Thank You for cleaning our hearts, washing us white as snow, making us new, and taking away our shame. We believe there is no condemnation for those in Christ. You have taken away our humiliation and regret. You have taken away the pain of our sinful choices. We hate the feeling of distress when we know we have sinned. We hate failing You. We are grateful that even while we were still sinners Christ died to cover our sins. Your love is transforming! Heavenly Father, please help us lay our shame at the foot of Your throne of grace. We don't want to carry the weight of shame. When we feel shame, we petition You to renew our minds, in Jesus's name! Please retrain our thought patterns and give us a new path to tread, a path that leads to righteousness. Lord, please keep us from intentionally embarrassing each other by mentioning past sin or mistakes that were made. May we refuse to bring up these faults to hurt each other or stir up condemnation. Make us careful to protect each other's hearts, knowing that it is only because of You that we are able to walk in victory. In Jesus's name we pray. Amen.

For the Scripture says, "Everyone who believes in him will not be put to shame." **(ROMANS 10:11)**

HOPE FOR BETTER DAYS

Dear Lord, Hope is an amazing gift! Hope encourages us to persevere through hardship with joy still intact. Hope is beautiful. We praise You for all the times You have given us hope in our despair, helping us to hang on just a little longer! Hope for better days helps us carry on in our marriage! When we feel like we can't continue in our relationship because we are at a loss for what to do, Your hope gives us something to look forward to. Hope binds us together in unity, equipping us to stay committed to each other. Lord, will You please help us remain hopeful all the days of our lives? Help us resist complaining about the messes or chaos in life. Increase trust in our hearts that You are working faithfully in us and holding us up with Your righteous right hand. In moments of weakness, when our souls ache under the pressures of this world, will You help us encourage each other to keep a tight grip on the hope we find in Your Word? Remind us to worship You for all the miracles You have worked in our marriage. Lord, increase our faith, believing that You have more in store for us! May we strive to experience extraordinary hope as You give us the strength to press on without giving up! May Your power and divine Spirit carry us, renew us, and provide opportunities for us to experience the power of oneness in our marriage. In Jesus's name we pray. Amen.

For God alone, O my soul, wait in silence,
for my hope is from him. **(PSALM 62:5)**

SAYING THE HARD THINGS

Dear Lord, As much as Your Word is full of encouragement, it is also full of commandments and expectations You have made known so that we can walk in Your ways. You have taken the time and effort to say the hard things that go against our flesh. Thank You for speaking the truth in love. Thank You for being honest in Your Word, because it challenges us to become the people You created us to be. Will You teach us how to be brave in saying the hard things to one another? When we need to confess a sin or confront our spouse with their sin, will You give us the boldness to say what should be said? When we need to share how we've been hurt or frustrated by each other, will You fill us with courage, for the sake of growing together? When we have to say something challenging so that we feel understood and so that change can take place, will You make time for us to talk without interruptions or distractions? Heavenly Father, please tear down any walls in us that keep us from knowing one another more deeply. Please give us the right words to say when we need to say hard things. Lead us to confess any sin in our lives so that we may be cleansed of all unrighteousness. May our hearts be able to receive correction from one another, even when it is hard to hear. Please help us to make our marriage a place to be known and loved. In Jesus's name we pray. Amen.

If we confess our sins, he is faithful and just to forgive us our sins and to cleanse us from all unrighteousness. **(1 JOHN 1:9)**

KEEPING A STEADY PACE

Dear Lord, Thank You for the encouragement in Scripture to lay aside every weight and sin that entangles us so that we can run with endurance the race set before us. Inspire us to encourage one another to evaluate our lives and examine our hearts, considering what weight or sin we need to remove from our lives. Enable us to run with endurance, especially through the circumstances we face in marriage. Teach us to set a steady pace in life and to find balance between all our priorities. We recognize that being constantly busy leaves us frazzled and upset. Please show us what causes us to get burned out and how to make adjustments to our schedules as needed. Lord, we ask You to help us slow down and rest. Help us to find a rhythm that blesses our family and encourages growth. When we do feel tired, stretched, or as if we can't continue on, please help us to lean on You for wisdom and rely on You for strength. Lead us to discover ways of recuperating and to make them a priority. When it comes to supporting each other, show us how to have a good balance of pushing each other to press on but also encouraging one another to rest well. May You equip us to run this race of life, including our marriage, at a steady pace, with all endurance. In Jesus's name we pray. Amen.

Therefore, since we are surrounded by so great a cloud of witnesses, let us also lay aside every weight, and sin which clings so closely, and let us run with endurance the race that is set before us. **(HEBREWS 12:1)**

HONESTY

Dear Lord, Thank You for the powerful impact of honesty. When we are honest with ourselves, we can clearly see weak areas where we need to grow. When we are honest with one another, trust is built. When we are honest with You, we are able to get our pride out of the way so that You can work in us. May our marriage be known by our decision to walk in transparency and honesty. May our courage to share openly with each other also inspire others to have the bravery to be transparent and honest in their marriage. When we choose to do the right thing, it usually encourages others to step up to do the right thing. Lord, please show us how to be brave. When our heart races with anxiety and feels like it is going to beat out of our chest, remind us to take a deep breath and rely on You to help us speak the truth. Please help us to be truth tellers. Please help us to be willing to confess our sin. Please help us to have integrity. Please help us to be trustworthy. As we mature in honesty, please keep foolishness far from us, especially in our marriage. Lord, we ask You to intervene if we are about to do something foolish. Our desire is to be virtuous, blameless, and well intentioned. We yearn to be sincere and free of deceit. In Jesus's name we pray. Amen.

Better is a poor person who walks in his integrity
than one who is crooked in speech and
is a fool. **(PROVERBS 19:1)**

CONTROLLING OUR EMOTIONS

Dear Lord, We are deeply and profoundly grateful for emotions. Our emotions are like a film score—without them life would be sorely quiet and would not have the same impact. We trust Your design of our bodies and the ability to feel emotions. It is good and necessary for us to have them. Lord, please help us to embrace and appreciate our range of emotions. May we never devalue our feelings because of embarrassment or pride. We also pray we would never use our emotions to justify poor behavior. Having emotions helps us understand You, ourselves, and the world around us. As much as we appreciate our emotions, they can sometimes lead us to sin. Lord, please help us to have self-control over our emotions. When we feel strongly about something, especially in our marriage, keep us from being overwhelmed by those feelings. Please help us remain steady, not hurting each other with our words or actions. Please help keep our emotions under control so that You are always glorified through us. In Jesus's name we pray. Amen.

A fool gives full vent to his spirit,
but a wise man quietly holds it back.
(PROVERBS 29:11)

PREPARING FOR ACTION

Dear Lord, Thank You for the wisdom and warning You give us in Your Word about our minds and our thoughts. We understand the importance of protecting our minds and guarding our thoughts so we are not easily tempted. If we're not careful, temptation can lure us to dwell on desires of our flesh, which, if we do not extinguish them, give birth to sin. Please train us to take every thought captive and operate in self-control. Many times we are focused on the wrong battle. We fight against each other. We fight to be right and have our own way. All the while, Your Word says that the fight is not against flesh and blood but against the Enemy! We must remember our spouse is not the enemy! The Enemy seeks to divide us so that we are useless for battle. We ask You to prepare our hearts for the true battle. Prepare our minds for action as we set our hope on Christ. Make us ready and equipped with the full armor of God, determined to battle the Enemy together. Please help us to defend and protect our marriage while we serve You. In Jesus's name we pray. Amen.

Therefore, preparing your minds for action, and being sober-minded, set your hope fully on the grace that will be brought to you at the revelation of Jesus Christ. **(1 PETER 1:13)**

MARRIAGE IS A MOSAIC

Dear Lord,   Thank You for the millions of marriage moments You have gifted to us that make up our love story. Thank You for the colorful mosaic that has been created with all of the light and dark moments we have shared. Sometimes it is hard to see how You are working in us and helping our marriage grow. Yet as we stand back with a heavenly perspective, we see Your work in us. Thank You for taking the good, the bad, and the ugly to make a masterpiece of our marriage. Whether we experience great moments or more challenging ones, please remind us of the truth that our marriage is a work in progress— You're still at work! We ask for endurance to walk through highs and lows and everything in between. May we embrace the times of joy, sadness, frustration, and peace. We are confident that the millions of moments we spend together make up a beautiful picture of marriage. Please help us to remember this when our hearts feel heavy. Fill us with Your peace. May the mosaic of our marriage reflect the power of Your love and inspire others to draw closer to You and closer to each other as they taste and see that You are good. In Jesus's name we pray. Amen.

> Oh, taste and see that the LORD is good!
> Blessed is the man who takes refuge
> in him! **(PSALM 34:8)**

DANCING TOGETHER

Dear Lord, Thank You for the dance that is marriage. We appreciate the friendship and camaraderie, the love and intimacy, the joy and tenderness we experience in our relationship. Thank You for Your Word, which directs us in our roles in marriage and shows us how to love each other well. May we never lose sight of marriage being a dance that we have the privilege of sharing with each other. Enable us to pursue regular date nights so that we enjoy quality time together. We ask You for wisdom on how to prioritize and align our schedules so we can have even more time together. Lord, help us to maintain our marriage by asking each other how we are doing, taking time to listen well, simply sitting with one another quietly, consoling each other in sadness, crying together when there is pain, and laughing together when happiness is abundant. We pray we would catch each other in the kitchen, the bedroom, or on the patio and invite each other to dance, to hold each other in a warm embrace, or to remind each other that we are near. Please teach us other ways to cultivate our relationship and strengthen our bond of intimacy. Please help us to dance gracefully in a way that honors You and blesses each other. In Jesus's name we pray. Amen.

For everything there is a season, and a time
for every matter under heaven: . . .

a time to weep, and a time to laugh;
a time to mourn, and a time to dance.
(ECCLESIASTES 3:1, 4)

NO MORE OFFENDING
EACH OTHER

Dear Lord,   Thank You for the way marriage refines us. The closeness we experience amplifies the way our choices affect each other. There is nowhere to hide our imperfections, such as selfishness, negative attitudes, or our desire to be in control. The day-to-day interactions provide too many opportunities for us to show who we are—the good and the bad. We do not want to hurt each other. We do not want to be a source of pain or contention in each other's lives. Instead, we desire to be reliable, trustworthy, and a source of joy. Please help us evaluate how we have been walking in marriage and show us if our thoughts and attitudes have been kind or unkind, respectful or disrespectful. If any part of us is contributing to pain, frustration, or sadness in our relationship, please radically change us right now! Help us to clearly see the impact of our choices and resolve in our hearts and minds to choose differently, to choose better. Sometimes it is challenging to let go of past hurt. Yet we know that if we already resolved those past offenses, it is only right that we truly let them go. Lord, make us able to sincerely forgive and move forward. We also pray we are never quick to be offended by each other. If an offense happens, please help us to recognize our responsibility, repent of our sin, and be reconciled so that peace abounds. In Jesus's name we pray. Amen.

Whoever covers an offense seeks love,
but he who repeats a matter separates
close friends. **(PROVERBS 17:9)**

SERVING GOD TOGETHER

𝒟*ear* ℒ*ord,* Thank You for strengthening our relationship and giving us the fortitude to carry on no matter what circumstances come our way. Thank You for helping us improve our character over time by making small changes according to the direction given in Your Holy Word. Thank You for our marriage relationship, which blesses us immensely. We desire to use our marriage to serve You. May You use us to do great things for Your kingdom. Lord, please use us physically to bless our neighbors and community through service projects and hospitality. Please use us mentally to help others experiencing problems by providing a fresh perspective or solution. Please use us emotionally to partner with each other to use our words to encourage those around us. Lord, please use us spiritually as a team to spend our prayer time lifting up our family and our friends, petitioning You on their behalf to move in mighty ways in their lives. Lord, we pray we would always be in a good place emotionally so we can serve side by side. May our marriage be a ministry to those near to us. We surrender our lives and our marriage so You can use us to fulfill Your purpose and spread Your gospel far and wide. In Jesus's name we pray. Amen.

If anyone serves me, he must follow me; and where I am, there will my servant be also. If anyone serves me, the Father will honor him. **(JOHN 12:26)**

MANAGING TASKS
TOGETHER

Dear Lord, Thank You for the tasks You have given us to accomplish. Thank You for the plans You have placed in our hearts and the ministry You have given us to fulfill. We know You trust us with the responsibilities You have given us. Make us good stewards as we seek to achieve the goals set before us. Lord, show us how to cooperate and contribute to the areas we are strong in and encourage each other through the areas where we feel weak. May our conduct glorify You and benefit one another. As we seek to manage our many responsibilities, we pray we would organize our time so that we are efficient. If there is anything in our lives we are chasing after, spending resources on, or concerning ourselves with that is not of You, will You open our eyes and help us to adjust to Your will? Please help us to prioritize the many tasks we are trying to complete. Equip us to work together and use our talents to accomplish these things. May the work we are doing, the many tasks we are managing, and the way we interact bring glory to Your name. In Jesus's name we pray. Amen.

*Look carefully then how you walk, not as unwise
but as wise, making the best use of the time,
because the days are evil.* **(EPHESIANS 5:15–16)**

LEAVING NOTES FOR EACH OTHER

Dear Lord, Thank You for sharing Your love story through the gift of the Bible. We are grateful to have a record of Your mercies and miracles. Lord, please write Your words on our hearts. Shape us so that we love as You love. We have learned so much about communication in marriage from the wisdom poured out through Scripture. Please continue to mature our understanding of how best to communicate with each other. We specifically pray we would perk up and get creative in expressing our love for each other. Please help us take the initiative to leave short and simple notes around the house or stuffed into each other's pockets to surprise each other with affirmation. Holy Spirit, infuse us with words of encouragement to pour out onto paper to share with each other. Inspire us to record the miracles we have seen in our marriage and share our gratitude with one another regularly. We ask You to gently remind us to send a text that says, "I love you!" or to make a call to say, "I'm just thinking of you!" Give us the right words to declare our love and loyalty, our adoration and respect, our attraction and delight for each other. Lord, help us to express ourselves in fun ways. May our love for each other never be quenched. In Jesus's name we pray. Amen.

Many waters cannot quench love,
neither can floods drown it.
(SONG OF SOLOMON 8:7)

A MARRIAGE BLESSING

Dear Lord, Thank You for the gift of love. Thank You for blessing our marriage and being the force that holds us together. We ask Your Holy Spirit to inspire us to care for each other in a special way today. May the smiles on our faces and the light in our eyes convey our desire for each other. Lord, soften our hearts toward one another so that tenderness pours out of us with every word and action. We also pray You would help us walk humbly with one another, being slow to speak and slow to become angry. We ask You to continue to deepen our relationship as we pursue each other in love. Give us a vision for our future together that will inspire our hearts and fill us with excitement for the potential growth we will experience. Bless our marriage today, in Jesus's name! Lord, please bless our intimacy, bless our conversations, bless our finances, and bless our getting up and our going to bed. We invite You to bless all the plans we have for our marriage, but ultimately, we ask for Your purpose to stand. Please use us to bless each other every day we are given. In Jesus's name we pray. Amen.

Many are the plans in the mind of a man,
but it is the purpose of the LORD that
will stand. **(PROVERBS 19:21)**

MAKING MEMORIES

Dear Lord, Thank You for the incredible ways our minds, hearts, and bodies experience memories. Thank You for the feelings associated with memories. Thank You that our brains hold on to interactions we have encountered in our marriage. Please help us keep a catalog of memories we share that remind us of how good our marriage truly is. May these memories never fade. Protect these memories from being overshadowed by the hard times we experience. Lord, may Your Holy Spirit draw up these memories in moments that we need them most. Help us to dwell on these recollections to affirm our love, while they also inspire us to love well today. May our reminiscing propel us forward, giving us momentum to persevere in our marriage. Lord, teach us to number our days so that we don't waste any opportunities to love. Give us wisdom to never put off expressing our love for each other and be intentional in making new memories together. Lord, help us consider the ways we can have fun loving each other today. May our marriage reflect the love and compassion You have for all. In Jesus's name we pray. Amen.

Teach us to number our days
that we may get a heart of wisdom.
(PSALM 90:12)

342

HAVING OPEN HEARTS

Dear Lord, We praise You for incrementally opening our hearts and teaching us how to trust one another. We have come a long way since the beginning of our relationship. Our desire is to keep growing in our love for one another. Please keep our hearts open toward each other. Help our minds to dwell on the reasons we appreciate our relationship. Search us and show us areas we need to submit to You, Lord. Where there is sin, we ask for the conviction of Your Holy Spirit to lead us toward repentance. Teach us how to expose what is going on in our lives to one another, as well as how we are feeling about it all. May trust build up between us so that we can confide in each other. We ask You to help us encourage one another through whatever the situation may be. In a world that seems to be changing quickly and at times feels unstable, please be our source of security. Lord, please help us to never harden our hearts in rebellion toward one another. Keep us from slamming doors shut both physically and emotionally. May we refuse to walk away from each other unreconciled. Holy Spirit, lead us to seek peace in every circumstance. In Jesus's name we pray. Amen.

Do not harden your hearts as in the rebellion,
on the day of testing in the wilderness.
(HEBREWS 3:8)

PLAYING TOGETHER

Dear Lord, Thank You for the way You designed life, including the way humans interact with one another! We are in awe of You! We specifically praise You for the wonderful gift of laughter! We praise You for humor and fun! Thank You for creating in us a silly side. Please show us how to fully embrace our silliness. Thank You also for creative games people have invented and the opportunities to play them together. Thank You for the abundance of enjoyable activities we can do together. Thank You for our intellect and wittiness that come out when we are having fun together. May we be determined to maintain a childlike wonder, playing together and engaging in a little fun. Lord, make us a couple who goes on adventures together, even if it is a short walk after dinner. Our desire is to be an active couple who enjoys outdoor activities together. Lord, help us to be thoughtful in how we incorporate play, building up our relationship through amusement. Lord, please help us to measure the days of our lives, reminding us how fleeting our time is and how to make the most of it. In Jesus's name we pray. Amen.

> *O Lord, make me know my end*
> *and what is the measure of my days;*
> *let me know how fleeting I am! . . .*
> *Surely all mankind stands as a mere breath!*
> **(PSALM 39:4–5)**

BEING STRONG FOR EACH OTHER

Dear Lord, Thank You for Your might. Thank You for being our strong tower. Thank You for comforting us when we are down and strengthening us when we are weak. Thank You for reminding us of Your Word, which gives us hope. Lord, we know You are our source of spiritual strength, helping us to withstand adversity. You sustain us by giving us Your peace and filling us with Your wisdom. In addition to our desire to be spiritually strong, we pray You would help us to be physically strong so that our bodies don't give up under stress. Instill in us a passion to take care of our bodies and exercise regularly. Encourage us to pursue strength training, growing our muscles by lifting heavier weights. We pray we would understand this same truth when we encounter trials of many kinds: that trials strengthen our resolve. May our hearts receive everything we need from You to endure. Inspire us to share Scripture to remind each other of where our strength comes from. When we feel out of control or desperate for our circumstances to work out in our favor, please show us how to be strong for each other. Please help us to stand firm today with hopeful hearts. In Jesus's name we pray. Amen.

Be strong in the Lord and in the strength of his might. **(EPHESIANS 6:10)**

DO NOT BE HARSH

$Dear Lord,$ Marriage is a beautifully complex relationship. We love each other greater than anyone else on earth, and yet we tend to frustrate one another the quickest. As much as we love and adore each other, we still have rough days. We aren't immune to arguing, disagreeing, and bickering. These situations rouse harsh feelings toward each other. We get irritable, we get angry, and sometimes we get ugly in the way we express our feelings with one another. We are sorry for this! Please transform us and enable us to talk to each other about what we are thinking and feeling without being mean or spiteful. Holy Spirit, please help us to communicate our differences of opinion with gentleness and self-control. May our perspectives align with Yours. Whenever frustration swells within us, we ask You to lead us to surrender those feelings to You. We ask You to help us navigate every situation. Please show us how to be understanding of each other. Restrain us from being harsh or selfish in our responses toward each other. May we love with gentleness, meekness, and peace. In Jesus's name we pray. Amen.

Husbands, love your wives, and do not be harsh with them. **(COLOSSIANS 3:19)**

DO NOT SHAME

Dear Lord, We thank You for teaching us how to reconcile! As we use Your wisdom to walk through situations together, we trust and hope for resolution. We value our marriage more now than ever before. After gaining understanding and insight as to what You desire of us, please help us to obey Your commandments. Keep us from pointing the finger or blaming each other. Lord, help us never to burden each other with our words, causing shame. Blame and shame will cripple us and keep us from ever reaching the potential You designed for us. We ask You to make us self-aware so that we quickly recognize the impact of our words. If we need to redirect a conversation to avoid making each other feel the weight of shame or embarrassment, we ask You to guide us. Holy Spirit, please go before us in conversation and convict our hearts when we are shaming one another. Keep us from struggling with or dwelling on feelings or thoughts of condemnation. Lord, please encourage us daily to walk in excellence so that shame has no hold on us. Let mercy and grace wash over us and cleanse us from negative feelings of failure. Lord, we lift one another up and ask that You affirm in each of us who we are in You. In Jesus's name we pray. Amen.

An excellent wife is the crown of her husband,
but she who brings shame is like
rottenness in his bones. **(PROVERBS 12:4)**

OUR APPEARANCES

𝒟ear 𝒧ord, We appreciate our bodies and all that we have been able to do with them. Thank You for creating us to be attracted to each other. Attraction draws us close to each other and invigorates our desire to experience intimacy. Please help us to take care of our bodies so we remain healthy. We also pray You would motivate us to maintain our physical appearances—to be mindful of how we present ourselves, but without vanity. As we age, will You help us to walk humbly with each other, understanding how our bodies change over time? May we never allow prideful thoughts to rest in our minds. We also ask You to protect our hearts from being discouraged about our appearances. Lord, give us eyes for each other, and make our attraction for each other strong. May we cheer each other on, daily encouraging one another to choose a healthy lifestyle. Keep us from being overly concerned with our looks, but rather to accept our bodies. Help us to be modest in our appearances, reserving for each other the exclusive rights to view and enjoy every part of us. May we honor You as we care for our bodies and in how we present ourselves to each other. In Jesus's name we pray. Amen.

The Lord sees not as man sees: man looks on the outward appearance, but the Lord looks on the heart. **(1 SAMUEL 16:7)**

SHARING THE WORKLOAD

Dear Lord, You have carried us through some extraordinary times. We are grateful that we can put our trust in You. We ask You to bless our relationship as we seek to fulfill Your will. Please keep us close to You and close to one another. Lord, bind us tightly together so that nothing can separate us from each other's love. Shape us to become an even better team than we have been. May the purposes You have for our marriage be accomplished through us. Lord, will You make us mindful of our responsibilities? Will Your Holy Spirit please show us how to share the workload in our lives? We ask You to supernaturally infuse us with the ability to support each other physically, mentally, emotionally, and spiritually. Our desire is to bring You pleasure as we seek to hold each other up under the weight of obligation. Please keep complaints and grumblings far from our minds. Prepare us and make us ready to serve You. May our love for You and each other drive our persistence and energy as we share the workload of all the responsibilities You give us so that we bring You honor. In Jesus's name we pray. Amen.

It is God who works in you, both to will and to work for his good pleasure. **(PHILIPPIANS 2:13)**

HOLDING HANDS

Dear Lord, Thank You for the experience of physical touch. The message of affirmation sent throughout our bodies and our minds when we experience physical touch is an extraordinary gift. We are also grateful for the way intimacy makes us feel close to each other and for the way it spurs us on to serve each other selflessly. We feel affirmed when we initiate physical intimacy and it is reciprocated. Lord, please help us to be mindful of the way we respond to physical touch. Help us never to reject each other in selfishness. Instead, give us an insatiable desire to take every opportunity to hold hands, hug, and accept each other wholeheartedly. Make us quick to use every small and big opportunity to cuddle, snuggle, and caress each other. Lord, thank You for holding all things together, especially our relationship! You are powerful and worthy to be praised! We know we have come this far in our marriage because You are holding us in the palm of Your hand. We cling to You and to Your truth. May our marriage continue to prosper and grow stronger as we hold each other in a secure embrace. In Jesus's name we pray. Amen.

He is before all things, and in him all things hold together. **(COLOSSIANS 1:17)**

GAINING UNDERSTANDING

Dear Lord, Thank You for the various resources from which we can increase our knowledge and understanding of many things in life. Thank You for the plethora of books and devotionals from which we can gain insight into faith and marriage. Most importantly, we thank You for Your Holy Word, which teaches us all sound wisdom. Please help us to consume information through a biblical perspective, filtering what is truth from what is not truth. Keep us humble learners, in Jesus's name! Stir up an eagerness to know more about the world around us and apply that knowledge to marriage as we make informed decisions and walk in wisdom. Lord, please lead us to gain understanding about each other as well, through our interactions, by being good listeners, and by paying attention to the way we operate daily. Lord, make us a studious couple who takes mental note of everything we learn about each other. Inspire us to ask good questions that will guide us in how best to bless and love each other. As You impart Your truth to us, may we gain understanding in marriage and faith so that we can better serve You as a light. In Jesus's name we pray. Amen.

The unfolding of your words gives light;
it imparts understanding to the simple.
(PSALM 119:130)

RALLYING TOGETHER

Dear Lord, Thank You for the growth we have experienced in marriage and the love we have for each other. May our love for one another be a continual source of passion that inspires us to rally together. Lord, will You give us a desire to pursue one another today in a special way? Will You show us how to maintain our unity? May the goals we have set in our marriage be met today. As we concern ourselves with the aspects of our relationship that most need attention and improvement, please fill us with positive attitudes toward one another that will help us move forward in our relationship. Lord, don't let our flesh hinder us from experiencing camaraderie in marriage. Help us recognize the work You are doing in our marriage and remember that You are for us. We know You want our marriage to thrive. We believe You want the best for us. So we petition You to make our marriage experiences be an abundant dose of joy and life. May we experience Your power and love in our marriage. Refresh us and awaken us to new life in our relationship. Please bring us to a place where our love can inspire other couples to surrender their marriage to You and experience true peace. Make them confident in the love they have for their spouse, and let them experience the extraordinary because of their faith in You. In Jesus's name we pray. Amen.

If God is for us, who can be against us? **(ROMANS 8:31)**

DRAWING NEAR TO GOD

Dear Lord, Thank You for drawing our hearts close to Yours. We acknowledge that our intimacy with You deepens with time. Please put in us an urgency to read Your Word every day, with the intention of abiding in You. Make ready our hearts to pray, and help us to be slow to complain about our circumstances. Lord, may we draw near to You, not only individually, but also together as a couple. We ask You to help us spend time talking about Your Word and explaining to one another all that You are teaching us. May our conversations about Scripture become some of our favorite moments together. Heavenly Father, help us never to be swayed in our beliefs by the temptation of doubt. Will You safeguard our thoughts and keep us from being double-minded? Lord, reinforce Your truth in us! Secure in us what we believe, and give us the ability to encourage one another at any moment toward love and faith. May we endeavor to cultivate a stronger relationship with You and with each other. In Jesus's name we pray. Amen.

Draw near to God, and he will draw near to you.
Cleanse your hands, you sinners, and purify
your hearts, you double-minded. **(JAMES 4:8)**

FAITHFULNESS

Dear Lord, You are faithful in every way. Your character is upright, Your love is genuine, and Your compassion is life-changing! As we draw closer to You, please purify us and make us holy! Transform our character, increase our faith, and set our hearts against sin. We ask You to build up our faithfulness to You and to each other. Rouse our hearts to initiate prayer time together, and please give us the words to say as we pray for one another. As we strive to be conscientious and consistent in our relationship with You, we pray the overflow of our faithfulness would pour into our marriage. Please help us adhere firmly to the boundaries we agreed to in order to protect each other's hearts. Make us responsible to keep each other accountable to walking in righteousness. May our faithfulness grow in abundance and produce incredible hope! Hope that will never cease! Hope that will carry us through every circumstance. In Jesus's name we pray. Amen.

Many a man proclaims his own steadfast love,
but a faithful man who can find?
(PROVERBS 20:6)

EXCELLENCE

Dear Lord, We praise You for Your everlasting love! Thank You for the special relationship of marriage. We are both thankful for our relationship, and we hope to experience incredible days to come. Although many areas of our lives still need growth, You consistently address these areas, leading us to mature in holiness. We submit to You, Lord! We ask You to help us never to tire of responding to the conviction of Your Holy Spirit. Please help us to strive for excellence in our character and in our marriage. Equip us to do everything in our ability and in Your strength—to help each other, serve each other, love each other, take care of each other, and cherish each other. Make us a couple who is diligent to fulfill our expectations in marriage. May we satisfy each other all the days of our lives. As we grow closer together and our appreciation for one another increases, may we fully grasp the value of having each other in our lives. In Jesus's name we pray. Amen.

An excellent wife who can find?
She is far more precious than jewels.
(PROVERBS 31:10)

OUR LEGACY OF LOVE

Dear Lord, Thank You for Your faithfulness. Thank You for never giving up on us. We praise You for being our King! Thank You for loving us despite our inability to be perfect. Thank You for Jesus Christ paying the price for our sin and covering us in His righteousness. We are deeply grateful for His perfect sacrifice. We rest in Him! May we always look to Jesus as an example of how to love each other unconditionally. Lord, extend grace from our hearts to cover each other. When the world tries to convince us to give up on each other, may we have the uncompromising faith to lay down our lives for one another. Lord, shape in our character a determination to make sacrifices for the sake of our marriage. Will You show us just how great our legacy of love truly is? Will You please give us a vision for our future together? Heavenly Father, help us to see the greater picture of our love story, which involves all our failures and how You have helped us overcome our brokenness. May our legacy of love positively impact other marriages. In Jesus's name we pray. Amen.

Greater love has no one than this, that someone lay down his life for his friends. **(JOHN 15:13)**

OUR VOWS

Dear Lord, Thank You for designing and establishing marriage. Thank You for inspiring us in the creation of and commitment to our wedding vows. Thank You for bringing us into a covenant where we are responsible to uphold our devotion and love for each other. We praise You forever! Lord, please remind us today of what we pledged to each other on our wedding day. We ask You to bring to our minds the very words we spoke. Make our commitments to one another a pillar of solid rock to hold up the foundation of our marriage. If parts of our foundation are broken, weak, or need mending, will You please help us to repair them? When demanding times press in around us or struggles come our way, will Your Holy Spirit remind us of our vows, encouraging us to hang on to every word we said? We know we can't hang on to our marriage in our own strength. Our grip is faulty because of our flesh. Yet You are the cord that binds us together and makes us capable of enduring together. We stand on Your truth and ask You to give us the strength to be faithful and loyal to the commitments we have made. May You be honored and our marriage be blessed as we seek to fulfill our vows day after day. In Jesus's name we pray. Amen.

> *So will I ever sing praises to your name,*
> *as I perform my vows day after day.*
> **(PSALM 61:8)**

MARRIAGE AFTER GOD

Dear Lord, Hope is a treasured gift that helps us confidently look to the future. Thank You for the hope we have in You! Thank You for establishing plans for our future. We are grateful for our marriage and the friendship we get to enjoy all the days of our lives. Lord, continue to expand our understanding that marriage is also a gift from You and that we are a gift to one another. Teach us how to treat each other with utmost respect and kindness. As we unwrap the gift of marriage, insist that we hold our vows in high esteem. Give us the ability to trust the plans You have for us and walk in the way You are leading us, even if it collides with our ideal hopes for our future. When Your will being different from our wills causes friction, please cover those wounds with Your peace. Transform us and help us recognize the places You are inviting us to join You in ministry. Lord, may we embrace all that You have for us, knowing You will use us to do good in this world. May we lay down any fears and have the fortitude to say yes to You. Lord, You are the bedrock of our marriage, allowing us to stand firm in this world. Our desire is to have a marriage after God, where we pursue You and eagerly and boldly chase after Your purpose for our life together. In Jesus's name we pray. Amen.

> *For I know the plans I have for you, declares the*
> *Lord, plans for welfare and not for evil, to give*
> *you a future and a hope.* **(JEREMIAH 29:11)**

PRIORITIZING OUR MARRIAGE

$\mathcal{D}ear\ \mathcal{L}ord,$ Thank You for today. Thank You for showing us what is truly important and worth investing our time and effort in. Lord, please show us how to prioritize our marriage. Please help us find balance in meeting the demands of our relationship and schedules. Create in us the ability to steward well all that You have entrusted to us. Put us on the same page as we identify our priorities and acknowledge what is less important. Lord, we plead for You to unify us more than we ever have been before. Will You guide us in organizing our responsibilities and knowing what strategy to use to fulfill them? Lord, please instill in us a resilient work ethic and a desire to assist one another in doing good work. We ask You to flood our thoughts with ideas about how we can love each other better. If there are areas we have been neglecting or need to put effort toward, please direct us in addressing those areas. Keep our hearts from settling into complacency in our marriage. Please mature us and give us discernment so that we put our marriage in the right place. In Jesus's name we pray. Amen.

Solid food is for the mature, for those who have their
powers of discernment trained by constant practice
to distinguish good from evil. **(HEBREWS 5:14)**

OUR MARRIAGE IS
A MINISTRY

Dear Lord, Ministry is the incredible work You are doing in this world, caring for people spiritually and physically. Thank You for the invitation to join You in Your work, using our marriage to minister to others. We hope our love for and devotion to each other are a testimony of Your power working through us, leading others to surrender their lives to You. Lord, we ask that our ability to honor You and serve each other selflessly is evidence that we don't rely on our own strength. Our boast is in You alone! We pray we would never get in our own way, lessening the impact of Your ministry. When we doubt that our marriage has divine purpose, when we are overwhelmed with shame, or when we are tempted to live in apathy toward Your will, please correct us and reaffirm our belief. Lord, bless others through us as we seek to be hospitable, as we offer to be prayer warriors, as we generously supply others' needs, and as we cultivate strong friendships. We desire our marriage to be a light in this world and a beacon of hope that points others to follow You. May the ministry of our marriage draw other couples to Your throne of grace, where they will discover that their marriage has a ministry purpose too. In Jesus's name we pray. Amen.

As for me and my house, we will serve the Lord. **(JOSHUA 24:15)**

FILL OUR HEARTS WITH PASSION

Dear Lord, We are deeply grateful for the purpose of Christ's suffering and passion when He faced crucifixion. His humble sacrifice and the power of His resurrection have transformed our lives, which is why we aim to honor You in everything we do. Our desire is that Christ's redeeming love would continue to transform and refine us. Thank You for all that You do in our lives to equip us to do Your will. We also thank You for the ability to love one another with intense affection. You have filled us with excitement in our marriage. You continue to teach us how to grow in our devotion to each other. Please knit us together, and never let us weary in doing good for each other. We also ask You to fill us with passion to complete the work You have for us to do today. Ignite in us an enthusiasm to work together as a team for Your glory. May our zeal motivate us to enjoy the time we spend collaborating to carry out Your will. May our passion for marriage and our faith in You be contagious, sparking a freshness in the lives of others, increasing their faith in You. Lord, set Your seal upon our hearts, and may Your Holy Spirit flow from us to touch this broken world. In Jesus's name we pray. Amen.

> *Set me as a seal upon your heart,*
> *as a seal upon your arm,*
> *for love is strong as death,*
> *jealousy is fierce as the grave.*
> *Its flashes are flashes of fire,*
> *the very flame of the Lord.*
> **(SONG OF SOLOMON 8:6)**

OUR EXTRAORDINARY ADVENTURE

Dear Lord, We acknowledge today as another opportunity to embrace and embark on the adventure of marriage. We thank You for this journey we have been on together. Thank You for all the highs and lows. We know we have grown in these moments, as well as all the in-between ones. Lord, we petition You to help us wake up every morning to see our marriage as an adventure we have the privilege and pleasure of sharing together. Show us how to leave margin in our day so that we can be interrupted by Your divine appointments. Make us a couple who is flexible in our plans, always holding our desires loosely. Lord, we ask You to surprise us today! We ask You to move in an extraordinary way. Keep our eyes on the lookout for how You will show up, and reveal how You are working in our lives. Heavenly Father, lead us to put our trust in You and You alone! We petition You for an extraordinary adventure in our marriage today. Please help us to receive one another as a gift and explore Your purpose for our marriage. In Jesus's name we pray. Amen.

> *Whoever gives thought to the word will discover good,*
> *and blessed is he who trusts in the Lord.*
> **(PROVERBS 16:20)**

OUR EXTRAORDINARY INTIMACY

Dear Lord, You give us life abundantly! We specifically thank You for the intimacy we experience in having a personal relationship with You. Prayer has changed our life for the better! Thank You for letting us come to You and offer our hearts to You in this special way. Please help us recognize the gifts in our lives and be grateful for all of them. Encourage us to express our thankfulness to You and to each other every day. Help us to be transparent with one another, whether we are struggling or doing well. Make us brave in sharing exactly where we are and exposing the areas where we need to be encouraged. We desire to continue to experience extraordinary intimacy with each other, that we may know each other fully. Will You keep us from holding back anything from one another? Will You teach us how to confidently initiate intimacy and romance in our relationship? Please inspire us to consider one another's needs and help us to find ways to fulfill and satisfy each other completely. May our choices to cultivate more love and trust in our marriage bring You joy. In Jesus's name we pray. Amen.

This is eternal life, that they know you,
the only true God, and Jesus Christ
whom you have sent. **(JOHN 17:3)**

363

OUR EXTRAORDINARY FAITH

Dear Lord, Thank You for the Bible and the truth of Your testimony. Thank You that we can repent of sin and believe that Jesus Christ died and was resurrected, making a way for us to be with You forever. Thank You for increasing our faith. We ask You to make our faith even stronger. Please give us assurance for the things we hope for and the conviction of things not seen. Make our faith extraordinary as we abide in Your Word. Will You show us how to courageously live out our belief in You? Especially during trials and challenges, please help us to cling to our faith, in Jesus's name! Help us walk in righteousness every day. Lord, please protect our faith from the flaming arrows of the Enemy. May our conviction and confidence in You encourage one another to trust You more. We also pray that our faith would impact those close to us. We hope our assurance in You and what You are doing leads us to help others and love others just as You do. In Jesus's name we pray. Amen.

Now faith is the assurance of things hoped for, the conviction of things not seen. **(HEBREWS 11:1)**

OUR EXTRAORDINARY ONENESS

Dear Lord, Your extraordinary design of oneness in marriage is a gift to us. Being unified is a beautiful testimony to Your marvelous presence in our lives. We ask You to help us never to lose sight of our extraordinary oneness. Remind us daily of the purpose You have for us—to be a team, to be of the same mind, and to be agreeable in marriage. Will You please show us how to be quick to support and encourage each other, especially during tough times? May our oneness reflect the unity among You, Jesus, and Your Holy Spirit. We appreciate the comfort of not having to experience life alone. You make it clear in Your Word that we are not alone and that You are with us. Thank You for never forsaking us! Thank You for the bond of friendship we experience in marriage. Lord, we ask You to help us take advantage of our time together by being emotionally present with each other. Protect our oneness so that it does not deteriorate from decisions we make or from the attacks of the Enemy. When we experience moments of brokenness, we ask You to mend us and strengthen us. May our extraordinary oneness paint a picture of Your love, mercy, and grace, evident for all to see. In Jesus's name we pray. Amen.

Holy Father, keep them in your name,
which you have given me, that they may be
one even as we are one. **(JOHN 17:11)**

THE MARRIAGE GIFT

Dear Lord, Thank You for our love story and for the days ahead that You are writing for us. Thank You for the times we have struggled in our relationship, as well as for the victories we have celebrated. We are deeply grateful for the gift of prayer and the ability You have given to us to pray continually for our marriage. Thank You for teaching us how to humbly bring our thanksgiving and requests to You. As we submit to You in prayer, please help us hear Your voice clearly when You respond and when You lead us through every circumstance. May we continually believe our marriage is extraordinary, that the purpose You have for our relationship is extraordinary, and that the gift of praying together is extraordinary. Give us eyes to see how each of us affects the oneness we experience. Please help our hearts understand the influence we have in each other's lives. Make us confident in knowing that You purposed our marriage to have a positive impact in this world, in Jesus's name! Mature our marriage by stimulating growth in areas of our lives that You are refining. Urge us to cling to one another every day and embrace closeness. We yearn for You to use us as vessels of Your glory and grace, sharing Your love and testimony wherever we go and in all that we do. In Jesus's name we pray. Amen.

"Therefore a man shall leave his father and mother and hold fast to his wife, and the two shall become one flesh." This mystery is profound, and I am saying that it refers to Christ and the church. (EPHESIANS 5:31–32)

ACKNOWLEDGMENTS

A book like this does not happen without dedicated support throughout the process and constant encouragement to rely on the Lord until it is completed. We would love to use this opportunity to acknowledge those supporters who have cheered us on, enthusiastically supported our vision for this book, and prayed for us throughout the writing process. Without you this book would still be just a seed in our hearts.

Our parents—You have always cheered us on to do good work. You have always believed we could do anything. Thank you for encouraging us when times felt challenging. Thank you for always being there for us and for our children. We appreciate you and we love you dearly.

Joshua and Melissa Smith—Our family and our friends! Words cannot express the deep gratitude we have for you and your children. We love that we get to live close and raise our children together. We appreciate the ways you have supported us with words of affirmation, as well as the times you help with the kids. Thank you for always being reliable, loving, and considerate of our needs. We love you!

Cody and Stacy Mehan—Your surprise hello in the middle of the park changed our lives for the better. Thank you for building our friendship over the years and sticking closer than family. We love and appreciate raising our children alongside you. We found best friends in you, while our children found best friends in your children. It has been a perfect gift from the Lord. Thank you for reminding us of the truth every day. Thank you for supporting our marriage. We love you forever!

Jordan and Nikki Deiro—Loyalty, love, and a whole lot of fun! We feel so blessed to share the gift of friendship with you guys. We appreciate the many ways you have encouraged us and supported us, not just through writing this book but in life. You are always prepared and willing to provide for us, to pray for us, to give and give and then give even more. We appreciate the late nights, the deep chats, the games we've played, and the camping trips we've taken together. Thank you for your words of wisdom and encouragement. We love you to the moon and back. You are amazing friends.

Chris and Cassidy McBride—You came along when we didn't expect it, and you've stuck like glue ever since. We value our friendship, and we appreciate that God has allowed you to join our ministry team. We are grateful for the ways you have helped us maintain our social media. More than that, we love that we get to hang out together. We love you guys.

Stan and Jessica Shvets—Neighbors! We love that even in our recent moves, we have moved together. Let us keep the trend going and remain forever neighbors! We adore living so close to you, but more than that we love doing life with you guys. You have become like family to us! Thank you for your loving friendship. We love how spontaneous you are. We love the times spent around a firepit and the many memories we have of laughing together. Thank you for being quick to support us with childcare at any moment. We value the trust in our friendship. We adore you and your family.

Our church family—Thank you all for the invaluable ways you love and support us. Thank you for the countless hours you have spent in prayer over us, our family, and this book. Your continual encouragement means the world to us. We could not do what we do without your support and love. We hope you know we enjoy and look forward to Sundays because we know we will see you and fellowship with you all. May the Lord continue to do great work within our church and the legacy He is building because of our faithfulness to meet together and worship Him.

Our online community—You make the Marriage After God ministry possible. Our desire is to work heartily unto the Lord, but we are confident God uses our work to impact you. Thank you for following along. Thank you for encouraging us to write and podcast. Thank you for supporting us in our ministry by purchasing our resources. We value you!

The Zondervan team—Thank you for seeing the potential this book has to impact marriages across the world. Thank you for being a pillar of support throughout the production of this book. Thank you for being our team to get this book into the hands of other married couples. We appreciate you!

GO DEEPER WITH
more encouraging and inspirational marriage resources by Aaron & Jennifer Smith

Please Visit
MARRIAGEAFTERGOD.COM/godeeper

Check out these 30-day
marriage devotionals

Also look for the
prayer books

WOULD YOU LIKE MORE?
Check out the Marriage After God weekly podcast by the authors!

Visit
MARRIAGEAFTERGOD.COM/podcast

"I'm a **Christian counselor** in California where I address much of what you guys talk about... I love what you are doing and believe you are spot on biblically..."
- *Dr. Jen Andersin*

"I'm obsessed! This podcast is so amazing! Please please do more of them ASAP! As a young **newlywed** I am LIVING for this podcast right now. God bless xoxo" - *kbraat*

"Great encouragement! I've been **married for over 20 years** and I'm really loving the reminders of what the vision for my marriage is." - *Readrc*

Marriage After God

Chasing Boldly After God's Purpose for Your Life Together

Aaron and Jennifer Smith

What if God has purposed your marriage for something so much more than "happily ever after"?

Since the very beginning, God's design for marriage has been for husbands and wives to be ambassadors of holy love to a hurting world. Still, too many couples stop short at happy and wonder why they feel unsatisfied. Rather than "you and me against the world," God calls each couple to the rich and meaningful mission of "you and me for the world."

In *Marriage After God*, Aaron and Jennifer Smith, popular marriage bloggers at HusbandRevolution.com and UnveiledWife.com, transparently share their own journey of turning a marriage in crisis into a marriage built on Christ's redemptive love. With fresh biblical insight and intimate stories of their own struggles and victories, this book will guide you toward a God-centered, ministry-minded, and thriving marriage. Throughout *Marriage After God*, you'll learn to:

• Discover the signature marks of a marriage after God
• Find principles for building an unshakable marriage foundation
• Let God's story take the lead in your love story
• Recognize the tools God has already equipped you with for a missional life together

Filled with timeless wisdom, this thorough and practical book will empower you and your spouse to dream, decide, and do as you step hand in hand into God's ultimate purpose for your marriage.

God has created your remarkable, romantic, and redemptive relationship to be a powerful light to a dark and hurting world. Let *Marriage After God* be your invitation to marriage as God intended—a lifesaving, hope-inspiring, and transforming force of God's love.

Available at shop.marriageaftergod.com and Amazon.com.

ZONDERVAN®

From the Publisher

GREAT BOOKS
ARE EVEN BETTER WHEN THEY'RE SHARED!

Help other readers find this one:

- Post a review at your favorite online bookseller

- Post a picture on a social media account and share why you enjoyed it

- Send a note to a friend who would also love it—or better yet, give them a copy

Thanks for reading!